THE CLOCK
WITH
FOUR HANDS

By the Same Author

THE RED FORT

THE MILLIONTH CHANCE

THE CLOCK
WITH
FOUR HANDS

BY JAMES LEASOR

Based on the experiences of
General Sir Leslie Hollis, K.C.B., K.B.E.

REYNAL & COMPANY
NEW YORK

Library of Congress catalog card number: 59-9120

Printed in the U.S.A. by American Book—Stratford Press

This book is

dedicated

by permission

to

SIR WINSTON CHURCHILL, K.G.

the greatest Englishman of all

THE CLOCK
WITH
FOUR HANDS

All that is necessary for the triumph of evil
is that good men do nothing.
—Edmund Burke

If you will not fight for the right when you can easily win without
bloodshed; if you will not fight when your victory will be sure and
not too costly, you may come to the moment when you will have to
fight with all the odds against you and only a precarious chance of
survival. There may even be a worse case. You may have to fight
when there is no hope of victory, because it is better to perish than
live as slaves.
—Sir Winston Churchill, *The Gathering Storm*

FOREWORD

by

General Sir Leslie Hollis, K.C.B., K.B.E.

Before I explain what this book is about, I would like to say what it is not about. It is *not* a history of the war, nor is it my biography. It simply contains some of my experiences and the impressions I gained during the nine years from 1936 to 1945; years which, in my view, have had a more decisive effect on the world's destiny than any other similar period of time.

During these years, I attended more than 6,000 meetings of the Chiefs of Staff, and also most of the decisive conferences abroad between the Allies, and while I had no direct responsibility for the plans made or the decisions reached, I formed my own judgment about them and the men who made them.

The idea for this book took shape early last year when James Leasor and I were walking through the labyrinth of passages under Great George Street in London, better known to us as "The Hole in the Ground," which housed the Cabinet War Room, the nerve center of British war direction.

I had not been there for some years, and I was moved to see how faithfully everything had been preserved. Yet it was really but a ghost of the headquarters I had known, for the War Cabinet Ministers, Chiefs of Staff, Staff Officers and Civil Servants who used to scurry along the passages like busy ants had all gone.

The empty Cabinet Room was just as I remembered it; chairs drawn up at the baize-covered table, with blotting pads and name cards in front of each place: Mr. Ernest Bevin, Sir Stafford Cripps, Mr. Bracken, Sir Dudley Pound, Sir John Dill; they were all ghosts, too. Only the aftermath of their decisions, often reached in the early hours of the morning, after long and bitter discussion, lives on.

As I stood in this empty room, remembering the discussions that had taken place and the personalities who had clashed here, I communicated my thoughts to Leasor, who suggested that we should write the story of this place—or as much of the story as we are allowed to tell.

So much for the background to the events we describe; now for the cast who play out the drama.

First, the man who dominated every meeting—Winston Churchill. My working days during the war had two beginnings; one was around seven-thirty in the morning when we started to deal with reports that had come in overnight, and the other was around ten-thirty in the evening, when Ministers would invariably be called to discuss some supply or manpower problem. And in the early war years, for reasons this book makes plain, we were nearly always desperately short of everything needed to wage war successfully: men and women in the Services and the factories, ships, cement, steel, guns and tanks.

By the time the atmosphere in the Cabinet War Room was blue with smoke and possibly sharp with acrimony, Mr. Churchill— the "Old Boss," as we called him—would trundle in wearing his siren suit, with dragon-decorated slippers and a cigar. At once each Minister would passionately press his claim to priority. The "Old Boss" would pass by, unruffled, to take his seat, and then ask Ismay what was on the agenda.

As Ismay replied, Churchill would toss the butt of his cigar in the fire bucket behind him. He never took aim, but he rarely missed. The Marines on guard outside the room made considerable sums selling these butts as souvenirs. Frequently, Churchill would quell the clamor of the Ministers by one wisecrack. I remember once, when everyone was pressing their own claims for war material, he grunted: "Same old story. Too many little pigs and not enough teats on the old sow."

Or, again, when Ernest Bevin kept interrupting a meeting to say how he *must* have half a million extra men, although it was perfectly obvious that this number could not be raised, Churchill stopped him by asking quietly: "What do you expect me to do? Go out into the streets and make them?"

It is impossible to recall Churchill without remembering Beaverbrook, who was nearly always present at these meetings. I liken him to an old eagle perched high on some rocky crag, surveying the scene beneath him, ready to swoop on the instant one of his projects became involved. He was Churchill's closest confidant, and so powerful was the influence of his buoyant spirit upon the Prime Minister that once, when Churchill was in ill-health, Sir Edward Bridges, now Lord Bridges, not one of Beaverbrook's closest friends, said earnestly: "We'll do *anything* we can to get Churchill right again. We'll even send Beaverbrook, if necessary!"

This Canadian millionaire was both a goad and a guide to the Prime Minister. Tireless, although sometimes almost consumed by asthma, he drove himself to the limit of endurance and frequently beyond it; as indeed he drove his subordinates. His contribution to victory was prodigious.

Then there was General Ismay. As head of the Prime Minister's Defense Office he held a position of unique authority and responsibility. He could easily have fallen foul of the Chiefs of Staff, but he never did; in fact, they would have been lost without him and his amazing gift for smoothing over clashes of temperaments. He got on equally well with Ministers, Service Chiefs, Civil Officials, Americans—everyone, in fact. He knew everything and he said little. As one who served as Ismay's No. 2 for thirteen years, I think I can say I knew him pretty well; he was indeed the wisest of old owls.

Next, we introduce General Sir Alan Brooke—now Viscount Alanbrooke—resolute, volatile, vibrant, versatile and sharp tempered. He would speak so quickly that Churchill sometimes said he couldn't follow what he did say. From my experience it was usually something he didn't want to hear! Alanbrooke was not, in my view, quite so omniscient as his Boswell, Sir Arthur Bryant, would have us believe, but he was still a very good war-time C.I.G.S.—Chief of the Imperial General Staff. He was an equally good general in the field.

From the Army to the Navy and the imperturbable Sir Dudley Pound, who often looked half asleep (for he suffered from a grave illness of which this was one symptom). Then someone would mention the word "ship" or "sea" or "Navy," and he was at once wide awake. Churchill deeply admired him, and he carried on his slight shoulders the terrific burden of the war at sea when the Germans virtually had everything their own way. It was ironic that he did not live to see this state of affairs entirely reversed.

Sir Charles Portal, Chief of the Air Staff, was another calm character with a brain like a rapier. I never saw him ruffled, even under vicious and uninformed attacks on the Air Force. He would sit, surveying the critic coldly from beneath his heavy-lidded eyes, never raising his voice or losing his temper, but replying to rhetoric with facts. A great man, Portal, who enjoyed the complete confidence of the U.S. Air Chiefs.

Montgomery was, in my view, the best and most successful general in the field in either the British or American camps. (I can't vouch for the Russians.) He was a master of his profession and a born leader: beside him Bradley and Patton were only good amateurs. He used to say that war was a rough and dirty business, and from his close experience of it I would not challenge that remark. Strangely enough the two and a half years I spent as Chief Staff Officer to the Minister of Defense after the war were without any question the most miserable and wretched of my life. That this should have been so was largely due to a clash of temperament with Montgomery, who had become Chief of the Imperial General Staff.

The Labor Party were then in power and were expected to make slashing economies in defense expenditure, and so the three Chiefs of Staff—for there were three and not only one as Montgomery seemed to think—were each very properly determined to extract as much for his own Service as would be possible in some very lean years.

Had the Minister of Defense, Mr. A. V. Alexander, now Viscount Alexander of Hillsborough, been a strong character he would still have had a hard job to reach a fair and constructive balance between the three Services at this time. But he was not a strong character. While he gave an outward impression of ferocity and strength of purpose, in the event he was always much milder than his utterances would suggest. Alexander was frequently brow-beaten by the Chancellor of the Exchequer, Dr. Hugh Dalton, who hated the Services, and had it not been for Ernest Bevin, the Foreign Secretary, who supported us on all occasions, we would have all come off worse than we did; and so would the country.

In the deep, dank waters of this muddy political pond Montgomery lay like a huge pike, with snapping jaws and voracious appetite, determined to have the biggest share of everything for the army.

This determination could be defended, but it was the way the C.I.G.S. went about it that infuriated us all. His method at a meeting was to place on the table a paper—which had not been previously circulated and which demanded everything for the Army—and then ask us peremptorily to read it. Then he would ask in short staccato tones: "Do you agree, do you agree, do you agree?" As a result we seldom reached agreement on anything—as Montgomery states in his memoirs. But the cause of this I lay largely at his door.

Then there was Roosevelt—an enigma; a great President, and a good friend to Britain when we needed help most in 1940-41. But after America's entry into the war, when her strength grew, he showed frequent suspicion of British Imperialism. His championing of Chiang-Kai-Shek nearly wrecked the Cairo Conference. But worse was to follow, when he failed to see through Stalin at Yalta. Churchill visualized so clearly what would happen between Russia and the West after the war if Roosevelt's policy prevailed, but with Britain's coffers almost empty, and America dis-

posing four-fifths of the men, equipment and ships of the Western
Alliance, what could he do? I fear that history may tend to minimize Roosevelt's good points and magnify his errors.

He acted sometimes in a way which we British just could not
understand. He was frequently, of course, under heavy political
and other pressures about which most of us knew too little at the
time, and he was not always well advised, but he always remained
a man of the highest personal integrity, and a genuine friend of
this country. We remember him now not by his statue in Gros-
venor Square, but by his courage: first, in overcoming his enormous physical disability, then in pouring arms and aid to Britain
in the early days of the war when America was also dangerously
short of fighting equipment, and he could so easily have done
nothing at all to help us.

Of the American Service leaders, Eisenhower was the leading
soldier-statesman; only he could have held together the vast
amalgam of U.S. and British Armies, Navies and Air Force. Eisenhower was no strategist, but then he did not have to be one. There
were quite enough, if not too many, without him.

General Marshall was the best military "logistic" organizer on
our side. He started from scratch, and in a couple of years or so
built up a huge U.S. Army and Air fighting machine. Marshall,
like Eisenhower, was no strategist, and would probably not have
made a great field general, but he was a man of charm and integrity. He and Sir John Dill did a tremendous job in ironing out
Anglo-American differences before they could become public.

The American Admiral King, rough, ruthless and unbending,
on the other hand, was anti-British, and particularly anti-Royal
Navy. He regarded the Pacific as his own personal war, which was
one of the reasons why he built up such a huge "private army"—
the U.S. Marines. A pity our Admirals did not think along the
same lines. King was one of the most difficult of all the Allied
leaders to get on with. I managed fairly well, principally because
I was a Marine.

Then there was de Gaulle: tall, austere, aloof, very touchy and
difficult to handle. Roosevelt never forgave him for occupying
the islands of St. Pierre and Miquelon without first asking permis-

sion. De Gaulle showed his own opinion of the American President on several occasions. Once, when Roosevelt cabled that he was going to Casablanca and would like to see him, the French General replied that there was no point in their meeting; he had nothing he wanted to discuss with him. Churchill had to put up with a lot from his tantrums, but treated him like a boy who has had an unfortunate background and needed both encouragement and the occasional stick. That de Gaulle had the makings of greatness, present events have proved.

I would also like to add here a few words in praise of an almost unknown but frequently maligned body of men who appear but infrequently in the memoirs of the great captains of the war, and even then are only referred to in a rather disparaging way as Whitehall Planners.

These were not—as might be inferred—a lot of doddering incompetents ambling about the corridors of "The Hole in the Ground" intent on nothing but making their returns, but officers of all three Services, with representatives of other Government departments; men of the very highest caliber.

We all met regularly, often several times a day, in "The Hole in the Ground," and so I knew them well. There were the Joint Planning Staff which consisted of the Directors of Plans of each of the Services, plus such groups as Strategical Planning Staff, the Executive Planning Staff, the Future Operational Planning Staff and, later on in the war, the Post-Hostilities Planning Staff, together with the Joint Intelligence Staff. They had to examine every operation suggested by the Chiefs of Staff who did not lack any fervor in off-loading every possible problem on to them. Indeed, the guidance of the three Chiefs of Staff was—to be kind about it—extremely woolly and vague, and sometimes almost useless, and it was the ineluctable task of the Defense Ministry planners to translate these vague instructions into something workable.

The advice they rendered to the Chiefs of Staff about some of their pet schemes was not always palatable, and I remember occasions when officers of great distinction were dismissed forthwith because they were honest enough to point out that some plan was quite impossible and hopeless, even though their honesty was proved in the event through some unusually grave fiasco of arms.

These planners, so often dismissed contemptuously by people who knew nothing about them, have their own memorial; the Americans modeled their system on ours, which is the greatest possible tribute that could have been paid to these largely unknown men who labored fantastic hours with me in "The Hole in the Ground," and who translated so many schemes from their seniors into action—and pointed out the folly of so many more.

Well, such is our cast. Let us begin the story, for they have long parts to play; and the curtain has still to come down on the last act of the drama.

Haywards Heath
Sussex
October 1958

Mr. Burgis and General Hollis in the map room of the Cabinet War Room

On board H.M.S. *Duke of York*, Washington Conference, 1941. General Hollis is fourth from the left and Averell Harriman is between him and Lord Beaverbrook; Mr. Churchill, Admiral of the Fleet Sir Dudley Pound and Sir Charles Portal are on the right.

Mr. Churchill and President Roosevelt on board U.S.S. *Augusta*, Atlantic Charter, 1941

Chiefs of Staff meeting, H.M.S. *Prince of Wales*, 1941; General Hollis
on the left

Chiefs of Staff meeting, 1945

After lunch, Downing Street Garden, V.E. Day—*l to r*. Portal, Alanbrooke, Churchill, Cunningham; *standing*, Hollis and Ismay

The Potsdam Conference, 1945

The Cabinet War Room

The Cookhouse

General Hollis' bedroom

The Little Mess Room and Waiting Room

The Map Room

Marine guard outside the Map Room

CHAPTER 1

There is no such thing as an inevitable war.
If war comes it will be from failure of
human wisdom.

BONAR LAW, Speech
July 1914

As the flying boat soared up and turned above the glittering bay,
weeping tears of sea-water from her wings, Leslie Hollis had a
quick last view of Government House, with the gray shape of the
battleship *Duke of York* in Bermuda harbor, and beyond, the
white surf breaking on the beach.

Then she righted herself, spray scudded past the windows from
the ends of the floats, and she was off east towards Britain. A
few American airplanes flew with her out to sea and then fell
back, and she was on her own, starting the strangest and most
crucial flight of the war.

At that precise moment, and 2,800 miles east—in the nursery
of a Devonshire mansion then in use as Control Room for Ferry
Command, dealing with American bombers flying across the Atlantic to Britain—a Wing Commander announced casually: "The
British Airways flying boat *Berwick* from Baltimore, was airborne
from Bermuda at fourteen forty-five hours Greenwich Mean Time.
Kelly Rogers is Captain. No information about passengers or
freight. E.T.A. in England oh-eight twenty-three hours tomorrow."

With a red crayon an airman orderly carefully chalked this information on a blackboard under the date, *January 17, 1942*.

11

A bored W.A.A.F. telephone operator looked up from filing her nails as he did so.

"Why does anyone want to leave Bermuda these days?" she asked.

A teleprinter girl shrugged her shoulders.

"Search me, dearie," she replied and started to tap the keys.

The Wing Commander began to give the details of the next plane expected over the West Country: a Lockheed bomber being ferried from the United States. . . .

As the chain of islands fell away like a lost necklace in the sea behind the *Berwick* the men inside her large saloon glanced at each other, the same uneasy thought in their minds: would they ever reach England?

Unconsciously, they all looked at Mr. Churchill whose idea this flight had been, as he stretched out in his easy chair, piercing the end of a new cigar. He appeared not to notice their stares, and applied himself to lighting up, as though that were his only worry.

Admiral Sir Dudley Pound, First Sea Lord, took off his braided cap and placed it carefully in the rack above his seat, smoothing back his thinning hair. He looked out of the window rather wistfully at the shrinking picture of the British warship. Untried though the *Duke of York* was, with her tests unfinished, gunners who had never fired their guns and many of her crew who had never even been to sea before, at least she seemed safer than this flying machine for a mid-winter crossing of the Atlantic.

In the back of the airplane, enigmatic, calm and bland as a Buddha, Lord Beaverbrook sat staring straight ahead of him towards the control cabin. No one could even guess his thoughts. As a son of the Manse, he was, in fact, repeating to himself the 23rd Psalm: "The Lord is my shepherd. . . ."

Air Marshal Sir Charles Portal, Chief of the Air Staff, glanced at his watch involuntarily to check their take-off time, gave a little sigh at the thought of the boring flight ahead, and then produced a pack of cards.

"How about a game?" he asked Hollis.

"A little later, if I may," Hollis replied. "I've got all the reports to catch up on first."

Portal nodded, and began shuffling the cards on the small table in front of him.

As Military Secretary to the War Cabinet, Brigadier Leslie Hollis had accompanied the Prime Minister and the Chiefs of Staff to the Washington Conference, called immediately after Pearl Harbor to decide strategy since America was involved in the war. Now they were all on their way home. While at the Conference, news came of the fall of Singapore. The tide of war was flowing so strongly and ferociously against Britain, both in the Far East and in North Africa, that Churchill, away from London for four weeks already, yearned to be back, and fretted at the thought of a further seven days at sea aboard the *Duke of York*, which had brought them from Britain to Bermuda.

He flew back in this flying boat from Washington to Bermuda to rejoin the battleship, occupying the honeymoon suite in the tail, and on the way a solution presented itself: why not fly the Atlantic in the *Berwick*?

When Captain Kelly Rogers, who commanded the aircraft, conducted him round the machine, the idea took hold of him. Mr. Churchill was most impressed by the fact that engineers could actually walk inside the wings to adjust the engines during flight, and he accepted Rogers's invitation to try the controls for himself, and flew for about twenty minutes, putting the flying boat into a couple of slightly banked turns and remarking on the vast difference between it and the first airplane he had flown in 1913 —an early Short's biplane in which he had taken some flying lessons. By the time they had landed in Bermuda harbor, Mr. Churchill's mind was made up: he *would* ask Rogers to fly him home in this flying boat.

A launch waited to take him to Government House, and he called for the Speaker of the Bermuda Parliament and announced that he wished to address the members. It was Thursday—a half holiday in Bermuda—and everyone had dispersed to their homes, but runners were sent after them. When they reassembled, the

Prime Minister, unwearied, buoyant and brilliant as ever, stood under the portraits of King George III and his Queen which hang on the walls of the Bermuda Parliament building, and spoke to the members.

While all this was going on, and naturally quite unaware of Churchill's intention, Rogers remained in the *Berwick*, preparing for his return flight to Baltimore. He was therefore surprised when the launch that had so recently taken Churchill ashore came out on the Prime Minister's instructions to ferry him to Government House.

He found Mr. Churchill waiting with one question: Could the *Berwick* carry him on to England in the morning? Astonished at the request, Kelly Rogers thought for a few moments, and then nodded. Yes, she could.

Satisfied, Mr. Churchill announced that he was calling an immediate conference between Sir Charles Portal and Sir Dudley Pound in the drawing-room, at which he also desired the presence of Kelly Rogers. The pilot sat down at the oval table, not knowing quite what to expect. Beyond the windows, the sun shone on the *Duke of York*, riding at anchor in the harbor, and following their gaze, Churchill lit a cigar and addressed the meeting.

"Outside, lies the *Duke of York*, waiting to take me to England, which I can reach in seven days," he began. "During that time I have ears to hear but no lips with which to speak. On the other hand, Captain Kelly Rogers here assures me that in the airplane in which we have just flown here, we can fly to England tomorrow—and in not more than twenty-two hours. This means many days saved, and during that time many things may happen."

He paused, looking round at his colleagues.

"Such a flight cannot be regarded as a war *necessity*," he added. "But as a war convenience."

The others did not share Mr. Churchill's view that such a flight, in such an unsuitable aircraft, and in mid-January, was at all convenient. They thought it was entirely unnecessary and an incalculable risk, and said so.

An aircraft of this type had never flown the Atlantic before in mid-winter, and was not intended for the journey on which they would encounter severe icing, and very bad weather nearer the British Isles. Since the *Berwick's* ceiling was barely 8,000 feet, they would not be able to fly above the weather and escape its ferocity. Further, although the flying boat could normally carry seventy-four passengers, she would now only be able to take seven with any reserve of petrol, for Rogers wisely insisted on carrying 5,000 U.S. gallons—making his flying boat an all-up weight of 87,784 lb. at take-off. Worst of all from a safety point of view, they would have to maintain radio silence for most of the journey because of the secrecy of their flight. This meant that, should they be forced down on the bitterly cold Atlantic, they would have no way of guiding in any rescue craft.

Kelly Rogers therefore came under some hard and prolonged questioning as to the feasibility of the flight. He was one of Britain's most experienced civilian air pilots: less than a month before the outbreak of war he had flown the Imperial Airways, flying boat *Caribou* 3,000 miles from Southampton to New York, to inaugurate the first trans-Atlantic air mail service between Britain and America. Then in January 1940, he had travelled to the Belgian Congo to salvage another Imperial Airways flying boat, *Corsair*, which had come down in the jungle—a task that took him nine months. He knew the risks involved in flying the Atlantic in such a plane, and gave immediate replies to all the questions that were put to him. At last Mr. Churchill turned to the others, taking the cigar out of his mouth, beaming with satisfaction.

"He seems to have all the answers, doesn't he?" he said approvingly. Rogers replied that he was confident in speaking as he did because "merchant airmen" (as the pilots of civilian airliners were then called) had gained confidence enough to regard a flight from Bermuda to Britain "as an everyday occurrence."

Without more ado, Mr. Churchill therefore announced that if weather conditions were suitable for flying next morning, he would fly home to England. If they were not, he would travel in the *Duke of York*. Portal would act for him in all matters relating to the flight, but the final decision as to whether or not they would make it would be left to Kelly Rogers.

"We all knew we had to reach home base or die," writes General Hollis. "As the meeting broke up, the general view seemed to be that the latter alternative would be our fate. All the cards seemed stacked against us, but since the Prime Minister's mind was set on making the journey by air, no one was courageous enough to appear cowardly before him. Secretly, we hoped the weather might be bad or some defect would be found in the aircraft, and then the whole mad flight would be abandoned, but to our alarm and disappointment neither of these hopes materialized. We *had* to go. As I shaved next morning I knew how the old Roman gladiators must have felt when they saluted Caesar on entering the arena, saying 'We, who are about to die, salute thee.' . . ."

After an early breakfast, they assembled without enthusiasm on the jetty harbor for the launch to ferry them out to the *Berwick*. Mr. Churchill sat in a deck chair, anxious to be away and increasingly impatient of the delay caused by the fact that by mistake, their luggage had been loaded in a tugboat which was already half-way across the harbor on its way to the *Duke of York*, lying in the Roads. They were forced to wait in the growing heat for several hours before this mistake could be rectified, and then the luggage had to be stacked carefully aboard the Boeing.

"With a full load of petrol on board, we did not clear the land by overmuch," recalls Hollis. "But we were soon flying at a medium height above a huge carpet of ten-tenths cloud, and I started work on my report of the Conference."

Churchill alone appeared in great spirits, ebullient and irrepressible, and after lunch he lit a cigar and invited Kelly Rogers to join him for coffee. He was enjoying his journey and also savoring the surprise with which his Cabinet colleagues would see him return a week before he was expected.

In the rainy darkness outside the Control Room in Devonshire, the sentries buttoned their greatcoat collars against the bitter wind from the Atlantic. Inside, the air felt stale and used up: against the friezes on the nursery wallpaper showing gnomes and fairies, the cables, boards and complicated electronic equipment appeared incongruous and unreal. The Wing Commander gave another brief report on the *Berwick's* progress: "Kelly Rogers is just halfway over and only a mile off his course. He's a great one, riding the weather fronts beautifully."

"He'd need to, in this gale," remarked another officer who had just come in from the black-out, pulling off his soaking raincoat and hanging it up on a peg behind the door.

Nearly 1,500 miles away, the *Berwick* struggled east through the cold darkness. Dinner was served: wines, roast chicken, a sweet, and brandy. No one felt very hungry; now and then the aircraft dipped and rose again in an air pocket, and the roar of the engines came up with a new harshness, making those unaccustomed to flying look at each other quickly.

"The best case I can make for this meal," said Pound drily, "Is that at least we're getting rid of some of the weight this ship's carrying!"

"It was like a dinner on the night before execution," says Hollis now. "I don't know how we all got through with it."

Churchill lit another cigar: he seemed impervious to the danger, unaware of the fantastic risk they were running; the thought of it certainly did not spoil his appetite—or his enjoyment of the food.[1]

"After dinner, Portal invited me to play cards. We had two hands of picquet, both of which he won," continues General Hollis. "As night descended, a glorious moon arose, and the whole scene was one of very great beauty. This, however, was no time for admiring the scenery, and I excused myself from a third game

[1] On a subsequent flight across the Atlantic, which was scheduled to last twenty-seven hours, Mr. Churchill called the steward as soon as the plane was airborne.

"Funny things happen to the clocks on a voyage like this," he said. "They go back or they go forward. Let me tell you that my stomach is my clock. I eat every four hours."

The only available meal on board was dinner: on that flight Mr. Churchill and his colleagues ate six dinners.

and worked on through the night. I had hoped to write my report during the week we would have been at sea. Now I had to do seven days' work in one."

As the evening wore on Portal showed card tricks to Pound; and Churchill and Beaverbrook went up on to the flight deck looking at the star-sown sky and the pale, fluffy carpet of clouds beneath them. On they flew into night and ice, while frost traced white lacy patterns on the windows. Kelly Rogers worked the crude mechanism that split the ice from the ailerons, for the flying boat had no modern de-icing gear, and he flashed a spotlight so that the Prime Minister could see the hard white ice crusts being broken from the wings. Lower and lower the flying boat came down over the dark sea; now and then the wind flung handfuls of rain against the small portholes.

In the saloon, thick with cigar smoke, the shaded reading lights glowing redly on the little tables, Hollis kept on working. From time to time he looked up, thinking of a phrase, and saw his colleagues playing cards, relaxed, talking among themselves, with darkness and eternity only a few feet away.

"Several times the absurdity of the whole situation struck me," he wrote later. "Here was I trying to do a week's work in a night —and for what purpose? I seemed to be working in vain. So far as I knew a machine of this type had never flown the Atlantic before. We had nothing to defend ourselves with, if any enemy plane found us, no rubber dinghies to survive in if we came down. And we were losing height as the bad weather forced us nearer and nearer the sea. We had to keep radio silence, of course, lest any German air or sea patrol should pick up our signal and locate us. The odds against us ever reaching home seemed enormous."

They flew on past the point of "three engine no return"; then the last milestone of the sky, the point of "four engine no return," which meant that the nearest way home was the way ahead.

"At five o'clock I felt too tired to do any more work and lay back in my chair and slept," says General Hollis.

When dawn came it was so cold that Mr. Churchill's valet warmed his master's shoes in the kitchen oven. Radio reports began coming in of worsening weather over England, for although

the flying boat was not sending messages, it could receive them.
The black cloud-tops beneath them grew purple and then the
sun brushed the sky with pale pink and orange, and soon after
first light an officer, whom Portal took to be the navigator on
duty, told him that their position had been checked by the sight
of a star about five o'clock in the morning. But even so, they did
not appear to be where they hoped they would be by that time.

"I did know from experience what could happen to dead reck-
oning in a relatively slow aircraft after five or six hours without
a chance of checking drift," Portal admitted later. Within seconds,
everyone else also knew what had happened—and the danger they
were in: they were due over German occupied France at any
moment.

The telephone rang on the desk of Air Commodore H. V.
Rowley, Acting Air Officer Commanding No. 10 Fighter Group,
and responsible for coastal defense from Southampton in the
south to Milford Haven in the west.

"Fighter Command here," said a voice over the miles of wire.
"Just thought we'd tip you off. A V.I.P.'s flying in from the west
in the morning. And when I say V.I.P. I mean a V.I.P. He expected to land anywhere between Plymouth and Milford Haven.
Just thought you'd better be in the picture. O.K.?"

"O.K."

The line went dead; Rowley walked into the Group operations
room and by first light had fighters airborne over Fairwood
Common, Cornwall and Exeter. Every half-hour they were replaced by others to make sure that both pilots and planes were
kept continually at the utmost readiness. Hours passed, but still
no aircraft was sighted from the west.

Back inside the *Berwick,* Hollis awoke slowly and rubbed his
eyes: the sky was pink and fresh through the round windows, but
the air in the saloon seemed sour.

"There was a great deal of coming and going between the
control cabin, chiefly affecting Sir Charles Portal," he wrote afterwards. "He wore a strained look on his usually calm and unruffled

countenance, and we subsequently learned that, largely due to his advice—he could, of course, give no orders—we made an immediate turn to the north-west. Thus, by a matter of minutes, we avoided coming out in a clear sky right over Brest, the most heavily defended French occupied port in the Channel. We were so low and so slow that the German gunners could not have failed to bring us down. I seriously considered tearing up my report and burning the whole thing in the aircraft kitchen, rather than risk its capture."

Portal later apologized to Churchill for what he feared might have been a lack of politeness in his suggestions.

Churchill grunted.

"In war you don't have to be polite," he replied, "You just have to be right!"

As the *Berwick* turned north-west a plot appeared on the radar screens of No. 10 Fighter Group Control Room showing an aircraft approaching thirty miles west and slightly north of Brest. It was immediately marked "Hostile" and Rowley, seeing it was laying a direct course for England, thought it must be a single enemy bomber, and put up a flight of fighters to intercept it.

Meanwhile, in the Ferry Command control room in the West Country, the Wing Commander looked at his watch.

"Time to feed some weather dope to Kelly Rogers," he said, and as he spoke, Rogers's voice came over the radio for the first time in clear speech.

"I elect to go into Mount Batten, Plymouth," he announced briefly.

The British fighters passed very close to the returning *Berwick*, but the fact that it was not spotted and shot down—after escaping the Germans—by its own side was largely due, says General Hollis, "to the heavy cloud conditions, and also to further changes of course. We were all very thankful, too, that we missed the planes sent up to search for us. Only a few days previously a British general had been shot down in similar circumstances and we did not want to repeat this performance." Air Commodore Rowley adds: "By the grace of God and the difficult weather conditions the fighters failed in their mission. Fighter pilots at that time were apt to be light on the trigger, and a Boeing was not a very well-known type of flying boat. I retired to the officers' mess and soothed my jangled nerves with some light refreshment."

The travellers from the *Berwick* were soon soothing their own nerves in the same way, on the train to London, more relieved than they would admit at being again on land.

"I was glad then that I hadn't destroyed my report," writes General Hollis. "It was a unique document, for our journey had actually begun on Sunday, December 7, 1941, when Churchill asked John G. Winant, the American Ambassador, and Averell Harriman down for dinner at Chequers. Harriman had ingratiated himself with Mr. Churchill's family, and then with the Prime Minister, who accepted him as a confidant and friend, and they travelled a great deal together.

"Harriman had been a rich playboy in his younger days, but later devoted himself to the interests of his country and was also very friendly to the British. He had the ear of President Roosevelt, but in my view he did not, in fact, help us as much as Harry Hopkins did."

He and Churchill appeared to have the highest regard for each other, until one day at the Washington Conference General Marshall came into the room and beckoned to him, saying, "Come in and tell me what you know." Hollis calls this "our first intimation that Harriman was gathering news to relay to his own colleagues in the States. He sent Roosevelt a great many telegrams, but they contained little of any importance. The President thought very highly of them, although they were mostly made up of snippets of gossip about personalities in British public life—such as the number of glasses of brandy certain British politicians might drink after dinner . . ."

On this occasion at Chequers, Churchill, half listening to his companions and half to the nine o'clock radio news, heard some vague references to Japanese attacks on American shipping at Hawaii, and on British ships in the Dutch East Indies. Harriman leaned forward and said he was sure there had been a reference to Japanese attacking the Americans. At that moment Churchill's butler, Sawyer, came into the room.

"It's quite true," he said. "We heard it outside ourselves. The Japanese have attacked the Americans."

The three men at the table sat looking at each other, remembering Churchill's words at a Mansion House luncheon the previous month when he had said that should Japan attack America a British declaration of war would follow "within the hour." Churchill walked to his office, and asked them to put through a call to the President at the White House immediately. Winant, at his elbow, asked him anxiously: "Don't you think you had better get confirmation first?" Mr. Churchill shook his head and stood waiting, cigar in hand, until the President was on the line.

"They've attacked us at Pearl Harbor," said Roosevelt. "We're all in the same boat now!"

Churchill thereupon decided to go to Washington to discuss plans with him, taking with him Lord Beaverbrook and the Chiefs of Staff, and Brigadiers Ian Jacob and Leslie Hollis.

This Washington Conference had been, in Hollis's view, the most difficult of all the conferences, for "the Anglo-American alliance was still untempered steel. The Americans were reeling under the disaster of Pearl Harbor, and possibly a little nervous that the war-tried British might try to tell them what to do. We, on the other hand, were anxious to show that we had no desire to act as senior partners in the new-formed alliance, but as equals. We had no pattern to guide us, and the discussions were therefore long and wearisome."

Hollis had brought his civilian secretary Mr. Jones with him, and during a lull in the conference Jones said that he would be very grateful if Hollis could help him to realize a life's ambition: to set foot in the White House. Could he possibly give him a paper which he could deliver there and so be able to tell his wife that he had achieved his aim?

This was quite easy to do, and Hollis gave Jones some documents to take to Mr. Churchill's secretary. He duly presented his pass at the heavily guarded entrance to the White House, and, having stated his mission and been scrutinized, was ushered upstairs to the first floor where Mr. Churchill had his rooms. To his alarm, as he stood in the corridor looking around him, the great door of one of the main bedrooms began to open slowly, and President Roosevelt emerged in his wheelchair. Mr. Jones had no idea what to do, and therefore pressed himself against the wall in the faint hope that he would not be noticed. Mr. Roosevelt noticed him, however, and seeing that he was obviously English, wished him "Good morning," and asked whether Mr. Churchill was ready to receive him.

Mr. Jones had no idea, but said he would find out. Roosevelt nodded towards another door behind which Mr. Churchill presumably had his secretariat. Jones knocked on this door and a gruff voice, unmistakably the Prime Minister's, grumbled something within.

"Please open it for me," said Roosevelt, and Jones did so and stood to one side. To his horror, Mr. Churchill was revealed standing within a few feet of him freshly emerged from his bath, wrapping a towel around himself and looking with some surprise at the entry of the American President. He was, however, entirely equal to the occasion.

"Come in, Mr. President," said the Prime Minister grandly. "England has nothing to hide."

The President later invited Mr. Churchill to accompany him to a special church service that Christmas, and with some difficulty Hollis managed to acquire a ticket for this historic occasion; but all through that morning the Niagara of memoranda and instructions and orders and telegrams proceeded without respite, and at last Mr. Churchill's valet came into the bedroom where Churchill and Hollis were working to say it was time to prepare for church.

The Prime Minister announced that he wished to wear a white waistcoat with his dark suit. The valet replied that he did not think this would be in keeping. Mr. Churchill told him to fetch the white waistcoat. The valet then made the point that the church would probably be overheated, and so the white waistcoat would be doubly inappropriate for such an occasion. Mr. Churchill persisted that he wanted his waistcoat. At this a look of despair crossed the face of his faithful valet. He admitted that the white waistcoat had not been packed: it had been left behind in London.

"Sawyer," asked Mr. Churchill sadly, "How could you?"

Because of his work General Hollis was despairing of being ready for church himself, but Churchill, seeing his disappointment on his face, patted him on the shoulder.

"Never mind, my boy," he said generously, "You will watch while I shall pray."

So busy were they at the conference that the Prime Minister even worked in his bath, and once he sent for Hollis to read him some secret reports that had just arrived. Hollis began to read, and suddenly Mr. Churchill gripped his nose between thumb and forefinger and disappeared like a pink, plump porpoise under the surface of the bath water.

Hollis stopped reading for a few seconds until the Prime Minister surfaced again, wiping water from his eyes and hair. Accusingly, he looked over the rim of the bath at Hollis.

"Why did you stop reading?" he asked in an aggrieved tone. "Don't you know that water is a conductor of sound?"

All these memories crossed Hollis's mind as the train took them through the snow-bound English countryside towards London.

"Thinking about your report?" asked Admiral Pound in the silence.

"No," replied Hollis, "As a matter of fact, I was thinking about how I got involved with this set-up in the first place—how it all began . . ."

It began, so far as Leslie Hollis was concerned, nearly six years before, on a March afternoon in 1936. As a Royal Marines major who had been attached to the Plans Division of the Admiralty for the past two years, he was in his office preparing for his next posting to command the Royal Marines Detachment in H.M.S. *Hood*. The telephone rang on his desk; he picked up the old-fashioned ear-piece.

"Hollis, Plans," he said crisply.

"Burgis here," said the voice at the other end of the line. "Sir Maurice Hankey asked me to telephone you. Would it be convenient for you to come and see him this afternoon at five o'clock?"

"Of course."

The strange wording of the request both surprised and disturbed him. In 1936, Sir Maurice Hankey, now Lord Hankey, held three positions of immense political power. Since 1922 he had been Secretary to the Committee of Imperial Defense, the governmental body charged with the task of advising the Cabinet on the safety of the Empire; for seventeen years of this time he had also been Secretary to the Cabinet, and, in addition to these appointments, for the past eleven years he had been Clerk to the Privy Council.

During the First World War, Hankey was said to be the only man to attend every political and inter-Allied conference, and afterwards, when he was given the thanks of both Houses of Parliament, praise galore, and, more usefully, a gift of £25,000, Lloyd George declared he was the best Chief of Staff he had known. Mr. Baldwin called him "the ablest Civil Servant any country could possess," and A. J. Balfour gave him the highest praise of all. "Without Hankey," he said, "We should not have won the war." Hankey owed much of his success to his ability to draft superlatively good minutes of meetings, to record clear-cut conclusions and to prepare memoranda on a variety of subjects, as required by the Government; all this when the Ministers themselves were not always very clear about what they *had* resolved.

At the Peace Conference in 1919, for instance, when many controversies and much friction disturbed the atmosphere, Clemenceau would rise from the table and say: "Gentlemen, it is luncheon. Let us leave Monsieur Hankey to tell us later what we have decided." After lunch, Hankey would table a list of "Conclusions," to all of which all the delegates would exclaim that that was *exactly* what they had been trying to say *all* the time.

Hankey had built up the system of the Cabinet Secretariat, by which records were kept and procedure made. Some might call him a soldier in peace and a secretary in war, but he did not mind: while his physical stature was slight, his power in 1936 was prodigious. He wore his responsibilities easily, however, often ate a two-shilling vegetarian lunch and travelled by bus whenever possible instead of taking a taxi.

Although Hollis had seen Sir Maurice when accompanying his own Director to meetings of the Overseas Defense Committee, and other Sub-Committees of the C.-I.-D., between a Royal Marines major on a staff job of limited tenure and a man of such eminence there was fixed a great and seemingly unbridgeable gulf. Surely a summons from such a man could only mean one thing: the sack.

Hollis looked at his watch; it was already after four. He took down his bowler hat and umbrella, left the office, and walked into the first men's outfitters he saw.

"A stiff white collar, please, size fifteen," he told the assistant. If he were going to be dismissed from the Service—and try as he might he could think of no other reason why Sir Maurice should send for him so suddenly—then he would go out smartly, and as befitted an officer of the Royal Marines.

He put on the new collar in the shop, crammed the old one into his pocket, and walked over the road to Westminster Abbey. The nave was nearly deserted. Here and there a few figures knelt in prayer; in the background an organist conducted an unseen choir at practice. Leslie Hollis, a clergyman's son, knelt down for a few moments, convinced that his career was at end. He prayed that, somehow, whatever disaster might befall him, his wife and two young daughters would not have to face privation. Nineteen thirty-six, with two million men unemployed in Britain, and the number rising, was not a hopeful year for an ex-Regular Marines officer of forty to begin looking for another job.

Then, feeling more composed and resigned to whatever the meeting might bring, he walked smartly across to Whitehall Gardens to Sir Maurice Hankey's office. Burgis met him in his outer room, looking rather sharply at Hollis's pale, set face.

"I suppose you know why you are being sent for?" he asked.

Hollis shook his head. As Burgis started to explain, a secretary entered the room.

"Sir Maurice will see you now," she said, and held open the door. Hollis followed her into a room that was far more luxuriously furnished than the usual Government office. A fire burned discreetly in a burnished grate. Beyond the wide windows the

Thames glittered in the afternoon sun. Hankey stood up, a slight, austere figure.

"Hollis," he began at once, "I've sent for you because I want you on my staff. We're re-organizing the Joint Planning Sub-Committee of the Chiefs of Staff Committee. I want you to be Secretary. How do you feel about it? You can have twenty-four hours to think it over."

This was indeed the reverse of all Hollis's forebodings: suddenly the world seemed a brighter, happier place.

"I don't need any time at all, sir," he replied. "I'll take the post now."

"Good. Sit down and I'll tell you what it's all about."

Thus, quite unexpectedly, began the career that was to bring Leslie Hollis into the closest contact with all the political and Service leaders of the 1939-1945 war, in which he became assistant secretary of the War Cabinet and the Chiefs of Staff Committee, and attended no less than six thousand meetings of this body, an average of three every day. He was privy to all the great decisions, and, working with his friend and colleague, Lord Ismay, at Winston Churchill's elbow, endured the clash of temperaments that frequently provoked them.

His was the strangest war of all: largely fought, as we shall see, 150 feet beneath London, in the troglodytic world he later built for the War Cabinet, the Chiefs of Staff, and their advisers. Against the background hum of fans, pumping in filtered air from miles away, Hollis, Ismay and others worked for eighteen hours a day, week after week, month after month, year after year.

During these years Hollis was to employ relays of secretaries and typists, who arrived every four hours; but frequently he himself would work around the clock. Night, day, morning and evening were only hours to fill with work. Frequently he had to spend days on end without coming up to breathe fresh air. Eventually, missing regular exercise, for he had been an excellent hockey and tennis player in the Royal Marines, he engaged a masseur, who pummelled him for an hour at seven o'clock every morning. But even through these visits Hollis would dictate his memoranda to a stenographer.

On that March afternoon in 1936, however, these things belonged to an unimagined and undreamed of future: the present was absorbing enough. It appeared that Hankey had been anxious for some time to have a Royal Marines officer on his staff—he had served in the Marines himself—and he wanted a man who would understand his thinking and his outlook but he feared lest such a move would be criticized as favoritism. Now that this new Governmental Sub-Committee was being formed, however, with a Naval Captain, a Group-Captain from the R.A.F., and an Army Colonel to advise the Directors of Plans of the three Services and the Chiefs of Staff on defense plans, it provided the opportunity he needed.

Because the estimates for expenditure to defend Great Britain and His Majesty's Dominions beyond the seas were so small,[2] competition for the available money was great between the three Services, and tempers frequently ran high over financial discussions. At such times, a neutral Royal Marines officer could be very valuable in keeping the balance—and the peace between them.

The Chiefs of Staff Committee at that time consisted of Admiral Sir Ernle Chatfield, Air Marshal Sir Edward Ellington, and Field-Marshal Sir Cyril Deverell, Chief of the Imperial General Staff. In addition to their professional responsibilities as heads of the three fighting Services, these officers also held the corporate responsibility of advising the Government on strategic matters, either if the Government asked—which was rare—or if the Chiefs of Staff Committee felt that the situation warranted such a step. But as heads of the three Services they were kept busy on a variety of problems affecting their own Service, so any strategical plans required were first drafted, not by them, but by three junior officers known as the Joint Planning Committee. In 1936, this Committee consisted of Captain Tom Phillips, Royal Navy; Group Captain Arthur Harris, and Colonel Ronald Adam.

---

[2] Mr. Chamberlain, as Chancellor, gave a stern warning to the Cabinet when defense expenditure reached £78,000,000 a year, saying that this "might lead to economic ruin." The alarm was unjustified. When war came, more than this was spent *every week* for nearly six years.

These three officers were also the Directors of Plans for the Admiralty, the Air Ministry and the War Office respectively, and were kept so busy on planning matters concerning these departments that they had little time to prepare any plans for their superiors. Nor could responsibility for national defense be passed further down the line; they were the end of the line.

By this extraordinary duplication of jobs everyone was so busy with their own affairs that the whole reason for having fighting Services at all was in danger of being forgotten. Indeed, after a decade of refusal to rearm, and an almost pathological inability on the part of successive governments to admit the increasing danger from Germany, no plan of any kind existed for the defense of Britain in the event of war. But by March 1936, when Hitler marched on the Rhineland in his first act of repudiation of the Versailles Treaty, even Mr. Baldwin, the Prime Minister, known more widely to the public for his pipe[3] than for his grasp of foreign and defense problems, felt that this policy of vacillation and drift must end. Since all the officers appointed to produce defense plans were seemingly too busy to do so, three *other* officers—Captain Charles Daniel, Royal Navy, Colonel Dick Dewing, and Group-Captain Hugh Frazer of the R.A.F.—were chosen to form this entirely new Sub-Committee of the Joint Planning Committee, of which Hollis would be the Secretary. Hankey had specifically arranged that these four officers would have no other Service responsibilities; it was sufficient responsibility to produce a plan to save their country.

As an earnest of the seriousness of his intentions, Mr. Baldwin appointed Sir Thomas Inskip, the Attorney-General, to be Minister for the Co-ordination of Defense. This appeared an excellent appointment, but Inskip, a brilliant lawyer who later became Lord Chief Justice of England, was given no powers and, since he was the first to hold the post, he had no precedents to which he could refer. Worse, apart from his own small secretariat he did not have

[3] He gave his name and photograph to an advertisement for pipe tobacco which quoted him as saying: "My thoughts grow in the aroma of this particular tobacco." He did not say what thoughts these were.

even an office from which to work. He was, in effect, completely in Hankey's hands. Afterwards he admitted to General Sir John Kennedy, when the latter was Director of Military Operations, that "it had taken six months to learn what the job was, nor could he get any guidance. . . ."

Worst of all, the Minister for the Co-ordination of Defense had very little defense to co-ordinate. More than three-quarters of the Navy's fighting ships were obsolete and of little more use than showpieces at Navy Weeks, or to be reviewed by King George in the Royal Yacht at Spithead once a year. The Army was equipped with guns and vehicles of First War design; its transport was still on a horse-and-limber basis. The Air Force was in a similarly ill-equipped state; its bombs were mainly left-overs from 1919.

This was the background when, on April 1, 1936, shortly after Hitler's unopposed march into the Rhineland, the Cabinet asked the Chiefs of Staff for advice on plans for military action, should it be deemed necessary or advisable to take any. The Chiefs of Staff were forced to admit, with some embarrassment, that no plan for hostilities existed; but they promised to arrange for a report to be submitted at short notice. The Joint Planning Committee, in turn, sidestepped their immediate responsibility, and referred the query to the new Sub-Committee which at that date had not even met. To these four officers sitting together for the first time round a table in a room in Whitehall Gardens, with thick pads of paper and carafes of water in front of them, the problem seemed insoluble. They were strangers to each other and by no means sure of the extent of official backing behind them— or how their decisions would be received by their seniors. Further, they had no idea at all of the extent of the forces available for Britain's defense, nor how they were disposed. Under these conditions, plans seemed difficult to make. Some decisions had to be reached, however, for the Cabinet was waiting, and, as they sat making small talk and hoping someone else would take the initiative, Leslie Hollis, as Secretary, felt that this was a time to bring into operation what he had learned on many staff courses.

"Well, gentlemen," he began a little diffidently, "I think we should set out exactly what *we* have and what *they* have. I suggest we put down the entire resources open to the French and us on one side of a sheet of paper, and, on the other side, the men and weapons that the Germans can command."

At this first positive suggestion the other three officers rose thankfully to their feet, relief showing on their faces.

"I agree entirely," said one of them, and looked round at his colleagues. "Gentlemen, this chap's going to write the plan for us. I suggest that we therefore adjourn for lunch."

"I second that proposal," replied another officer.

"Carried unanimously," announced the third.

Thus, on All Fools' Day, with Baldwin's Cabinet desperate for a solution to a problem that should have been faced nearly a generation earlier, Major Hollis received his baptism in the ways of Whitehall, and spent his first lunch hour in his new job producing a few headings about the position of troops in Europe and their probable movements.

Hitler's successful reoccupation of the Ruhr, and march into the Rhineland, gave the British Government much indigestible food for thought. It meant that war was, if not imminent, at any rate looming, and as the days and weeks went by, the Junior Joint Planning Sub-Committee completed their appreciation of the situation.

They calculated that, at the rate of build-up of German troops, and the successes they were likely to achieve before Britain and France were finally forced to take some action, war was due in September 1939, which was the month in which Germany would reach her peak of truculence and expansion short of actual fighting.

When the four officers had finished the report, which declared that unless there was an immediate drastic reorganization in all three Services, and unless the greatest urgency was given to defense, then Britain could expect to lose any war with Germany and Italy, they remained in some doubt as to whom they should send it. Major Hollis, knowing little of the inner workings of the Government, and the etiquette involved, decided that the best thing would be to send copies to everyone who could possibly be concerned with the defense of the country. He therefore had a number of copies stencilled and sent them off himself. One naturally went to Mr. Baldwin, and others to the Ministers in his Cabinet, and, of course, to the Chiefs of Staff.

For a few days this pronouncement produced no reaction, and Hollis and his colleagues began to wonder whether they had labored in vain. He was abruptly disabused of this when he received an urgent message to report to Sir Maurice Hankey's office. On the way he met Colonel Henry Pownall, Secretary to the Chiefs of Staff Committee.

"You've put your foot in it, Jo," said the Colonel, not without some glee. "There's a dickens of a row going on. You'd better put a piece of cardboard in your pants, for Hankey's after your blood."

This intelligence did nothing to cheer up Hollis, nor did his meeting with Hankey give him any comfort.

"Did you send this report round to all the members of the Cabinet, *including* Mr. Baldwin?" Hankey asked him, hoping for a denial. Hollis admitted that he had done so.

"What on earth possessed you to do such a thing? You've let me down badly," said Hankey. "I don't know if I can keep you on. I've told him that you were newly arrived, and didn't know the ropes, but I'm not sure whether he is satisfied with that."

Colonel Pownall interrupted this gloomy monologue.

"After all, we *asked* these fellows to tell us the truth," he said reasonably. "Hollis's only error has been to give the truth such a wide circulation—and especially to let the Prime Minister know it!"

For some days Major Hollis's future hung in the balance, and then the incident was allowed to be forgotten. But when the Chiefs of Staff commented on the report, they complained that it was "too watery," and made their own assessment correspondingly stronger. The First Sea Lord, the chairman, ended it with the words: "We cannot ignore the writing on the wall."

Until 1936 Mr. Baldwin and Mr. MacDonald before him had managed to ignore it without much difficulty, but after these reports, it became clear that there was indeed a grave risk of war, and the Cabinet therefore decided to make some arrangements so that they could continue their work, even though London should be bombed from the air—a fate that many felt would be as final as to suffer an H-bomb explosion today.

With Germany building her air force at the rate of 750 airplanes every month, many of which were capable of carrying bombs a distance of 450 miles from their bases, the Government was forced to admit that the southern part of England, at least, would be subjected to severe air attack in the event of war. Since the railways and telephone lines had their heart in London, it was reasoned that a few bombs at such strategic points could completely dislocate work in the capital, as well as communications and the transport of men and supplies over a vast part of Britain. Under such chaotic conditions, the ordinary running of the nation's affairs by the Government would become impossible, because they had no meeting place capable of withstanding a bombardment, no special telephone lines laid, and no plan to carry on in the event of invasion.

It was suggested that the basement of the War Office—which had a certain psychological attraction, since it was the lowest part of the building—would be a suitable place for such a Cabinet headquarters in war-time. Investigation proved, however, that the safety was illusory, and it was indeed more dangerous than an upper room, for it had no protection or concreting of any kind. Thus it remained all through the war, when it served as an air-raid shelter for thousands of Civil Servants, clerks, officers, secretaries and messengers, who had nowhere better to hide.

On July 28, 1936, Mr. Churchill led a deputation of Conservative members of both Houses to Mr. Baldwin and Sir Thomas Inskip to explain their concern for Britain's defense. He ended a long and devastating statement on the inadequacies of national defense and the danger from Germany with a question: "Have we organized and created an alternative center of government if London is thrown into confusion? No doubt there has been discussion of this on paper, but has anything been done to provide one or two alternative centers of command, with adequate deep-laid telephone connections and wireless, from which the necessary orders can be given by some coherent thinking-mechanism?"

By March 1937, nine months later, the Cabinet felt that some permanent arrangement *should* be made to safeguard their work in time of war, and accordingly asked the Chiefs of Staff to work out a plan for the organization and construction of a war-time headquarters. The Chiefs of Staff passed this task to their deputies. Sir Maurice Hankey, as Chairman, passed it on to Colonel Ismay, who, in turn, handed it over to Major Hollis. There being no officer more junior to whom Hollis could delegate the task, he was forced to accept it himself, and set about finding a suitable site near the center of London where the Cabinet could meet and work in war. He received the assistance of Lawrence Burgis, for Hollis realized that, as a Service officer, he would be up against difficulties working with Civil Servants if he was simply acting on a military requirement. The two men soon became close friends.

Burgis was a short, rotund and rubicund person, who loved a good story and a glass of wine. He was also very interested in horsemanship and later became an authority on judging gym-khanas in Oxfordshire, to which county he eventually retired. "We had many good times together," recalls Hollis. "Not always to the benefit of our health."

Colonel Ismay relieved Pownall as Hankey's deputy shortly after this, and in the following year succeeded him as Secretary to the Committee of Imperial Defense. It was then decided to divide the appointments that he had held. Sir Edward Bridges, now Lord Bridges, became Secretary to the Cabinet, with Ismay as Deputy Secretary. At about the same time, Lieutenant-Colonel F. B. Webb, who had been Senior Assistant Secretary in the Committee of Imperial Defense, completed his service in the appointment, and, being the next senior Assistant Secretary, Leslie Hollis was appointed in his stead to be Ismay's Deputy. So began an association between Ismay and Hollis which lasted, unbroken, for nearly nine years, including all the war years.

One of the reasons they both worked so well together was that they both shared a highly developed and specialized sense of humor, illustrated by a story Colonel Ismay would tell that both enjoyed regardless of the number of times it was repeated. It concerned an old Irishwoman who complained to her doctor of the

poorness of her blood. The doctor advised some port wine, and
so the old lady went to her grocer's and asked how much a bottle
would be. The grocer explained that the best port cost six shillings
and ninepence a bottle. A cheaper brand was four shillings and
sevenpence, and the cheapest was as low as two shillings and six-
pence. The old lady asked whether the half-crown port was good
for the blood—and by this time Ismay would be in paroxysms of
mirth.

"I don't know whether it's good for the blood," retorted the
grocer, "But it's bloody good port for half a crown!"

Ismay had been born in India, the son of a High Court Judge,
and great-grandson of a Military Secretary to the former Viceroy,
Lord Hastings—from whom he took the Christian name of Hastings. He was known to his friends and intimates as Pug, due to
the set of his features, but it could also be a shortened adjective
to explain his whole pugnacious demeanor and his refusal to be
browbeaten.

In addition to a sense of humor, Hollis and Ismay shared another characteristic of immense value: the ability—possibly in
part absorbed from Hankey—to pick the flesh from some unusually diffuse document, or inconclusive meeting, and produce
within the compass of a few crisp sentences what had taken others
hours or days to try and resolve.

"But while Hankey would often say, in a spirit of compromise,
when presented with several plans or men of almost equal merit:
'Do not let the best be the enemy of the good,' Ismay was never
interested in anything less than the best—in work, in men or in
wine and food," recalls General Hollis.

"I remember, early in the war, that Pug asked Burgis and me
to lunch with him at the Ritz. We all arrived rather late and the
head waiter explained most deferentially that, owing to our late-
ness and the war, some dishes were unfortunately not available.
General Ismay took no notice of this, and we began with a dozen
oysters each and then a most delicious souffle. We followed this
with cold chicken and ham and French salad, and then we had
a huge bowl of strawberries and cream, plus a delightful savory
and the best champagne.

" 'Jo,' said Pug, as we sat back, 'This is pigging it: *pigging it*. I cannot imagine how we are going to survive the war under these ghastly conditions, with such poor food.'

"At this Lawrence Burgis spoke my thoughts.

" 'Well, Pug,' he said bluntly, 'If this is pigging it, I don't mind pigging it through with you!' "

*   *   *   *

The basic requirements for a protected Cabinet war room appeared deceptively simple: offices for the Cabinet and Chiefs of Staff, with bedrooms, plus lighting arrangements, and a kitchen and sick bay that could keep functioning under a direct hit from a bomb, and even if the buildings above were demolished.

The site had also to be in or near London, and Hollis and Burgis spent many dreary days examining railway tunnels, and old abandoned underground workings. Eventually the choice was narrowed down to four sites in London and one outside. The first was a large basement beneath the Office of Works—now the site of the Ministry of Defense at Storey's Gate, overlooking St. James's Park, and used as a depository for old files and records. The second was a disused tube station, Down Street, between Hyde Park Corner and Piccadilly Circus, about ninety feet under the ground. This had been one of the original stations when the Great Northern, Piccadilly and Brompton Railway—now the Piccadilly Line—was opened in 1906. The station had been closed since May 1932, and in 1937 it had no access to the street, the only way to reach it being by train. Special identity discs were issued to anyone who needed to stop there, which were shown at the previous station to the driver of the train, who would allow him to travel in his cab. When the visitor wanted to leave, he pressed a button which lit a red light on the platform, which was a signal for the driver of the next train through to stop.

The third choice was the site of a disused gasholder in Horseferry Road; the fourth, the General Post Office Research Station in Dollis Hill, North London. This was rather far out for everyday use, and, although war-time petrol rationing did diminish the volume of traffic on the roads, hold-ups and delays still occurred at many bottlenecks. It was unthinkable that the direction of the war should suffer because of a holdup in the Kilburn High Road. Indeed, when Mr. Churchill became Prime Minister he had a huge bell fitted to his car which could be rung to clear the road in just such an emergency.

A fifth place of safety, a country house in Worcestershire, was also considered, in case London should fall to an enemy invader. Here the Cabinet could have worked in the event of London's total destruction. Security arrangements for this house and reinforcements against possible bombing were reduced to a minimum, for Hollis felt safe in relying on its distance from London, and the fact that only a small circle of officers knew its exact location.

Of all these sites for protected headquarters, the most promising—because it was also the most central—was beneath the Office of Works, and later in the year work began on what soon became known as "The Hole in the Ground." Steel girders were not available for such work, and so Hollis had to find woodworking firms that specialized in supplying huge oak beams, at least nine feet long by six inches deep. These were used to shore up the 'ceilings of the cellars, and, even when steel became available in 1940, they still remained, and stand there to this day, white-washed and as strong as when they were first put in.

From the modest cluster of rooms which housed the mellowing records of the Office of Works, "The Hole" grew ever larger and larger, spreading down to a deeper level, and out until it covered six acres underneath Whitehall. At such a nerve center, it was essential that communication with other Government offices and Service Commanders should not fail under any foreseeable conditions. Thus a network of tunnels ran from it like a spider's web beneath the heart of London. Along these permanently lit channels were grouped clusters of armored telephone cables, so thick that a break in the wires was considered virtually impossible. Even if the whole capital fell in ruins above them, these cables would not be affected, and news could still go out to other command posts and to a hidden radio station. London might fall, but Leslie Hollis was determined that her voice would not die. To make doubly sure of this, engineers patrolled these passages continually on cycles or on foot during the war, testing the wires.

Most of the telephone conversations in "The Hole in the Ground" were spoken into receivers fitted with scramblers, a device that rendered the message meaningless and just a jumble of noise, until it could be unscrambled at the receiving end. Usually a scrambler of adequate security is contained in a box about two feet square, which can be concealed easily in any office. When Mr. Churchill became Prime Minister in 1940, however, he arranged for a special line to be run to President Roosevelt at the White House, in Washington, and the complicated scrambler fitted to this to ensure complete security for their frequent calls was the size of a battleship's boiler. Even with one hundred and fifty rooms, and more than a mile of twisting corridors in the "Hole" by that time, it was impossible to find space for this gigantic scrambler. Eventually, engineers fitted it in the cellars of a department store in Oxford Street.

Because nothing like this underground headquarters had ever been constructed in England before, Hollis had no precedent to follow, and no idea of the total services required, apart from the bare essentials of safety, food and communication, and the ability to sustain life for at least a week should all exits be blocked by bombing. It soon became clear that there must be some central office where all information could be pooled, and from this modest beginning grew the Map Room, into which flowed all information from every front, and which was the nerve center of the war. The walls were papered by maps, with colored pins to represent the passage of British convoys and individual ships around the world.

Although "The Hole" was believed to be secure from any known weight of bombs, there was one danger which remained until the end of the war: flooding. The depth of the main floor was about one hundred and fifty feet below the streets, far beneath the level of the bed of the River Thames, and should any of the tunnels crack under bombing and allow water to enter, little could save the whole labyrinth of rooms and passages from being completely flooded. In an attempt to minimize this grave danger, the doors of the various rooms, like doors in a battleship, had ledges over which people climbed so that some depth of water could rise in the corridors without flooding every room, and give time for pumps to come into action.

A further difficulty was to provide fresh air for the hundreds of men and women whose lives were to be lived for weeks on end so many feet beneath the ground. The easiest way was to build giant air intakes overhead, but this would arouse comment and could also be dangerous. An enormous underground metal duct was therefore constructed under Whitehall, between Westminster Abbey and the Houses of Parliament, and on to Horseferry Road, where it ended in what was called "The Rotunda"—one of the alternative sites for "The Hole." Here pumps drew in fresh air and blew it back along this duct to the cellars of the Office of Works, an underground journey that tainted the air with the reek of raw metal. Adjustable nozzles of the kind found in ships' cabins were fitted in each room and through them a stream of this air could be directed in any direction, or cut off altogether.

When the air-pumping engine was fitted inside "The Rotunda," the occasion was used to strengthen this structure in case "The Hole" should be irreparably damaged. First, a twelve-foot steel and concrete crust was constructed, thought to be strong enough to protect it even against an atomic bomb. So strong was it, indeed, that when, in July 1944, a flying bomb fell within thirty yards of the main entrance, only surface damage was caused.[4] Under this protection were built three miles of corridors connecting nearly a thousand rooms with their own power plant, water supply and radio station. Four diesel-electric engines, working sixty feet below street level, generated light and power, and worked an air-conditioning plant which, at the touch of a button, would give protection against poison gas.

As "The Hole" also progressed in size and complication so did the requirements increase, and no sooner had Hollis added another room, than he found that two more were required. He had to provide accommodation for guards and orderlies to look after

[4] When a bomb fell near Storey's Gate, Churchill remarked rather wistfully to Ismay that he wished it had landed nearer "The Hole" so that they could have "tested their defenses."

the Ministers and senior officers, and he organized a platoon of Royal Marine pensioners, under a Captain of Marines, who became Camp Commandant, with a color-sergeant, two sergeants and six corporals, to work in watches day and night. These men guarded the headquarters and also looked after the Ministers, senior officers and other officials of high rank. They ran two messes, one for Cabinet Officers and Ministers of the Crown, and the other for junior officials.

The civilian Custodian of "The Hole" was Mr. George Rance, chosen for the task less than a year before he was due to retire from the Office of Works. He was sworn to secrecy on the nature of his duties, and all through the war he kept silence. Neither his wife nor his grown-up family had any idea of the exact nature of his work. He was a popular character, and the Royal Marines became known jocularly as "Rance's Guard."

The strictest security precautions were necessary to prevent any unauthorized person from bluffing the guards. Every Marine was issued with a wooden tally so that in an emergency his identity could be established immediately. Members of the guard who left the building also carried a wooden token to show on their return. All were under the strictest orders to allow no stranger in, no matter who he claimed to be. General Hollis remembers one exception to this rule. He had just taken on his staff a young officer, Major Antony Head, later Minister for War in the first Conservative Government of 1951. Hollis's personal assistant, a Mr. W. R. Jones, who bore a striking resemblance to Mr. Robertson Hare, with similar diction, bald head and lugubrious features, was asked to escort Major Head to "The Hole" from the Cabinet Offices, at that time in Richmond Terrace. Jones for some reason assumed that Head had never been in London before, and, as they walked down Whitehall, he pointed out the Cenotaph, removing his bowler hat in salute to the glorious dead, and indicating the various points of interest in the way of the Londoner to the provincial visitor. Eventually they arrived at the outer door of "The Hole," and Jones produced his own pass and was about to lead the Major past the sentry, when the Royal Marine on duty stuck his tommy-gun in his stomach.

"No one's allowed here without a pass," he said, nodding towards Head, who had not yet been issued with one.

"But this officer is working for Colonel Hollis. It is *imperative* that he gets to his office," replied Jones. The sentry remained adamant: no one was allowed through without a pass. Argument raged between them as politely as possible, and suddenly Jones stamped his foot in annoyance.

"Look here, corporal!" he said in his most Robertson Hare voice. "You know who I am. We've not come here to be fagged about!"

A smile crossed the homely features of the sentry. No enemy could speak like this; this was the language of a true-born Englishman. He removed his tommy-gun from the Major's stomach at once.

"Pass, friend," he said.

❖   ❖   ❖   ❖

The seeds of Britain's military weakness in 1937 that forced such an unsatisfactory compromise as a converted cellar for War Cabinet meetings, were sown in 1919. The Government decided in that year on the grounds of economy that Service Departments should draw up their estimates on the assumption that "The British Empire will not be engaged in any major war during the next ten years, and so no Expeditionary Force will be required." This so-called "Ten-Year-No-War-Rule" had the gravest consequences, for it colored all thoughts on defense.

In 1924 Churchill became Chancellor and asked the Committee of Imperial Defense to review it, but without success. In July 1928, the matter was discussed again, and it was agreed "that the basis of estimates for the Service Departments should rest upon the statement that there would be no major war for a period of ten years, and that this basis should advance from day to day, but that the assumption should be reviewed every year by the Committee of Imperial Defense."[5] Any Service Department or Dominion Government should be able to raise the issue as they thought fit. Until 1929, when he left office, Churchill was hopeful that peace would prevail, and therefore saw no reason to change this

[5] *The Gathering Storm*, Winston S. Churchill.

decision. In fact, there was to be no war till 1939, and, as he has written, "ten years is a long time in this fugitive world."

The reply that there will be no war for ten years, however, had become the answer to all proposals for modernizing or enlarging our forces. When the Navy suggested building a new battleship, for instance, it was said that this would take four years, and, since no war was expected for ten, the battleship would by then be obsolete. And the request would be turned down. The Army and the Air Force shared similar experiences.

When Ramsay MacDonald won the Election of 1929, he sent for Sir Maurice Hankey.

"Hankey," said the Prime Minister, "Why the deuce did you let those Tories have that Ten-Year Rule perpetuated? Every day I get telegrams from the Foreign Office about how quickly Germany's rearming, and our own wretched state. What did the Conservatives imagine they were doing? Did they ever think what *my* position might be?"

"Not to my knowledge, Prime Minister," replied Hankey. "I expect they thought you wouldn't be here!"

"Despite my record I've never *really* been a complete Pacifist," MacDonald replied. "Something *should* be done, but what *can* I do? My Foreign Secretary, Henderson, is President of the Geneva Disarmament Conference, and is deeply committed to disarmament, and has an enormous influence in the Labor Party. My Chancellor is in the same position. So is the whole Cabinet. They are nearly all Pacifists and are committed by their statements which they cannot go back on now. What *can* I do?"

In the event, Ramsay MacDonald, like so many other politicians, did nothing, because that was the easiest thing to do, and the Ten Year Rule was further extended. In March 1932, Stanley Melbourne Bruce (now Viscount Bruce of Melbourne), a staunch friend of Great Britain, who had rowed for Cambridge in the 1903 Boat Race, and who was then Australian High Commissioner, came to see Hankey privately.

"Look here," he said with characteristic directness, "This Rule really must be smashed, or we'll be smashed ourselves."

Realizing that he had a powerful ally, because Bruce sat on the

Committee of Imperial Defense, Hankey suggested that Bruce should put these views strongly to the Chiefs of Staff. He did so gladly, and from then on more vigorous and realistic thinking prevailed. A Defense Requirements Committee was formed to report on what was needed to repair the worst deficiencies. They issued their findings within six weeks. The Cabinet then set up their own Committee: they took six months to reach much the same conclusion. But it was one thing to agree that mistakes had been made; another to rectify them.

The strength of the R.A.F. had been agreed in 1923 as fifty-two squadrons for Home Defense, with a first-line strength of 550 aircraft. Insufficient financial appropriations backed this decision, however, and so the numbers were only academic.

The actual rate of construction was far below the recommendation: 495 airframes were ordered in 1929, but none at all in 1932 and 1933. By 1934, the Home Force of the R.A.F. was still ten squadrons below the minimum strength agreed ten years previously. Worse, most of the planes were as much as twenty years out of date, based on 1914–18 models. In 1935, the Gloster "Gauntlet" was the main "new" fighter—with a top speed of 230 m.p.h. The most modern bombers were the "Hind" and "Hendon," carrying total loads of only 500 lb. and 1,500 lb. for 920 and 430 miles respectively. The fact that so few airplanes were needed drove British aircraft firms to the edge of ruin; the Westland Aircraft Company tried to keep solvent by making stainless-steel beer barrels.

But of all three Services, the Army was the Cinderella. Four years before the Second World War began the most modern field gun in use was of first war vintage, mounted on artillery wheels, without even pneumatic tires. Up to 1937, the Vickers gun, designed in the 1880's, and the 1912 Lewis gun, were the main machine-guns. The 3.7 in. anti-aircraft gun, which was to be a prime defense against enemy aircraft throughout the 1939–45 war, had been originally designed in 1933, but the design was so complicated that it required over three thousand drawings. By the time of Munich, five years later, less than fifty guns were available, with only a few predictors. Of the 375 tanks in the Army, 300 were officially classed as obsolete. Most had been made between 1924 and 1925. And the newer tanks were only armed with machine-guns. In 1934, the cost of modernizing the Army was put at £50,000,000, to be spread over ten years. This was held to be exorbitant; the estimate was therefore halved.

Worse, lack of demand had driven firms that had traditionally supplied the fighting Services with weapons and equipment to find other markets and make other products. In 1934, out of eleven large concerns which had been active in 1914, only one could still manufacture the heavier munitions, and these only on a very small scale.

On St. Valentine's Day, 1938, plans for the Valentine tank, with a two-pounder gun and armor considered relatively heavy for that time, were proposed to the War Office, but both the proposition and the design were rejected. This tank was reviewed again in June 1939, and some orders were placed, but by then seventeen months had been lost. A tank took from three to five years to prepare for mass production and the successful German "Tiger" tank, which first appeared in Africa in 1943, was already in prototype form at the same time that the Valentine was being turned down by the British War Office.

Indeed, in June, 1943, when there was a lot of controversy about the merits and failings of the British tanks in the Middle East, Churchill told a member of the Defense Committee (Supply) meeting what he thought about the Crusader tank, which the War Office no longer required, but the manufacture of which the Ministry of Supply was unable to stop as quickly as they wished.

General Sir Ronald Weeks, who for the last three years of the war was Deputy Chief of the Imperial General Staff, suggested that all the extra—and otherwise useless—tanks that would be produced before the model was abandoned might be used without their turrets as gun-towers for seventeen-pounder anti-tank guns during the Second Front. Mr. Churchill shook his head at this proposal.

"General," he said slowly, "You remind me of a man who gets out of bed in the morning, goes to the cupboard, removes a box of biscuits, and wanders round the streets of London—trying to find a dog or dogs to give them to!"[6]

Before the war, fierce argument also raged between the Navy and Air Force. The Navy, supreme for centuries, saw no reason to fear aircraft as a decisive factor in a war.[7]

So fierce grew this unresolved controversy that Sir Thomas Inskip, as Minister for the Co-ordination of Defense, became chairman of a Committee to inquire into the whole question of the vulnerability of capital ships to air attack.

"This Committee," writes General Hollis, "discovered the fairly obvious fact that an aircraft costing only a few thousand pounds could sink a ship which cost £7,000,000, and that for the cost of one capital ship, forty-three twin-engined medium bombers could be built. However, in their wisdom they decided that the capital ship was the one remaining surface craft which, if hit severely by an aerial bomb, was not liable to be sunk.

"Of the airmen's views, they declared: 'If their theory turns out well-founded, we have wasted money; if ill-founded, we would, in putting them to the test, have lost the Empire.'[8]

"In fact, by refusing to admit the ascendancy of the air, the Government wasted money and lost most of the Empire . . .

"At our meetings, Captain Phillips was always convinced that warships could carry sufficient anti-aircraft guns to make any threat to their safety absurd. 'Bomber' Harris was equally convinced that this was a fallacy . . ."

One December day in 1937, before they began their usual discussions, Harris turned to Phillips and said, half jokingly: "I had the strangest dream last night, Tom. I saw your future so clearly. War was declared in the East and the Japanese had taken Siam.

[6] Recalled by General Sir Ronald Weeks in *Organization and Equipment for War* Cambridge University Press.
[7] Naval reluctance to admit any rival was not new. In 1804, Rear-Admiral Earl St. Vincent refused the offer of an American inventor, Robert Fulton, to build a submarine, on the theory that if Britain began such experiments, other countries would follow, which would be "the greatest blow at our supremacy on the sea that can be imagined."
[8] Report, H.M.S.O.

You'd been promoted Admiral, and you set off in your flagship up the East Coast of Malaya to deal with the situation. Suddenly, down comes a rain of bombs and aerial torpedoes. You look down from your bridge, and say: 'What a lot of mines we've hit!' "

"You're talking rubbish!" said Phillips with a grin and changed the subject.

"There was a most extraordinary sequel to this," says General Hollis. "It is the only case I know of a dream anticipating events with a most disturbing accuracy."

Four years later, in 1941, Admiral Sir Tom Phillips, Commander-in-Chief, Eastern Fleet, sailed to Singapore in H.M.S. *Prince of Wales* and called at Cape Town to refuel. He flew up to Pretoria where he had a long talk with the Prime Minister, Field-Marshal Smuts. Shortly after the visit Smuts cabled to Churchill: "If the Japanese are really nippy, there is here an opening for a first-class disaster."

Such a disaster took place within the month, and exactly as "Bomber" Harris had foretold it four years previously in White-hall Gardens.

The Japanese were landing on the north-east coast of Malaya, and in what the official historian has admitted was "a political move accepted reluctantly by the Admiralty,"[9] the *Prince of Wales*, 35,000 tons, and the *Repulse*, a battle-cruiser of 32,000 tons, sailed north to intercept them. Phillips was convinced that, with surprise and fighter cover, he could successfully intercept Japanese communications. Some time after midnight on December 8th, however, he was told that he could not have fighter escort in the Gulf of Siam. Thus denuded of one element for his plan, he unwisely decided to go ahead with surprise as his only shield. Before he went off the air, he signalled from the *Prince of Wales*: "We are looking for trouble. No doubt we shall find it."

At almost that moment, some water buffaloes strayed into a minefield near Kuantan, on the East Coast, and set off the charges. Indian troops opened fire, thinking a Japanese landing was in progress, and informed headquarters at Singapore that they were

[9] *The War against Japan,* Vol. I, by Major-General A. Woodburn Kirby. H.M.S.O.

being invaded. Singapore radioed Phillips to change course; as he did so, he was spotted by a Japanese submarine. Within the hour, dozens of Japanese planes were swooping down on these two great ships. Ninety minutes later, aerial torpedoes had sunk them both, and the sea was littered with debris and the bodies of the dead. British destroyers and airplanes combed the area, but, not for the first time, help arrived too late; 673 men lost their lives.

Ironically, the Japanese did not reach Kuantan for another month; and when they came, they travelled overland and did not come by sea.

* * * *

Added to the enormous physical difficulties of rearming were moral difficulties at least as great. An extraordinary confusion of mind prevailed throughout the country that did much to slow down rearmament, characterized by tragic irresponsibility and ignorance. After the First War, as an answer or reaction to Lord Roberts's pre-war campaign for National Service, the Pacifist element in the Labor Party asserted its ascendancy over the industrial element by securing the adoption of a policy of declaring a General Strike to check any warlike action by the British Government. An attempt was made to get a similar policy adopted internationally, so that a general international strike could oppose "all wars that may threaten to break out in the future."

Psychotic thinking prevailed in the nineteen-thirties over the question of rearming—and still does. As early as 1931, when the Japanese invaded Manchuria, Dr. Maude Royden, a well-meaning woman, formed what was called a "Peace Army." Idealists were expected to sail for the Far East, seek out the battlefield, and then intermingle with the opposing forces in such a way that the armies would not shoot at each other without shooting the soldiers of peace. It was claimed that both sides would be so astonished at the spectacle of unarmed men and women doing such a thing that they would stop fighting.

Clerics, then as now, were also not backward in preaching the gospel of peace—with which few would disagree had not their views been so harmful to its maintenance. The Rev. Dick Sheppard, for instance, Rector of St. Martin's-in-the-Fields, and a former Chaplain to the Forces, formed a Peace Pledge Union with the policy of non-resistance to any aggression. Nobody was to help any invader, but the conditions facing them would be of a universal general strike. It was claimed that the enemy would be so impressed by this show of moral strength that he would relent and retire. In Czechoslovakia and Poland and elsewhere it was later discovered that an invader also had a third course of action: to advance without pity or delay.

In 1933, the year in which Hitler came to power, the British Labor Party introduced the slogan: "A vote for the Tories is a vote for war," and Dr. C. E. M. Joad, who became a radio celebrity in the war on the "Brains Trust," expressed his views at a Universities Congress in Cambridge.

"If it be asked what course you would take in the event of your country being invaded," he said, "The answer is simply: 'Disobey all orders.' If a general strike were declared, if all goods were held up at the ports, if no taxes were paid, if the Civil Servants refused to obey orders, it would be impossible for any enemy power to overrun the country."

In the following year, Mr. Attlee stated in the House of Commons that: "The Opposition do not think that disarmament and security could be separated. We stand for a system of collective security under the League of Nations, and are entirely opposed to separate alliances. The Labor Party will oppose increase of armaments on the plea of either national defense or parity."

Later, he told the House: "We deny the proposition that an increased British Air Force will make for the peace of the world, and we reject altogether the claim to parity. We think that parity is an out-of-date conception of the balance of power . . ."

In October 1933, what Churchill called "a wave of Pacifist emotion" increased the Labor vote in a by-election at East Fulham by roughly 9,000, and decreased the Tory vote by rather more. The successful candidate said: "The British people demand . . . that the British Government shall give a lead to the whole world by initiating immediately a policy of general disarmament." If we replace the words "general disarmament" by "banning the

H-Bomb" we can see that the same refusal to face reality still prevails.

And as late as 1936, a month after the new Sub-Committee of Defense started work, the Labor Party newspaper, the *Daily Herald,* gave this opinion: "Mr. Baldwin's theory that this country will be safe if only it has a lot of airplanes is just the sort of dangerous nonsense that led to the last war. How are the airplanes to be used? To make Britain stronger than any other power, so that it may enforce its 'rights' as it defines them? If so, they will breed war, and will have to be used."

Such an amalgam of well-wishing, ignorance and a determination to make political capital out of their country's dilemma produced terrible results. MacDonald the Socialist, and Baldwin the Conservative, had inherited an Empire, supreme in arms and secure in liberty: together and separately, they conducted it to the edge of darkness and annihilation.

The million unemployed rose to nearly three: more than half a million workers left the land; the Air Force declined from fifth to sixth in world ranking. Cranks, vague do-gooders and pacifists were counted the sages of this strange inglorious time, and patriotism was out of fashion.

Thus only those called up to fight for their country in 1939 were surprised at the inadequacy of the equipment offered to them for their task.

The unpreparedness of Britain in 1914, when it was the only country in the world whose Army had field guns incapable of firing a high-explosive shell, was eclipsed by Britain's almost unbelievable lack of fighting material twenty-five years later in 1939. What had been obsolete in 1914 was still in use.

"We had no sub-machine-guns, no rimless cartridges, no percussion grenades," writes General Hollis. "There were, of course, no dive-bombers in the Air Force and the tanks were fit only for museums. The solar helmets issued to troops going East to defend India, Burma and Malaya, were remnants from the South African war.

"Nearly all the bombs the R.A.F. possessed in 1939 had been left over from 1919. In 1921, some attempt had been made to produce a better bomb, but work only started in 1938, and very few were ready in time for the declaration of war. The British bombs contained an explosive, amatol, which was far less destructive than the explosive used in German bombs. An attempt had been made to remedy this and use a more powerful explosive, RDX, but its production stopped in 1937. It was not until 1942 that British bombs contained RDX.

"British bombs were only 500 pounders—for the Air Staff thought that larger ones were no better; and, more important, the planes of the time had been so constructed that they could not carry single bombs heavier than 500 lbs. each, and to build bigger bombs would have meant building bigger planes, which the country was said not to be able to afford.

"Further, only about a quarter of the weight of each bomb was made up of explosive—a 500 lb. bomb therefore contained barely 125 lb. weight of amatol or RDX . . .

"It was never questioned, however, that the British Army's cavalry lances and swords, their saddles, horse-shoes, picks, shovels, and tent mallets were the equal of any in the world.

"Such were the conditions obtaining in 1937, when, emulating the ostrich which buries its head in the sand and foolishly imagines that its whole body is safe, Mr. Baldwin's Government ordered the digging of what we facetiously called 'The Hole in the Ground.' "

CHAPTER 2

> In war it is not permitted to make a mistake
> twice.
>
> LAMARCHUS, *Plutarch,*
> Apothegms No. 186.

"The Hole" was first tried out during the Munich crisis in 1938, when the Chiefs of Staff went down the stairs rather self-consciously with Colonel Ismay and Major Hollis to take notes of their deliberations.

"Various Ministers also went below, but the Prime Minister, Mr. Chamberlain, would not come. At the height of his euphoric popularity as the man who had assured Britain of 'peace in our time,' he shared the abhorrence of his familiar, Sir Horace Wilson, of whom more later, for anything connected with military matters, and refused to take any part in the rehearsal," recalls General Hollis. "Less than two years afterwards, out of office and a dying man, reviled by those who had applauded him as Prime Minister, Chamberlain was living out the few remaining months of his life at No. 11, Downing Street. This is traditionally the official residence of the Chancellor of the Exchequer, and Mr. Chamberlain had used it when he held this office. In 1940, after Mr. Churchill became Prime Minister, he agreed to allow Mr. Chamberlain to live there still. I remember how, night after night, the bombs from the country he had so desperately and pathetically appeased sent him down from his sick-bed to the cold, damp, unprotected cellars of the house—only a few yards away from the underground Cabinet offices he had declined to visit at the height of his power."

For this first test, the main entrance was used, which still survives, at the back of the front hall in the Ministry of Defense, overlooking St. James's Park. The casual caller today sees only a wall with a small slit, rather like a letter-box, about five feet up. No letter was ever posted here, however; Royal Marines guards with tommy guns used it to cover the entrance against all comers. They had a wide field of fire, and would have proved almost impossible to dislodge without the use of gas. Behind them, on a small landing, patrolled a Grenadier Guardsman similarly armed. At the far side of this landing, a green-painted metal door, several inches thick, leads to "The Hole in the Ground." Never lavish, its furnishings at the time of Munich were crude indeed, and this legacy of Government parsimony lasted throughout the war. The King, who would sometimes visit the Map Room, and General Eisenhower, as Supreme Commander, with other war leaders and the Dominion Prime Ministers, were entertained in a small anteroom which served double duty as an Officers' Mess and a waiting-room. There was no proper bar. For such occasions, a few bottles of whisky and gin were kept in a cheap metal cabinet painted dark green.

Behind a drab curtain across this room was a sink where the glasses could be rinsed, dishes washed, and cold water drawn from a brass tap for mixing with the drinks. Round the walls stood a line of odd chairs on which the distinguished visitors sat, while awaiting their appointments with the War Cabinet. No two chairs were alike; a second-hand salesroom had been ransacked to find easy chairs with soft arms, wooden chairs without arms, even kitchen and dining-room chairs of a surprising variety. On the walls hung bad prints of the English countryside, and in one corner, a gigantic photograph of a Royal house party at Balmoral in the reign of Edward VII. The sad, soft eyes of kings whose countries no longer existed peered from under stiff naval caps and top hats at the men who were waiting to re-apportion their old frontiers. And every day came a regular reminder of the changed status of the monarch. At ten o'clock precisely, a beautifully maintained brougham, varnished in maroon, picked out in gilt, arrived from Buckingham Palace at the entrance in Storey's Gate with two liveried men. They were given a red leather box, stamped with the royal arms in gold, which contained the latest reports from all war fronts. Winter and summer, daintily picking its way past the bomb holes and the rubble of ruined streets, the magnificently groomed horse would bring the brougham back to the palace where the King, more secure in his people's affection than any British sovereign had ever been, would study the secret dispatches.

In the main corridor of "The Hole," between the anteroom and the Cabinet War Room, a wooden holder was fitted against the wall, resembling the departure indicator at a railway station. These boards gave news of the weather in London 150 feet above: COLD, SUNNY, or FINE. This contraption was worked either by Mr. Rance, or a Royal Marines corporal, and was necessary, because, with upwards of five hundred people living and working underground night and day all through the war, without any idea of conditions in the capital above ground, they had to know what weather to expect when they ventured aloft. To give warning of any exceptionally heavy raid, an electric bell would ring, and then Mr. Rance, as his private joke, would put up the board that bore one word: WINDY.

At intervals along the walls of the main corridor hung storm lanterns containing candles, in case the electric lighting system failed. In a brave attempt to add color and break up the drabness of distemper, these walls were decorated with charts showing decorations of the various Allies as they joined the fight. No chart could be found to cover one particularly bare spot, however, and someone had resurrected a huge poster of Lord Kitchener in 1915 making his appeal for five million men. With unintentional irony it was headed "A Memento For All Time."

At the bottom of the stairs, Hollis had fixed a further black metal door with screw-bolts that recalled the fixtures on a warship's water-tight doors. Three capital letters—"C.W.R."—here stood for "Cabinet War Room"; and underneath were two words: "Keep Shut." The Cabinet Room itself was about forty feet square under red painted girders, eighteen inches across. On one wall, facing the Prime Minister, hung a Navy League map of the British Empire with a small desk by it for a Service Secretary; nearby was a similar desk for a Civilian Secretary to use while taking notes. Tubular metal chairs with green leather unholstery faced a huge hollow table covered in black baize.

In front of every member of the War Cabinet a white blotting-pad with a newly sharpened soft pencil was placed every day, with a pad for notes and a small round tin for paper clips made out of a dull metal. At each place around the table were sets of old-fashioned punches, shaped like huge pairs of pliers, so that holes could be made in sheaves of papers and tags quickly inserted. All waste paper was burned, lest any secrets should be disclosed.

The Cabinet War Room had double doors which were always locked when a meeting was in progress. Outside, a sentry patrolled, and another armed sentry stood on duty between the two doors. He had a small, glass-filled aperture in the inner door reinforced by fine mesh netting, through which he could watch the Cabinet, but not hear any of their deliberations.

The Prime Minister's chair was of dark brown wood, with rounded arms, the only one of its kind in the room; the sort of chair the father of a suburban family might use at the head of the table, when presiding over Sunday lunch; a chair of character and authority. Mr. Churchill sat on an old cushion, which still remains.

"Late one evening, in May 1940," writes General Hollis, "shortly after he became Prime Minister, when a German invasion was expected hourly, Mr. Churchill came into the War Cabinet Room with Sir Edmund Ironside, then C.I.G.S., and some other close colleagues. The complicated system of pointers and floodlit maps had still to be installed around the walls, and the room looked cold and uninviting. A few electric bulbs burned under their white china shades, accentuating its emptiness, and the gravity of their faces. This bare, unlikely room underneath London was at that time the most important room in the free world. Cut into the living earth, beneath the roots of the world's greatest city, it was the heart and core of all resistance, and I remember thinking how Winston Churchill symbolized the flame and spirit of this resistance and gave it immortality.

"As he looked around the empty room, the poignancy of the moment touched him. No one could say what the news would be within the hour, whether or not England was even then under her first invasion in a thousand years. The little group stood for a moment in silence under the humming fans, each thinking his own thoughts, and then Mr. Churchill took his cigar out of his mouth and pointed at the homely wooden chair at the head of the table.

" 'This is the room from which I'll direct the war,' he said slowly. 'And if the invasion takes place, that's where I'll sit—in that chair. And I'll sit there until either the Germans are driven back—or they carry me out dead.' "

Behind Churchill's chair was an empty fireplace, devoid of any fire or heating equipment, for, of course, no chimney could be fitted, but the empty, cheerless, useless hearth contained a fire bucket which was strategically placed every day to catch Churchill's cigar-ends, which he always threw backwards over his shoulder, without looking where they landed.

In front of him, beyond his blotter, stood four inkwells, two red and two black, set in a glass stand that also held half a dozen red pencils. On his blotting-pad was a small pile of red labels marked "ACTION THIS DAY." By these was an ornately carved dagger, used as a paper knife. He would remark jocularly that he kept it there against the day Hitler would be brought before him.

In front of Mr. Churchill, where he could read it, and where he could also show it to any who might appear despondent, stood a piece of cardboard about eighteen inches by six inches on which some unknown had laboriously printed Queen Victoria's remark: *"Please understand there is no pessimism in the house and we are not interested in the possibilities of defeat: they do not exist."*

By the Prime Minister's side was an ordinary black Post Office telephone with a cardboard ring pasted in place of the dial, with the warning: "Speech on this telephone is not secret." On the table before him stood two carafes of water and a number of soft india-rubbers, stamped S.O. (for Stationery Office). Two clocks on the wall bore the twelve hours of night in smaller figures above the other numbers. One of Mr. Rance's jobs was to set all the clocks in "The Hole" every morning by Post Office time, which might be one or two hours ahead or behind Greenwich time, a humble, routine task in which the Prime Minister took an unexpected interest. When the clock in the Cabinet War Room failed one evening in June, 1943, for instance, Mr. Churchill reminded Mr. Rance that three years before he had told him *never* to let the clocks tell the wrong time. Mr. Rance was suitably penitent.

"The Hole in the Ground," in which about one in ten of all wartime Cabinet meetings was held, and the majority of Defense Committee meetings, shared several similarities with a warship. As well as the watertight doors, there were raised sills for other doors, and square, cream-painted metal ducts, about eighteen inches in diameter, for ventilation. Set high up in the four corners of the War Cabinet Room, small black revolving fans circulated this air, and one electric extractor drew off the dense fumes of cigars and cigarettes which clouded the atmosphere by day and night. Above the door, two unshielded bulbs, one red and one green, showed whether an air-raid or the all-clear was in progress. Here and there, on long lengths of flex, other bulbs hung low over the table in white china shades. The atmosphere was of makeshift simplicity and a rather spartan efficiency. All cables, for instance, were carried along the bare walls on porcelain insulators, instead of being concealed, so that current failures could be traced more quickly.

Along the walls of the corridors that linked the Cabinet War Room with the mass of other rooms leading one to another, extending under the Park, under Whitehall, almost up to Nelson's Column in one direction, and down to the Houses of Parliament in the other, thick brown pipes lay like shiny snakes. These were for the rapid transport of messages, which were folded in circular canisters, and blown along by compressed air, much as salesmen in old-fashioned departmental stores receive change from a central accounts office.

In the main corridor was a small door with a wooden plaque above it on which were painted two words: PRIME MINISTER.

Here, in a narrow room, the walls covered by maps, Churchill made all his famous war-time broadcasts. He sat in a swivel chair at a desk at the far end, under whitewashed oak beams. The desk was unusually wide, and leather-topped, with a blotting-pad, and two candles in simple holders in case the electricity should fail while he was speaking. At his hand were three press-buttons in a small piece of wood. One was labelled *Inspector Thompson,* his detective; the next, *Sawyer,* his valet; the third was for his secretary. The room contained a single bed with a table by it and an old-fashioned bedside reading lamp.

A few steps more down the corridor was the smallest room in "The Hole," little larger than a telephone box, yet important out of all proportion to its size. It was fitted with a lock taken from a lavatory door, marked "Vacant" and "Engaged," and contained a seat facing the wall, with a clock to one side. This clock had four hands: two black hands recorded Greenwich time, and two red ones gave the corresponding time in Washington, generally five hours behind London.

"To many of us working in 'The Hole in the Ground,'" says General Hollis, "this clock and the time lag became symbolic as the war progressed and, despite earnest efforts on both sides, a tragic gap grew steadily between Britain and America.

"As well as the difference in time, this clock recorded a difference in our national outlook. America was five hours behind us according to the clock, and seemed sometimes to be behind us also in sizing up the relative importance of issues at stake. American leaders tended to preserve a naive—and to us more cynical Britons—a frequently unfounded belief in the goodness of their fellow men in other nations.

"They credited everyone with their own good intentions, and Roosevelt seemed convinced almost up to the hour of his death, that the Russians and the Chinese Nationalists could be trusted, whereas the British, for so many years a great Imperial and Colonial Power, could not.

"Looking back now across the years when British influence around the world has shrunk, and Imperialism comes from either American oil companies or Russian Communist infiltration—what has happened in the countries that the wicked British Imperialists left? In Ceylon, there is near Communism; in Burma, it is an event if a train can run from Rangoon to Mandalay without being ambushed by bandits. Pakistan is under military dictatorship; so is Iraq and Egypt, and India stands on the edge of bankruptcy.

"Over these remnants of Empire the shadow of Communism and slavery grows daily darker. Much of this could have been avoided had the Americans been less hostile to what they regarded as British Colonialism.

"Thus the clock with four hands recorded not only the physical difference in time, but a difference in outlook that has since cost the world dearly.

"Here, though, I must make plain one fact. Differences of opinion were not by any means confined to Americans against British, or British against French. Any clash between personalities certainly overrode national or political frontiers.

"My own relations with the Americans were all most cordial, and Sir John Dill, who did magnificent work in Washington, formed the closest friendship with General Marshall and the other American Service chiefs.

"It is always easy to look back and to say what might have been, but differences or not, there can be no doubt at all that today the Anglo-American alliance is without any question the strongest force for good in the world today. We speak the same language, we have the same customs, the same faiths and the same belief in individuality, human dignity and personal freedom.

"Thus, if I seem to criticize the Americans sometimes, I do so in a friendly way, because without the breath of honesty when one feels a friend is making a mistake real friendship is of little worth.

"The clock with four hands may have shown differences of opinion as well as differences of time, but it is needful to remember that at least those four hands were on the same clock! We did and have so much in common that we must never forget these bonds that unite us." On the wall in front of the seat where Churchill sat when telephoning the President was fixed a small shelf covered in black baize. This contained the telephone, and a stencilled sheet of paper giving the difference in times between

America and England. A card hung on the wall, with instructions for those unused to speaking on the trans-Atlantic telephone—then something of a novelty—and advising them not to shout "as this will distort reception." From this tiny hutch, unnumbered feet below Horse Guards Parade, Mr. Churchill had a direct line to President Roosevelt in the White House.

"I remember very clearly," writes Hollis now, "How Churchill would suddenly decide to speak to the President, regardless of what hour it might be in Washington. In his slippers with pom-poms, wearing his magnificent mandarin dressing-gown embroidered in red and gold dragons, the belt pulled tightly round him, his cigar clamped like some miniature torpedo between his teeth, he would stump along the corridor towards the telephone. Even in the unhealthy light from the electric bulbs that lit the corridor, his complexion seemed cherubic and as pink as if he had just risen from eight hours' sleep.

"The rest of us would be pale and unhealthy in that wretched light, but not Churchill. Day and night, long hours, bad ventilation, nothing seemed to affect his appearance; he was outwardly as unperturbed as the waxworks image of him in Madame Tussaud's . . .

" 'Put the President on,' he would say in an imperious way, waiting, head down, glowering under his brows, impatient of a second's delay. . ."

This was sometimes easier to say than to do, for Roosevelt, while willing to speak to Mr. Churchill, was not at all eager to come to the telephone until he knew for certain that the Prime Minister was actually waiting for him at the other end. Churchill was also reluctant to be closeted in the tiny, airless telephone room, wasting time, while the President was being wheeled to the telephone in the White House. So Hollis and his opposite number in Washington would pretend that their principals were actually on the line, when in fact they were not.

"The President is just coming, sir," the American would say over the miles of cable. "He is picking up the telephone at this very moment."

Hollis, for his part, would claim that Churchill was at that same second stubbing out his cigar, and reaching for the instrument. Eventually they would make contact, Hollis would leave the smallest room, and the indicator on the door would turn from "Vacant" to "Engaged."

Sometimes, when Churchill was in a heated argument over this telephone, still puffing his cigar, the blue smoke would curl up underneath and above the door, so that to a stranger it would seem as though the whole place was on fire. When he came out, the room would be full of smoke, and for the moment it appeared as though he were stepping from the heart of a furnace.

"Churchill's energy was inexhaustible," writes General Hollis. "When the generals, who in many cases were still geared to the regular hours of peace-time soldiering, with leaves at stated intervals, and week-ends free, explained to him that he would have to run the war without them for a few days while they went on leave, salmon-fishing, shooting, or bird watching, his amazement left him temporarily speechless.

"He would look at them with astonishment from across his desk. At his most Pickwickian—spectacles down on his nose, mouth agape with amazement, cigar clamped between the first two fingers of his right hand on the desk in front of him, he stared with incredulity at this pronouncement.

"Leave?" he would repeat, as though he had never heard of the word, and did not understand its meaning. "Leave? Aren't you *enjoying* the war? H'm, h'm, don't you want to *win* this war?"[1]

Mr. Churchill also had a dining-room in "The Hole" which he rarely used, with a small bedroom for Mrs. Churchill. Their daughter, Miss Mary Churchill, sometimes slept here on a camp-bed when on leave from the A.T.S.

The furnishings in these rooms, and in all others used by ministers and service chiefs, were simple; a ewer for washing water

[1] Churchill, never over fond of generals since his early experience with them during the Boer War, and the First World War, is said to have remarked to a friend recently, regarding some of the controversial memoirs written by generals during the last few years: "In war, generals usually lead safe lives. But in peace, how very dearly they sell their lives!"

on a table, a china soap dish with a lid, a mirror on a stand. Instead of being the sleeping quarters of the British Prime Minister, Mr. Churchill's room was as plainly furnished as an attic in an Earl's Court apartment house. Indeed, the bedrooms were all so small and narrow that they resembled prison cells, and since the occupants' names were on a list for extermination or life imprisonment should Hitler succeed in invading this country, one officer remarked to Hollis: "We should be all right, if he only *jails* us. We've got used to living like prisoners in cells!"

Beneath this floor were further dormitories for men and women employed on secretarial and clerical duties. These were at such a depth beneath London that gigantic sewers, water pipes and gas mains ran through the rooms, and, should any of these have been cracked by a bomb explosion, the fate of everyone beneath ground would have been terrible. These rooms were overrun with great rats that scuttled over the beds, making the nights alive with the clatter of their claws. Lights burned continuously, for so far beneath the ground the hours of the clock had no meaning, and day and night lost all significance. Sometimes, however, a bulb would fail, and then, in the darkness of this lower level, entombed beneath the capital, the gloom would be pierced by pairs of bright green beads; the eyes of the rats.

"Mr. Churchill's servant in 'The Hole' was a Marine Ives, a redoubtable character," writes General Hollis. "He was very worried because the Prime Minister insisted on going upstairs and into St. James's Park at all hours of the night to watch the effects of air raids. Eventually, the risk of being hit by falling shrapnel was so great that we told him that on no account must he allow Mr. Churchill out after dark on such expeditions. These orders poor Ives did his best to carry out—by hiding Mr. Churchill's boots.

"Then, one night, at the height of the blitz, Mr. Churchill rang for him.

" 'Ives,' he said, sitting on the edge of his bed in his bare feet, 'Ives, my boots.'

"Ives, mindful of his orders, gave him all sorts of excuses; the boots were not there, they were being cleaned, mended, anything.

"At last Churchill stood up, hand outstretched for his boots. Out of excuses, poor Ives had to produce them. Mr. Churchill put them on and then addressed himself to Ives.

" 'I would have you know,' he said, 'That as a child, my nurse-maid could never prevent me from taking a walk in the Park when I wanted to do so. And, as a man, Adolf Hitler certainly won't.'

"Then he was off up into the night."

       *   *   *   *

Thus the scene was set, the stage was ready. To the heads of the Services meeting on the morning of Sunday, September 3, 1939, in the underground War Room, an air-raid siren blowing a false alarm opened the world's strangest, and most unnecessary war—that would see them all replaced as defeat after defeat overwhelmed British armies; a war in which the major battles began in "The Hole in the Ground," 150 feet underneath London; where the large strategic conception was planned by the men in the tubular chairs in the Cabinet War Room, pale and sallow from their premature entombment, breathing in the tired, used-up air of underground; hundreds, perhaps thousands of miles away from the campaigns they conducted. Day and night had no meaning for them, distance was eliminated by radio and the scrambled telephone. The commanders in the field added smaller touches of initiative to their plans, brush strokes on the final canvas of action and victory.

It was a war in which the messages flowed in and out of this strange warren of cellars by radio, by code message, by agent—even by pigeon. Some generals thrived on this campaign by remote control; others were broken on the wheel of events. Montgomery offered spirited resistance to the London directives; Wavell was told to do too much with too little; Auchinleck's chances melted away like the shifting sands on which he fought.

This war was conducted from underneath the earth, and won in the clouds above it. By the time it ended, the British Empire, which was so clearly and proudly delineated in red on the Navy League map on the wall of the Cabinet War Room, would be almost completely changed. And Poland, the country over which it ostensibly began, would be in far harsher bondage than when it started. It was a war for justice and freedom, to solve all problems, that solved none, and resulted in many great nations losing both freedom and justice.

"On Monday, September 4, 1939, as I prepared for the first Chiefs of Staff meeting, a uniformed messenger arrived from the War Office to deliver a special letter, for which I had to sign with due formality," writes General Hollis. "Thinking it must contain information of the gravest importance to be delivered with such ceremony, I ripped open the envelope. It contained the following intelligence:

Office Memorandum, No. 1897.
The following information is circulated for Office use only.
H. J. Creedy.

The War Office,
4th September, 1939.

OUTBREAK OF WAR

Notification has been received from the Offices of the Cabinet and Committee of Imperial Defense that a state of war exists between the United Kingdom and Germany with effect from 11 A.M. on 3rd September, 1939.

"Thus, one day late, the War Office went to war. . . .
"The three men who sat with Ismay and me around the oval table in the Conference Room that morning were completely dissimilar to each other in character and outlook.

"General Sir Edmund Ironside, Chief of the Imperial General Staff, represented the Army. In the First World War, while commanding an Infantry Brigade, he was inevitably accompanied by his brindle dog, which wore the Mons Star and a wound stripe. On the Sunday, he had wanted to get into his office in the War Office, but the front door was bolted and barred. Finally, someone came and opened the door—but the rest of the War Office staff were hiding in the cellars because of an air-raid warning!

"Sir Dudley Pound, First Sea Lord, was the antithesis of Ironside, physically and in outlook; a slight, elegant man, while Ironside was like a huge woolly bear.

"The third was Sir Cyril Newall, Marshal of the R.A.F., sharp, alert and very much aware that his Service, as the junior Service by several hundred years, had still to prove itself."

Ironside was taking his place as C.I.G.S. for the first time, because he had only been appointed to this post on the previous day, replacing Lord Gort, who became Commander-in-Chief of the British Expeditionary Force in France.

As they all sat down, a message was received that the Cabinet were about to join them, and there was some scraping of chairs because nobody quite knew where they should sit. Ismay thought it would be an idea for the three Chiefs of Staff to sit together, but Ironside would not hear of this.

"No, no," he said testily. "We should be like three naughty boys. That won't do at all."

Eventually it was agreed that if the Cabinet arrived each Service member should sit next to his own Minister; but, in the end, the Cabinet did not appear, and so the problem of precedence was forgotten.

At one of these early wartime meetings, Admiral Pound announced that he considered the main Fleet, based at Rosyth, was too vulnerable to attack.

"I've decided to send the Fleet to Scapa Flow instead," he said. "We're making the best provisions we can for boom defense."

This meant, in fact, that three old ships would be sunk across the wide mouth of the harbor in the hope of preventing any submarines from entering. The news did not cheer the other members of the Committee, because no proper defense existed at all at Scapa, and it seemed that the ships were being moved for no good reason. Something of the sort was said, and the First Lord replied: "Well, I must have *some* air protection for my fleet. All I've got is one antique flight based on Wick, the northernmost part of Scotland."

He turned to Newall.

"Can't I have any modern aircraft to defend my fleet in Scapa?" he asked in desperation.

Newall shook his head. He knew better than anyone how short the country was of aircraft.

"Sorry," he replied. "I just haven't *got* any modern aircraft to spare. I didn't even know you were moving the fleet to Scapa, anyway."

Ironside was sitting next to Pound, and had all the old soldier's antipathy to the new arm of the air. At this news he laid his huge hand on Pound's shoulder in sympathy, and beating it up and down for emphasis, spoke up for the Navy.

"Newall, here is this poor wretched *whale* Pound sitting in his harbor with his ships, and you won't darn well help him! It's *disgraceful!*"

Pound visibly quailed under this tremendous beating on his back; but from then on he kept the most inappropriate nickname of "Whale."

"Three blockships had been ordered to safeguard Scapa from submarine attack, but only two were in position. The third was still being towed from London as Sir Dudley Pound was speaking," recalls General Hollis. "The Treasury apparently refused to pay the price asked for the third ship when it was first needed, and then, when consent was finally given, the cost had risen because of mooring and other charges, and the Admiralty was forced to state its case again. This parsimony nearly cost us the war, for at the same moment as the Chiefs of Staff were discussing the defense of Scapa, Grand Admiral Doenitz in Wilhelmshaven was briefing a submarine officer of the German Navy, Lieutenant Gunther Prien, for an attack on it. Had this attack failed—as it should have failed had the blockships been in position and our defenses alert—Hitler, not at that time very sure of the value of U-boats, might have been convinced they had no great part to play in his plan for victory. The operation was, unfortunately for us, completely successful."

It owed some of this success to an apparently unrelated happening sixteen years previously, in 1923, when Admiral Canaris, the father of the wartime German intelligence system, found a job for an ex-naval officer, Alfred Wehring, as a salesman for a German watch-making firm. Wehring was later apprenticed to a Swiss firm, and then emigrated to England under the name of Albert Oertel. He settled in Kirkwall, near Scapa, working for several jewellers, and eventually opened a small shop of his own. He also kept a close eye on naval events, and warned his superiors in Germany that all the blockships were not in position. This was the last message Oertel did send, but it justified all his years of waiting and watching. Doenitz studied the report and put the proposition to Prien: could he take his U-boat right into the heart of the harbor? Prien decided that this was possible, and set off in U.47, lay up for a day in the Orkneys, and noted in his log: "From 22.00 to 22.30 the English are kind enough to switch on all the coastal lights so that I can obtain the most exact fix. . . ."

He sailed down to Scapa, which he found "disgustingly light. The whole bay is lit up." At night he entered the harbor, between one blockship and the shore—actually scraping an anchor cable—and fired his torpedoes.

Through his periscope Prien saw a car racing along the shore, and thought he had been seen by the driver, but he escaped safely. Within three days he was back in Germany, driving in triumph through the streets of Berlin to be decorated personally by Hitler for his achievement in sinking the *Royal Oak* (29,000 tons) with a loss of 833 officers and men.

This was bad enough for British naval prestige, but the economic consequences were disastrous. The success of this daring operation "considerably enhanced"[2] Hitler's opinion of his navy and its value in war. He gave Admiral Raeder "virtual permission for unrestricted naval warfare against British and French merchant shipping."[3] On the same day the Russians were helpful enough to place at his disposal a well-situated base west of Murmansk, where a repair ship would be stationed.

This gallant attack by Prien, who died on patrol two years later, presaged the Germans' all-out U-boat onslaught against merchant shipping, which reached its peak in the Battle of the Atlantic, and nearly cost Britain the war.

[2] Führer's Conferences on Naval Affairs, 1939.
[3] *U-Boats at War*, Harald Busch.

News of the attack reached London on a morning in October. Hollis was at a meeting of the Chiefs of Staff. The message for the First Sea Lord was written on a small piece of paper that had been folded over once. Hollis handed the paper to Sir Dudley Pound, wondering how he would react to this disaster, so soon after moving the Fleet to Scapa before its proper defense could be ensured. The First Sea Lord looked at the message and then laid it face down on the table in front of him. No emotion or flicker of feeling showed on his face. He turned to the Chief of Air Staff, who had paused in mid-sentence, and the discussion went on. Only at the end of the meeting, when all other points had been dealt with, did he mention the grievous news he had received.

* * * *

In complete contrast to the Spartan conditions of "The Hole in the Ground" was the Prime Minister's house at Chequers, "the most extraordinary place from which to run a war," writes General Hollis, "a beautiful country house with none of the official amenities of Whitehall. It was, of course, a most gracious building with lovely rooms and pictures, but it had only two telephones, and all the work had to be transacted in one small office.

"At Chequers dinner was usually served about 9 P.M. and lasted till about 11, when the company would repair upstairs to see a movie, usually one of the latest available. If it was my duty weekend at Chequers I used to hope that I could take a back seat at the film and perhaps have a little doze before resuming the work which I knew would be required of me later in the evening. I was seldom able to achieve this respite because the Old Boss, as we called Churchill, would say, "Come and sit beside me." From time to time he would leave the room to see if there were any telegrams, and on his return he would expect an accurate recapitulation of what had occurred on the screen during his absence. Dire was the castigation one would receive if the report was not particularly accurate or informative. Churchill's favorite film was *Lady Hamilton,* and I think I saw this no less than eight times.

"On one occasion, he decided to have a little practice in the

garden at Chequers with various kinds of firearms he had acquired. I rather fancied myself as a good shot, having been to
Bisley for many years, but he usually beat me and most of the
others as well. At one time he took a great fancy to playing on a
pin-table. He never played against anybody, but always wished
to beat his own record score. Like everything else he did he took
the game as an intense form of skill (which it wasn't), but I suppose it was a form of relaxation from the multitude of worries
which he had on his mind, but which never allowed him to lose
his sense of balance.

"Churchill was always a charming host, but in spite of this, and
the good food and hospitality, a week-end at Chequers as duty
officer was by no means a picnic, and work was the prevailing
topic from early morn to dewy eve. It was almost a relief to get
back to the more ordered routine of Whitehall . . ."

At Chequers the Prime Minister was quite capable of—and indeed accustomed to—carrying an apparently social evening up to
what most people would regard as their bed time and then switch-
ing to matters of state for two or three hours. His powers of concentration were not subject to orthodox time or place and vast
was the quantity of the work put in by himself, his Chiefs and his
subordinates on journeys to and from important conferences.

In August 1941, for example, during the journey which was to
end in the signing of the Atlantic Charter, the Prime Minister
spent the whole of the first day on the train carrying the party to
Thurso working under a shaded reading lamp, surrounded by
despatch cases and boxes of papers, his glasses down on his nose,
while two secretaries sat opposite with notebooks on their knees.

In the evening, however, his work over for an hour, Churchill
became more relaxed and at ease. Beaming around his compartment, full by now of aides and advisers, he announced that he
had drunk one half-pint of champagne on almost every night of
his adult life. Turning to Professor Lindemann, who was his scien-
tific adviser, he said, "Now, Professor, you tell us how much that
would add up to—work that out for us."

Entering into the spirit of the thing, Lindemann produced a

slide rule, made some calculations, and gravely announced: "Prime Minister, you have drunk enough to fill this entire compartment."

"Exactly!" said Churchill, beaming round again like an amiable cherub. "What did I tell you?"

Not all the calculations made by the "Prof," as Lindemann—later Lord Cherwell—was known, were to be so simple, and later on in the war he made a serious miscalculation. "At a Defense Committee meeting in December 1943," writes General Hollis, "when reports of a German rocket or pilotless plane were discussed, Lord Cherwell was not inclined to place much weight on them. He argued that we had only been able to fit 650 automatic pilots on our aircraft in a month, and he did not suppose that the Germans could beat this figure.

"Anyhow, of all such pilotless planes or flying bombs to be launched, Cherwell was sure that only a few would ever reach their target area. He reckoned that the payload of such planes would be half a ton, and forecast that the launching of each flying bomb would result in no more than one casualty in London.

"In actual fact nearly 1,500 flying bombs equipped with automatic pilots came over in the first twelve days of attack; in the last six days—June 21 to June 27, 1944—275 flying bombs hit London out of a total of 594 launched. The weight of their war-heads was one ton, not half a ton as he had calculated, and each bomb caused an average of four casualties.

"On the morning after the first flying bomb landed, the Cabinet met at the House of Commons, when the Prof. was at pains to remark that one swallow does not make a summer. But the explosions had irreparably damaged his arguments against such missiles. Rather sadly, Churchill said to him afterwards, 'Why did you stick your neck out so far?' "

*   *   *   *

The first winter of the phony war passed, and spring brought the German invasion of Norway and the start of the fighting war.

"A main objective of this German campaign was control of the iron ore route from Narvik, but the significance of the invasion was far deeper; it was launched as a deliberate test of Allied war strength—a plot to discover how far the Allies were actually prepared to fight a total war," writes Hollis. The German plan was brilliantly executed, and had been set on foot long before by undermining the Government with German spies and Norwegian traitors. Nothing was left to chance. Merchant ships full of German soldiers had already docked in Norwegian ports; corrupt officials had been bribed with promises of power under the new regime, and all subversive elements were cleverly co-ordinated to act in cities and military centers at precisely the right moment. Beach-heads were held for the German troops to land, while the Luftwaffe kept the skies clear of British planes.

The British landing in Norway to defend that country against the Nazis was an example of how not to carry out such an operation. Almost everything was left to chance. They could not land their out-of-date heavy guns and tanks, because of German air superiority; the Norwegians were hampered by equipment of even greater age and uselessness. Barely twelve thousand British troops were put ashore—and these landed through their own skill, perseverance and determination, rather than through any feat of planning, to engage ten times as many Germans. Their commanders complained bitterly of the lack of accurate maps, or information about beaches and fjords. One transport sailed without either a barometer or chronometer, and with the wrong charts. Several commanders were issued with plans based on woodcuts of Norwegian beauty spots dating back to 1860—which obviously bore no relation to those same places eighty years on. Some jetties had been described as possessing cranes and heavy tackle; other possible landing beaches were said to be suitable for small boats. In fact, the jetties had been abandoned half a century ago, and the beaches were strewn with great rocks, and were unapproachable by anything larger than a canoe. This lack of topographical intelligence played a heavy part in the defeat. As a result of this débâcle, the Germans gained Norway as a most valuable air and submarine base on the North Atlantic coast, and also won control of the iron ore, for a loss of only 1,300 men. Most important, they now knew that Allied talk of welcoming attack was bravado; they knew how weak we were, and so did the rest of the world.[4]

The general public, lulled for years by misinformation, pacifist wishful thinking, and political lies about our strength, were less philosophical. Chamberlain resigned and Mr. Churchill became Prime Minister of a National Government.

One of the first things that he did was to set up a committee under Mr. Attlee, the Lord Privy Seal, to investigate topographical beach intelligence so that such a fiasco could not occur again so easily. Planners in the Admiralty, Air Ministry and War Office prepared maps of all coasts likely to be affected by the war, and Mr. Churchill demanded to see these maps urgently, with their attached intelligence summaries. Hollis explained to him that the Admiralty and Air Ministry maps were already in his possession, with the necessary summaries; but that he was still awaiting the map and summary from the War Office.

"Pray send for it at once," said Churchill.

A runner was therefore despatched immediately and returned with the map enclosed in a large sealed envelope. Hollis tore it open and saw to his horror that under the title of "Beach Intelligence" someone had pencilled in two letters—"F.A." However, nothing could be done about erasing these letters, for the Prime Minister was waiting with increasing impatience for the document, and so Hollis took it into his room, and placed it on the table before him. As he saw Churchill's eyes drop on these two initials in the middle of a blank page, he explained with some embarrassment: "Prime Minister, these initials stand for 'Fanny Adams.' " Meaning, in Service slang, "Nothing at all."[5]

---

[4] "Those of us who had access to all the information available," wrote General A. E. (now Sir Archibald) Nye, when he was Vice-Chief of the Imperial General Staff four years later, "who knew the full extent of our unpreparedness, were fully aware that it would take at least two years from the outbreak of war before we could organize, train and equip an army proportionate to our needs, well knew that during those two years we were bound to be involved in a series of disasters. . . ."–The Times, May 8, 1944.

[5] Fanny Adams was a prostitute who plied her trade on the Portsmouth Road in the late eighteenth century. In a Royal Navy mutiny in Spithead at about the same time, one of the contributory factors was said to be the bad food issued to the ships. The rumor was put about by the predecessors of

Churchill looked up at him long and carefully from under his heavy reading-glasses.

"I trust, Hollis," he asked gravely, "that you are not suggesting that I should place any *other* interpretation upon them?"

---

the Communists that Fanny Adams, who had not been seen on her beat for some time, had been killed and carved up by a naval contractor and issued as meat to the mess decks.

This absurd theory had great support from the men, but was, of course, quite groundless. She had in fact been murdered and her murderer was apprehended; the gibbet from which he was hanged still exists at Hindhead, Surrey. It subsequently became Service slang to refer to "Sweet Fanny Adams," "Fanny Adams" or just "F. A." as an expression meaning "nothing at all."

CHAPTER 3

How often things occur by the merest
chance, which we dared not even hope for!
(Quam saepe forte temere Eveniunt quae
non audeas optare!)

TERENCE, *Phormio* 1

"The strangest example of chance playing a very helpful part in
the war took place in May 1940," writes General Hollis.

"To prevent Germany supplying their forces in barges we decided to bomb the 170 miles of canal that linked the industrial
town of Dortmund 50 miles east of Dusseldorf to the River Ems.
In those days, with the bombers at our disposal, this was a very
hazardous task—and one of the R.A.F. officers was awarded the
Victoria Cross for his efforts. We had also to be convinced that
the risk of losing valuable bombers would be balanced by the certainty that the canal would be put out of action. The only way to
do this was to bomb the locks so heavily that they would take
weeks to repair, and hope that by then the Dortmund-Ems canal
would have lost its strategic significance.

"The question now arose—where exactly *were* these locks, and
which were the most vulnerable? This seemed to me a formidable
proposition to discover in a hurry, but I was assured that the
Inter-Services Topographical Department, so recently formed at
Mr. Churchill's command, would soon provide the answers.

"As we came out of the War Room into the spring air of St.
James's Park, after reaching this conclusion, I saw a fellow Royal

73

Marines officer, Colonel Sam Bassett, walking towards the Admiralty. I thought nothing of this then, but afterwards I thought a lot about the chance that brought Bassett there at that particular time. . . ."

Colonel Sam Bassett had joined the Royal Marines as a boy in 1907, and was granted one of the first two commissions ever to be given to rankers. He fought throughout the First World War, and in the Eastern Mediterranean afterwards. Between the wars, he served in many countries, and had also been seconded for security work. On that May morning when he passed his old friend and comrade Leslie Hollis, he was on his way to see the Director of Naval Intelligence to whose department he had just been posted. He assumed that this meant he would be working as before in connection with security, and the idea that he might have a part of incalculable significance to play in the conduct of the war would have astonished him.

Bassett was shown at once into the D.N.I.'s office in the Admiralty, and was just about to be briefed on his new job when the telephone rang. The First Sea Lord wanted to see the D.N.I. urgently; he was making a tour of Naval fortifications between Dover and Deal and wished the D.N.I. to accompany him.

"Look, Bassett," the D.N.I. explained as he replaced the receiver, "I've got to go on some inspection with the First Sea Lord, but I'll see you as soon as I get back. You'll be working from Room 30 across the corridor. All right?"

"All right, sir," replied Bassett.

Since nothing had been said about the nature of his duties, he was sure he would be dealing with security as before, and he crossed the corridor to Room 30 and opened the door expecting to find the usual office furnishings: a desk with several telephones, one green to show it was a secret line; the locked filing cabinets, the smaller desk for an assistant. Instead, the room was completely bare, save for two chairs up against the far wall, and a telephone in a corner on a pile of old directories.

It was, in fact, a disused lavatory, and had been hastily converted into an office, but still lacked even a table or any office furnishings.

In one of the two chairs a young man sat reading the midday edition of an evening paper. He looked up with interest as Bassett entered.

"Good morning," he said cheerfully. "Can I help you?"

This was not quite the greeting Bassett had been expecting.

"I don't know," he replied truthfully. "Are you doing secret work—security?"

"No, I'm not," replied the young man, who went on to explain that he was an Oxford don, seconded to the Admiralty.

"If you're not on security, then what *are* you doing?" Bassett persisted.

"Well, actually I'm working on Norway."

"On *Norway?* Do you know Norwegian?"

"Oh, no, not a word. But I know Latin and Greek and some High German."

"I see."

The two men looked at each other, not quite knowing what to make of their meeting, and then the don handed Bassett half of his newspaper, which he accepted gratefully and sat down on the other seat.

As he began to read, the telephone rang on the floor beside his feet. He bent down and picked it up. A voice asked urgently over the wire: "Is that the Inter-Services Topographical Department?"

"No," replied Sam Bassett. "You've got the wrong number."

The voice appeared annoyed at this reply and gave the number of the extension he wanted. Bassett saw to his astonishment that this number was stamped in the center of his telephone dial. The man had the right number. Was Bassett in the wrong office?

"Fellow here asking for the Inter-Services Topographical Department," he said to the don, holding his hand over the mouthpiece.

"Yes, that's us, all right," replied the don calmly, looking over the top of his paper. "What does he want?"

Bassett uncovered the telephone.

"What do you want?" he asked.

"I want to speak to the chairman," said the voice.

Bassett replaced his hand.

"He wants the chairman," he told the don.

"Well, he's got him. You're the chairman."

"Me?"

Surprised and puzzled, Bassett spoke into the instrument again. "Chairman speaking," he said.

"And about time, too. Don't you know who you *are* yet? This is very important. You're to come along to the Air Ministry at three-thirty this afternoon for a special conference. I can't say more now over this open line, but you can bring one expert with you. See you there."

The instrument went dead, and Bassett replaced it thoughtfully and turned to the don.

"Now what *is* all this?" he asked. "I thought I was coming here for security work. Now you tell me I'm chairman of the Inter-Services Topographical Department, whatever that may be. And *this* fellow on the 'phone says I've got to go to the Air Ministry this afternoon at half past three for a conference. The D.N.I.'s off on tour so I can't ask him what it's all about. Can *you* help?"

The don replied that he had only been in the office for a day or so, and knew no more about things than Bassett. The simplest solution seemed to be to go to the meeting and try and clear up the whole position then. He'd come along, too, as the expert.

"Well, if we've got to go," said Bassett, "We might as well look the part. We must have a brief case each. I've never seen anyone attend an Air Ministry meeting without a brief case."

They therefore went down to the basement to see the Administrative Officer, and asked him to provide them with a pair of black leather brief cases. He roared with laughter at this request, and explained that every new department wanted brief cases and so there was naturally a great shortage. It would be quite impossible to furnish brief cases for them, unless they were indented for in the proper way. As the man was speaking, Bassett noticed that a small pile of black brief cases lay, covered with dust, in a corner of the room.

"What's wrong with those?" he asked.

"Oh, they're no use," replied the Administrative Officer. "The locks are broken. I can't open them."

"They'll suit us," said Bassett at once. "We've got nothing to put in them, anyhow!"

They blew the dust off a couple of these useless, empty cases, and took them along to the Air Ministry that afternoon. To their astonishment they discovered that the conference was being held under the direct orders of the Prime Minister with the highest priority and secrecy. Their task was to discover in the shortest possible time the exact position of the most vulnerable locks in the Dortmund-Ems canal so that they could be bombed. But time was their worst enemy; if they delayed, the French Army might collapse before the canal could be bombed.

"We need your report on the location of these locks absolutely as soon as you can let us have it," an Air Marshal explained to Sam Bassett. "You'll have a great deal of work to do on this, so you can leave this meeting and begin now if you wish."

At this, Bassett and the don withdrew, completely baffled, and with no idea how to set about the task that faced them. They had not been given the opportunity of explaining their position; the thought of failure and its consequences was appalling—and yet what could they do?

The two men stood on the steps of the Air Ministry, discussing their next move. Bassett declared that he would stand there until the Air Marshal left the conference, and then explain to him that this was all a mistake; someone must have bungled his posting, and the sooner the error was corrected the better. The don agreed that this was the wisest course, and so they waited, watching the cars and buses going round Aldwych. Soon the sun went in, rain began to fall, and a bitter wind blew down Kingsway.

"At my college there was a professor who went on a hiking or canoe trip to the canal just before the war," said the don slowly, turning up his coat collar. "Instead of hanging about here, why don't we go up to Oxford and see him? He may be able to help us, and even if he can't, at least we'll have a good dinner and a glass of excellent port. Anyway, it will be better than hanging about here in the rain."

This reasoning appealed to Bassett, and they hailed a taxi for Paddington.

That night, in the Senior Common Room of the don's college, after a dinner and port that were both as good as he had promised, they explained their predicament to the professor.

"I know very little about it myself," he told them. "But I've a friend who knows a lot. He was an engineer in the company that actually built the Dortmund-Ems canal. He's living at Cardiff now and I've got his address and 'phone number."

Bassett asked for a trunk call to be put through to Cardiff; the operator explained there was four hours' delay unless they had priority. Bassett said that they had priority. The operator said they needed No. 1 priority. Bassett said they *had* No. 1 priority. The operator was still dubious, but eventually they were put through, and in guarded terms explained that they wished to see any pictures of the canal that might be available.

The engineer promised to have all his blue-prints and photographs ready, if they could come and collect them from his home. By then the time was ten o'clock, and, with strict petrol rationing, no one seemed very confident that they would find a vehicle to take them to Cardiff. Eventually, the College Bursar prevailed upon the owner of a local taxi to run them there on the assurance that he would be well rewarded and his petrol coupons refunded —though from where none of them knew.

So they set off in the back of an old Austin, still clutching their useless brief cases, and by two o'clock on the following morning, after a wearying drive through the black-out with dimmed headlights, they were sitting in the engineer's study at Cardiff, all the plans of the Canal spread out on the table before them—with every detail they wanted about the locks. All that now remained was for them to return to Room 30 in London with the information they had gleaned. At that moment they met their first difficulty; the taxi owner refused to take them on to London: he said he was needed for a job in Oxford that same morning. He demanded the money and the coupons he had been promised.

The two men argued with him, explaining the urgency of their errand, and eventually persuaded him to change his mind, first by appealing to his patriotism, and then by promising him an extra fiver above his fare.

Just after six o'clock that same morning, unshaven and red-eyed, they were back in their bare office in Room 30 at the Admiralty, nearly eighteen hours after they had left. The don volunteered to type out the intelligence report while Bassett pasted pieces of brown paper with figures, arrows, distances and so forth on the blue-prints and the maps.

They then realized that their office contained neither typewriter nor paper, and when they went into neighboring offices to try and borrow them, they found that the typewriters were actually fixed to the tables and could not be removed. Eventually, they prised one loose and carried it back with a folder of paper to begin typing, balancing the machine on one of the two chairs in their room.

By the time the cleaners arrived at eight o'clock, the two men were half way through their task, and persuaded them to find two cups of tea. By noon, their report was complete, and in the hands of the Air Staff. That night the canal was bombed—and in the following six months it was successfully bombed sixteen times.

The officer in charge of Air Intelligence was delighted with their report; so was the Air Marshal. As they left the conference room on this second occasion, praise still warm in their ears, Bassett took him on one side and explained that during the previous night he had done some terrible things. First, he had made a number one priority call—without proper authority; next, he had hired a car for which £15 at least would be payable through public funds, including a £5 tip. Lastly, he had promised the man some petrol coupons. The Air Marshal roared with laughter at this confession and pressed a button on his desk.

"Give me £20 in notes and some petrol coupons," he told a junior officer who arrived at his summons.

From such unlikely beginnings there developed the Inter-Services Topographical Department which assessed and collected Intelligence on all kinds of targets and beaches round the world. By the end of the war this Department employed 6,000 people—

Americans, Norwegians, French and Dutch—of all three Services, and played a role of inestimable importance in every amphibious operation of the war, culminating in the success of the D-Day landings in Normandy in 1944.

"As the weeks passed," says General Hollis, "And the news from France grew steadily worse, it became clear that Sir John Dill should become Britain's principal military adviser—Chief of the Imperial General Staff—in place of Sir Edmund Ironside, who barely a month before had been unwise enough to say 'we should welcome an attack.'

"The news was broken to Ironside one evening in late May at Admiralty House, when he was telling a group of us—including the Prime Minister, Lord Beaverbrook, Sir John Dill and General Ismay—of his experiences during a visit to France."

While visiting the British Expeditionary Force, the house in which he had stayed was hit by a bomb, and the explosion tore away one entire wall from the room in which he was sleeping, but left the other three intact.

"What did you do?" asked one of his listeners, for this was before any blitz on London, and few knew from first-hand experience what it was like to be under aerial bombardment.

"I slept on," replied Ironside calmly.

At that moment, as the laughter died away, Churchill told him that it had been decided to appoint Sir John Dill in his place as C.I.G.S. Ironside could become Commander of the Home Forces in Britain.

General Ironside was not only a large man physically: he was large in character and heart, and accepted this news of demotion calmly.

"Prime Minister," he replied quietly, "If this is the job that, in your opinion, I can discharge to the best advantage, then I accept it gladly."

In November of the following year, Sir John Dill was, in his turn, superseded by General Sir Alan Brooke, who by that time was Commander-in-Chief, Home Forces.

"The world is upside-down for me," Dill told General John

Kennedy. "I am to go. The Prime Minister told me last night." On the night Dill relinquished the post of C.I.G.S., he saw Lord Hankey.

"I want you to understand," he told him, "that never under *any* circumstances will I serve under that man Churchill again."

Hollis was sorry to see him go, but as the British Chiefs of Staff representative in Washington Dill had a task of the utmost importance to discharge.

"When the Chiefs of Staff particularly wanted to dissuade Churchill from some course on which he was bent, they would cable Dill to see General Marshall and ask him to advise President Roosevelt to cable Churchill to say that what he wanted just could not be done![1]

"Churchill's love of unorthodox working hours, his relentless, tireless energy and ever-constant flow of new ideas had wearied him," writes General Hollis. "Dill was a man of extreme sensitivity, but in my view he reached the height of his academic career when he was Commandant of the Staff College at Camberley between the two wars. When he became C.I.G.S. he was a physically spent force, and being such a sensitive man was quite unable to stand up to Churchill's jibes about the Army and the alleged unwillingness of the generals to fight. But so great was his contribution and so highly did the Americans regard him that when he died out there he was buried in Arlington War Cemetery—the only Englishman ever to receive this honor. Dill was a perfect gentleman, who could not bring himself to reply forcibly to Churchill's caustic comments, and the impact of the recurrent disasters to the British Army undoubtedly impaired his morale and wore him down."

In the few weeks remaining before France fell, and Britain was left on her own, Churchill flew across the Channel four times to try and instil some resistance into the French leaders. They were visits which, to many of those who accompanied him, seemed unreal and phantasmagoric. It was often difficult to believe the magnitude of the issues at stake.

---

[1] "A strange way to handle the strategy of a war indeed! But it seemed to work. . . ." *Strategy and Compromise,* Samuel Eliot Morison, Little Brown.

"Discussing plans to save both British and French Armies with Reynaud, the French Prime Minister, Marshal Pétain and General Weygand for instance, on one of these visits," writes General Hollis, "We met in a *chateau* near Orleans, where the center of government had retreated. These deliberations, requiring constant contact and reference to London and Paris, were not aided by the fact that the only telephone available in the whole place had for unknown reasons been set up in the lavatory. And despite the urgency of the hour it was subject to all the delays, crossed lines and confusion of the French telephone system."

By far the most important of Churchill's visits took place on June 13th, when he made a final desperate attempt to persuade the French to continue the fight, if not in their own country, then at least from North Africa.

Before he left London, he cabled to Roosevelt: "It seems to me that there must be many elements in France who will wish to continue the struggle either in France or in the French colonies, or in both. This . . . is the moment for you to strengthen Reynaud the utmost you can, and try and tip the balance in favor of the best and longest French resistance. I venture to put this point before you, although you must understand it as well as I do."[2]

Roosevelt later cabled Reynaud that his government was doing "everything in its power" to help him, and added that he was "personally, particularly impressed" by his statement that France would fight on even in North Africa. But he refused to allow Reynaud to make public this message so it was almost valueless. Roosevelt feared possible repercussions in America, where it might affect his chances in the 1940 Presidential Election.

"I remember the morning well," writes General Hollis. "It was a warm day with the sun shining. I marvelled at the calmness and serenity everywhere, and then realized with a shock that hardly anyone in the crowds of people out in the sunshine—the clerks, the typists in their summer frocks, the shoppers—realized what fearful danger faced Britain. I was already so used to living near calamity that I had imagined others felt as I did. . . ."

[2] Winston Churchill: *Their Finest Hour.*

The forecast was for bad weather ahead, and the Air Staff suggested that the flight should be postponed.

"To hell with that," retorted Churchill. "I'm going, whatever happens! This is too serious a situation to bother about the *weather!*"

Churchill flew from Hendon in a yellow-painted Flamingo airplane. With him on this last trip went Lord Beaverbrook, Lord Halifax and General Ismay. A Flamingo was not the ideal aircraft to choose, but the choice was small. How safe this particular plane was can be judged from the fact that it blew up later in the war over London with some senior Russian officers as passengers, who were all killed. The Government was worried lest the Russians should suspect sabotage, but this suggestion—which would have been completely wrong—was never made. Such was the Flamingo into which the Prime Minister now climbed; and soon it glittered above London like a flame in the sky. At the south coast, it was joined by an escort of twelve Spitfires, which flew six on each side, in perfect formation, across the Channel. A few clouds drifted between the airplanes and the sea like puffs of cotton wool, but, as they approached the French coast, the passengers could see great black smoke clouds rising from harbors and oil installations blazing in the ruins of war.

The French Government had withdrawn still farther away from the fighting, and were established, albeit temporarily, in Tours. The pilot brought down the little Flamingo low over Tours airfield, which was heavily pock-marked by bomb explosions, made in a German raid on the previous evening. He had a most difficult task, but managed to maneuver his machine skilfully between the great raw holes. They were still some distance from the central airfield buildings; too far away to walk, and the pilot taxied the Flamingo towards the buildings, taking care to avoid the bomb craters, and also the twelve Spitfires that were swooping down to land all around them.

No one had come to meet Mr. Churchill; no one even seemed to be expecting him and his party. "Immediately one sensed the increasing degeneration of affairs," he wrote afterwards in *Their Finest Hour*. The whole airfield was deserted, but at least they had landed safely without any attempts being made to stop them —as French locals had dragged carts and even gates across the runways of Marseilles airfield to prevent British planes taking off to bomb Italy, lest such activities should bring reprisals on them. Even so, this lethargy at Tours was only slightly less deadly. The airfield buildings were also deserted, but eventually a Citröen car was found and, crammed into this, sitting on each other's knees, the party set off for the town.

The road was choked with refugees streaming away from the war; cars had mattresses and suit-cases and all kinds of household belongings lashed on their roofs; men and women pushed perambulators laden with food and clothes; others trudged with bundles on their back, or wheeled handcarts, barrows, bicycles, anything that could help them carry away a few possessions. All were going west, as far away from the advancing Germans as they could. Symbolically, Churchill's car was the only vehicle in all this turmoil going against the tide of retreat, towards the center of action.

Policemen, trying half-heartedly to control this chaos of defeat, blew their whistles and waved their truncheons frantically at cross-roads, but nobody took any notice, and it was only by driving straight through hedges, and taking to the fields and bumping over ditches that the Citröen eventually reached Tours, and drove to the Prefecture, which was said to be the center of such government as remained. No one seemed to know where M. Paul Reynaud, the Prime Minister of France, might be. Since it was then just after two o'clock in the afternoon, and the party had been up since the early hours and were hungry, when they saw a café nearby Churchill decided to have a meal while they waited. The door was closed, but they beat on it until the manager came to answer their knocking. They explained that they wanted luncheon.

The manager spread out his hands, palms uppermost, to explain the emptiness of his larder.

"We have no food, M'sieur," he said. "We are absolutely stripped. There is nothing to eat in the place."

He made as though to shut the door again in their faces, but they pushed past him into the empty restaurant, where places were laid at the tables. Advertisements for Pernod and Dubonnet lined the walls; a few flies buzzed in the listless air. The manager shrugged again at the oddness of the English, and disappeared into the back premises. No one cared whether the British Prime Minister and his colleagues had a meal or not before they began negotiations that might save the whole French Empire.

Eventually, a French Under-Secretary, M. Baudouin, who had heard they were there, arrived and produced a few meager eatables of his own, which he placed before them.

While they ate, he began to speak with a most dreadful defeatism, pouring out a terrible list of setbacks and blunders, and orders which had never reached armies. "France was lost, England was lost, all was lost"; such was the theme of his discourse. Nothing Churchill or anyone else could do now would save matters—although if America declared war on Germany immediately, it *might* be possible for France to continue the fight. He asked for Mr. Churchill's view on this. Churchill said that he hoped America would come in on the side of the Allies, but that, in any case, Britain would fight on. "He afterwards," wrote Churchill in *Their Finest Hour*, "spread it about that I had agreed that France should surrender unless the United States came in."

Churchill paid no attention to this Niagara of doom; he might have been hearing an actor declaiming the decline of hope in some stage tragedy, His mind was made up; the defeatism of others could not change his intention.

As soon as he had finished eating, he turned to M. Baudouin. "Now, where's your Prime Minister?" he asked.

The Frenchman shrugged his shoulders; it was impossible to say. The Prime Minister *should* be in Tours. He was driving in from the country. He was due at any moment. He would join them later. Clearly he did not care where Reynaud was. He was piqued at Churchill's indifference to his recital.

Mr. Churchill and his party left the restaurant and went over to the Prefecture where it was hoped to hold the conference with the French Premier, but he had still not arrived; nor did anyone seem to know where he was.

Churchill lit a cigar and announced that he would stay there until Reynaud arrived. His time was, in fact, limited, because he had to take off again for England in daylight, since the airfield had no lights, and the fearful condition of the runway made a take-off in darkness impossible.

The Minister of the Interior, M. Mandel, a former secretary to Clemenceau, was the only Frenchman there who seemed to believe in the Allied cause. He gripped a telephone in each hand, and, too busy to eat the chicken lunch which lay untouched on a tray on his desk, he was doing his best to cope with the inertia of defeat and failure, desperately beseeching his colleagues to fight on as long as possible to give the French Army time to withdraw to North Africa to continue the struggle from there.

At last, M. Reynaud came in and sat down. He was joined by M. Herriot, the President of the Chamber, and M. Jeanneney, the President of the Senate.

"Where are your other Ministers?" asked Churchill.

Reynaud shrugged.

"They'll turn up, perhaps," he said, looking around the small room; it appeared of no great consequence whether they arrived or whether they stayed away. His eyes kept twitching from left to right with a nervous tic. At every untoward sound from the street outside, he gave a quick little look towards the window as though he wished to find out what it could be, but yet feared to show his feelings. As the conference began, a light rain began to fall.

Reynaud had one main question to ask: "What would be the attitude of Mr. Churchill and the British Government if France asked for an Armistice?"

He mentioned the pledge existing between Britain and France that neither would sue for peace alone, but he argued that France had nothing left to give; she had weakened Germany considerably, but in so doing she had exhausted herself. She was not physically capable of further fighting.

"We know *you* will carry on," Reynaud told Churchill. "We would as well, if we saw any hope of victory. But we don't see sufficient hopes of an early victory. We cannot count on American help. There is no light at the end of the tunnel. We cannot abandon our people to indefinite German domination. We must come to terms. We have no choice. . . ."

"No!" said Churchill. "There *is* a choice. Fly to North Africa and carry on the fight from there. We will help you with ships and transport in whatever way we can."

"What if we can't get to North Africa?" persisted Reynaud.

"In that case, move your navy to England or the French West Indies or even America," replied Churchill. "But whatever you do, don't make an Armistice now."

At the beginning of the conference he had lit a cigar, but it soon went out and he made no attempt to relight it or remove it from his mouth, as he spoke with a tremendous urgency, in a Churchillian mixture of English and schoolboy French. Those who were with him in the room declared afterwards that it was the most impassioned oration he had ever made.

Churchill explained that Britain quite realized the enormous sufferings that had overtaken France, but his only aim was to defeat Hitler. The French must hold on until Roosevelt replied to his message—and a reply would come very shortly.

"At all events, England will fight on," he said. "She has not, and will not alter her resolve; no terms, no surrender. The alternatives for her are death or victory. . . ."

Reynaud still appeared unconvinced; his little eyes darted right and left as though seeking a physical escape from the problem; a way out that the others had somehow missed. Standing by the door, watching this struggle of wills, stood a tall, austere French officer, visibly moved by the passion of Churchill's plea to fight on, and full of barely concealed contempt at the lack of response from his own Premier and his colleagues. This was General de Gaulle, whose own mind was already made up.

At last Churchill finished his speech, and suggested that the British group withdraw to the garden of the Prefecture while the French considered whether to fight on or to surrender. The garden was shabby and unkempt, with the flower beds thick with weeds; the rain had stopped and the stone paths were steaming in the sudden sunshine. They walked to and fro in this muddy confined space, discussing the situation, and when they returned,

Churchill pointed out to the French Cabinet that Britain could not agree to France making a separate peace with Germany. He suggested that Reynaud should send a further appeal to President Roosevelt, and this Reynaud promised to do. He also gave his word that France would hold on until Roosevelt replied. Herriot, with tears running down his cheeks, and Jeanneney also made a great appeal to continue the fight. Both were anxious to fight on, but no satisfactory assurance was forthcoming from the French Prime Minister. Churchill saw that further pressure on him was useless, but he put forward one last plea.

"You've got 400 Luftwaffe prisoners of war," he said. "Hand them over to us. Our pilots shot down most of them, in any case, and we need them so that they can be an assurance that our own R.A.F. men will not be roughly treated by the Germans. At present, we have no German prisoners at all, but they have captured a number of our pilots."

Reynaud agreed to this but he had not the power to implement his promise; when France fell, the Germans were liberated, and, as Churchill has written in *Their Finest Hour*, "All became available for the Battle of Britain and we had to shoot them down a second time."

Before Churchill left he arranged to fly over to France on the following Monday for a further joint Cabinet meeting. He could delay his departure no longer for already the daylight was limited. As his party went out to the cars that now waited for them in the courtyard, people who had heard they were there surged forward to see them. They might have been visitors from another world; in a sense they were. They fought their way through, and suddenly, above the roar and clamor of voices raised in anguish and despair, a woman's voice came clearly.

"Mr. Churchill! Mr. Churchill!" she called. "I wish to speak with you!"

Churchill pressed on to his car, his hat rammed on his head, cigar clamped in his mouth, pretending not to hear or see her.

She called again: "Mr. Churchill, my country is bleeding to death. I have a story to tell and you *must* hear me. You must hear my side of it. You must!"

Still Mr. Churchill gave no hint that he had either seen or heard her, and he shut the door behind him, completely ignoring the pleas of the Comtesse de Portes, Reynaud's intimate friend, whose counsels and pro-German views had helped to bring the French Prime Minister and France to this sad plight.

The cars of the British party forced their way through the crowds, hooters blowing continually, and by the time they reached the airfield, the twelve Spitfires were already airborne, flying round and round above the pock-marked field in the mild afternoon sky. All the while, Churchill never ceased pleading with Reynaud to change his views, giving him promises of aid without restraint if only he would stay in the fight.

"*Don't* give in, don't go over to the enemy," he kept repeating. "Fight on!"

Reynaud would have liked to assure him that he would do so, but it was clear that he could not carry his Cabinet; he was politically impotent.

At last an officer reached Mr. Churchill with the warning that they would have to be off.

"If we don't leave soon, Prime Minister," he explained, "The Spitfires won't have enough petrol left to reach the coast."

Churchill nodded, and made as if to leave—and then turned back to Reynaud, urging him once more never to give in. The Spitfires wheeled above them in the sky, while petrol and time alike ran low. Still Reynaud would show no answering spark of spirit or defiance, and at last Churchill and his colleagues climbed aboard their yellow Flamingo. Behind them, on the edge of the runway, stood the handful of men who had come to see them go. Churchill waved to them, and then as soon as the plane was airborne, he sat back in his wicker seat, pulled out a black scarf, and wrapped it round his eyes. Almost instantly, he was asleep.

At the British coast, the Spitfires went down, and the little Flamingo flew on to Hendon. The party drove back to London in silence.

Later, at a meeting of Ministers, Mr. Churchill gave a brief account of his journey, ending unexpectedly with his sight of the Comtesse de Portes.

"So," he said sonorously, "Paul Reynaud returned to Tours and the Comtesse de Portes." He paused and added: "She had comfort to give him that was not mine to offer."

At six o'clock on the following Sunday evening the same colleagues assembled at Downing Street to fly to France for a further joint meeting with the French. Churchill was in bed, for it was his habit to have a nap every afternoon: he was about to get up and prepare for the journey when the telephone rang. The news was that Reynaud was out of office: Marshal Pétain was now Prime Minister of France; he declined to receive Churchill.

At two o'clock that morning, after long and frustrating delays, Mr. Churchill finally managed to reach Marshal Pétain—by then in Bordeaux—on the telephone, and spoke very strongly to him, trying to infuse into his old bones the spirit of attack. But he had no success.

"It was the most violent conversation I ever heard Churchill conduct," says General Hollis. "He only spoke so roughly because he felt that anger might sway the old Marshal when nothing else would. But, like the journey, it was all in vain."

Within four days, France was out; Britain was on her own, and four years passed before Churchill and his colleagues again returned to France.

CHAPTER 4

9. And Moses said unto Joshua, Choose us out men, and go out, fight Amalek: tomorrow I will stand on the top of the hill with the rod of God in mine hand.
10. So Joshua did as Moses had said to him, and fought with Amalek: and Moses, Aaron and Hur went to the top of the hill.
11. And it came to pass, when Moses held up his hand, that Israel prevailed: and when he let down his hand, Amalek prevailed.
12. But Moses' hands were heavy; and they took a stone, and put it under him, and he sat thereon; and Aaron and Hur stayed up his hands, the one on the one side, and the other on the other side; and his hands were steady until the going down of the sun.
13. And Joshua discomfited Amalek and his people with the edge of the sword.

Exodus, Chapter 17

"It has always seemed to me that, if Churchill could be cast as Moses, holding up his hands to encourage Britain in the fight, then the two men to whom he turned most in times of crisis and who always helped and enheartened him, were Lord Beaverbrook and General Ismay," writes General Hollis.

"Except for this closeness to Churchill and a complete dedication to whatever task was in hand, the two men were utterly unlike each other. Ismay was born in India, the son of a High Court judge, and had been a good polo player and pigsticker and a professional soldier all his adult life. Beaverbrook, born in Canada, the son of a Presbyterian Minister, shrewd and often ruthless, made himself a millionaire by the time he was thirty, and enjoyed the freedom and independence bought him by his wealth and power as a newspaper proprietor. Both were an enormous comfort and inspiration to Churchill, as became abundantly clear in 1940. . . ."

The fearful state of the British Army, engaged, not for the first time in its history in a fighting retreat, aroused the sympathy and admiration of the world, but such emotions, while worthy, were of little practical help. In Whitehall, those who knew most, feared most. The Army's only hope seemed to be for some miraculous happening, or an inspiring gesture that could infuse the retreating troops with initiative and the desire for attack. This would crack the legend of German invincibility, and if the line could be held the French might keep on fighting.

Mr. Churchill was still conducting the Government and the war from his old room in the Admiralty, for he had not the time to move into Downing Street. Ismay and Hollis were both seeing him several times every day, and so many others also sought interviews with the Prime Minister that chairs had been set up in the corridor outside his rooms. Here generals, admirals, and ministers sat awaiting his pleasure, or paced up and down the strip of red carpet impatiently, looking at their watches. And still the lines of colored pins on the map of France in the Map Room marched steadily and ceaselessly towards the sea.

Late in the last afternoon before the evacuation of Dunkirk began, General Ismay suddenly turned to Hollis.

"I'm just going over to see the Prime Minister," he said casually.

Hollis nodded. They made these visits so frequently that there was nothing in this news; and yet for the very reason that the visit *was* so commonplace why should Ismay mention it at all? For a moment Hollis felt surprised, and then some more documents arrived, and he put the whole thing out of his mind.

These new papers occupied him until about midnight, and since he had not been out of the building all day, and there now appeared a temporary lull in work, he thought he would walk over to the Admiralty himself. He turned to mention his intention to Ismay, and saw that his desk was still empty. This again was unusual, for Ismay's hours were as arduous as his own—from 7:30 in the morning until one or two o'clock the next morning—and so he decided to see whether his friend had finished his interview with the Prime Minister.

The usual cluster of people waited outside Mr. Churchill's door, and the air was heavy with tobacco smoke. Under the dim electric bulbs, the officers looked pale and dull with fatigue. Hemmed in by black-out curtains, day and night had little meaning; it could have been any hour of the twenty-four. Hollis stood apart from the rest in the corridor, waiting for Ismay. Now and then dispatch riders would arrive, faces gray with dust, deliver their messages and leave. The noise of their motorcycles accelerating on the cobblestones of the Admiralty courtyard echoed from the gray walls like distant machine gun fire.

At last, about 12:30 A.M., the door of the Prime Minister's room opened and General Ismay came out. He appeared more cheerful than he had been earlier in the day, and there was about him an air of determination and buoyancy. He walked swiftly past the waiting officers and as he came to the door, Hollis touched him on the arm. Ismay looked surprised to see his colleague, and as Hollis opened his mouth to speak, he held up his hand to stop him.

"No, you're not going to prevent me going, Jo," he said at once. "I've just persuaded the Prime Minister to give me permission, and I'm going to go right through with it. Nothing anyone can say will make me change my mind."

Hollis had no idea what he was talking about.

"All right," he said. "If that's what you feel, I'm sure it's the best thing."

At this, Ismay's attitude eased slightly, and together they walked down the steps and out into Whitehall. The night was still warm, and sentries stood rigidly by sandbags that had spilled their sand on to the pavement. The moon showed up the strips of sticky paper that criss-crossed on the office windows to minimize the risk of splintered glass in a bomb explosion.

Something in the night air, with all the rush of London gone, put both men at peace, despite the urgency of the hour and the prospects of further bad news from France. Hollis lit a cigarette.

"Now what's all this about, Pug?" he asked easily.

Ismay stiffened.

"It's agreed," he repeated. "I'm going tomorrow."

"Where?"

"To France," replied Ismay quietly. "I'm flying to France. All my friends are out there fighting, either facing death or capture. That's where my place is, too. I think I might be able to do some good. Anyhow, I've talked Churchill into agreeing to my plan."

"Let's hear about it," said Hollis, and General Ismay began to expound the most astonishing proposal Hollis had heard. At dawn on the morrow, Ismay, who was then fifty-six years old, proposed to fly over the battlefields where the British troops were fighting their way back to the coast. He would parachute down onto the headquarters of the British Expeditionary Force—and fight with them. He felt that his sudden and unexpected arrival from the skies, plus his ability to size up the situation on the spot—instead of having to make do with the reports of other men—would put what he called "heart and hope" into the staff at Headquarters as well as into the fighting men. Such an example might make the difference between falling back further, or holding the line until reinforcements could be sent.

It was a suggestion in the great Army tradition of personal bravery and self sacrifice, and all the more courageous because it would almost certainly result in General Ismay being killed or captured.

"I tried to put the drawbacks to him as we walked together," writes General Hollis. "First, I felt that no matter how recent his reports of the situation in France might be when he left England, by the time he arrived above France, seventy miles away, the whole situation was likely to have changed. We had no static line as in the First War, nor had we any means of finding exactly where our Headquarters would be from one day to the next. We might pinpoint it in one place, but within twelve hours it could be thirty miles away. At best, General Ismay would be captured. At worst, he would be killed. He was irreplaceable, and much as I admired his courage, I felt it my duty to try and dissuade him from this mad scheme."

The argument raged between them as they paced up and down Whitehall. At first, Ismay refused to be dissuaded; he would not consider the danger to himself, but eventually, and with the greatest reluctance, Hollis made him promise to sleep on his proposal.

It was as well for Britain that he was thus persuaded, for in the years ahead, General Ismay became closest to Churchill of all his military colleagues. His contribution to victory—which would have been cut short immediately had he insisted on his plan—was immeasurable.

"The fruits of his experience would all have been lost had he been obdurate and refused to be convinced that his place lay at home," says General Hollis.

"The evacuation of Dunkirk followed immediately, and its success in bringing back 360,000 British troops to fight again owed something to the ubiquitous Colonel Sam Bassett of the Royal Marines and his newly formed Inter-Services Topographical Department.

"The First Sea Lord urgently wanted details of all the beaches of Northern France. He asked for routes so that the British Army could reach them by the quickest way, avoiding major towns and bad traffic intersections. He also demanded the fullest information on coves and inlets on the north coast of France where small vessels from England could lie up."

The routes were speedily dispatched by air to the various force commanders, but details of the beaches were more difficult to find. So inadequate was the Intelligence on these that Bassett, who by then had a staff of three surveyors, visited travel agencies, asking for brochures that would describe French beaches in detail. His request was received with astonishment, for it was obviously impossible for anyone to spend a holiday in France.

All that the agencies could supply were colored pamphlets of Le Touquet and Biarritz; they had no information about the depth of water, or the height of the tides. Bassett therefore suggested that three fast Navy ships should be sent immediately to the northern coast of France, each with a surveyor aboard. Each examined a section of the coast, and reported on the best site for a mass evacuation. Thus Dunkirk and the other points of evacuation were selected.

"We had hardly any anti-tank guns or ammunition and very little field artillery in the country to repel the Germans should they invade us," recalls General Hollis. "I remember that when Mr. Churchill visited the beaches of St. Margaret's Bay, near Dover, the officer in charge of the anti-invasion defenses explained rather apologetically that he had only three anti-tank guns in the whole brigade, which covered five miles of this coast nearest France, with six rounds for each gun. He wondered whether he was justified in firing one of these six to show the men how the gun worked.

"Winston replied that the fire should be held "for the last moment at the closest range."

"We looked out from Dover Castle across the Channel to France, and curiously enough this was almost the same day that Hitler was looking from the coast of France towards the Straits of Dover. Hitler's 'Operation Sea-Lion,' the invasion of England, never materialized, but the chances are that had he taken the risk the Germans could have landed large forces on the south coast of England with very little opposition. This Churchill knew, but it did not disturb his resolution. On the way back to London he told me that if the Germans crossed the Channel, those who were not drowned before they landed 'nous les frapperons sur la tête. . . .'"

So rudimentary were our defenses that some harked back to the Middle Ages and beyond. The London, Midland and Scottish Railway, for instance, made huge catapults that were able to fling a four-gallon petrol tin for a short distance, when it would explode. The Bank of England used its printing works to construct a 1940 version of the Roman ballista which could throw a Molotov cocktail (a home-made petrol bomb) for 100 yards. This instrument was known as "Larwood," after the Nottinghamshire fast bowler.

But the next phase of the battle, and the most important so far, was won not on land but in the air.

On July 2nd, an Oberkommando der Wehrmacht order, signed by Keitel, stated: "The Führer and Supreme Commander has decided . . . that a landing in England is possible, provided that air superiority can be attained and certain other necessary conditions fulfilled."

Hitler planned to complete this "Operation Sea-Lion" by the middle of September, for, as he told the heads of his three Services in July, "the weather in the North Sea and in the Channel during the second half of September is very bad, and the fogs begin in the middle of October. The main operation must therefore be completed by September 15th. . . ."

But these operations, against what he admitted was "a defensively prepared and utterly determined enemy," would only be possible if Germany had air supremacy. Everything hinged on victory in the air. Reichsmarshal Goering promised Hitler that the Germans would control the air, for the Luftwaffe would destroy the British airfields in Kent and Sussex and so establish domination over the entire English Channel.

The Battle *of* Britain was therefore the first—and decisive—round of the Battle *for* Britain. The Germans could not invade until they won this battle; Britain could not stay free if she lost.

The Royal Air Force victory in that amazing and immortal summer saved Britain from German invasion. Hitler, thwarted, turned his attention to the East and attacked Russia, and the danger of invasion passed—although not until February 13, 1942, did the German troops originally earmarked for the invasion of England finally stand down. Ever cautious, the British Invasion Committees remained in force for more than two and a half years following this, until November 1944, five months after the Allied invasion of France. Then the road blocks were finally removed and railway stations were at last allowed to reveal their names. But "the invasion of England was never again contemplated after the end of September 1940."

Goering seemed to be right in promising Hitler aerial supremacy over the Channel, for when Mr. Churchill became Prime Minister in May, Britain only had *five* airplanes in the Storage Units. That these five were increased within as many months to

704 first-line fighters with 289 in reserve stands to the eternal credit of one man who found his hour and saved the nation: Lord Beaverbrook.

The sequence of tragedy and ruin, had Beaverbrook failed to produce these planes to hold the Luftwaffe, would have been catastrophic and irremediable.

First, England would have been invaded; next, the Japanese would have seized Hong Kong, Malaya, Borneo and Burma at least a year earlier than they did—and probably India as well. Australia and New Zealand would then have been on their own with very little to save them. The Japanese, swollen with such easy conquest, would probably not have attacked America at Pearl Harbor, for there would have been no need to do so, and America would therefore have still remained a technical neutral.

Had the Japanese decided to attack her, however, America, with a regular Army of only 75,000 men, an Air Force a third of this size and a one-ocean Navy, would have fared even worse than she did in December, 1941.

Next, British intervention in Greece in that spring, which delayed Hitler's attack on Russia, would have been impossible. Moscow would almost certainly have fallen to the Nazis, and the world would have been faced with the Axis in control: Germans in Moscow, Italians in charge of the Mediterranean, Japan predominant East of Suez, and Fascists in South America and elsewhere ready to seize power. That this picture remained only a nightmare is due to the Royal Air Force and to Beaverbrook's organizing genius. This is his abiding triumph and the memorial by which he will be best remembered.

How did he perform this fantastic task? By a ruthless program of improvisation and drive.

When Lord Beaverbrook became Minister of Aircraft Production in May 1940, he ordered the immediate "cannibalization" of all wrecked machines, for between 1,500 and 2,000 British planes had already been shot down or had crashed in these islands, and were written off as being beyond repair. Beaverbrook had them broken up, and from every two or three ruined planes one airworthy machine was constructed.

The Air Ministry, with true bureaucratic caution, had provided enormous stocks of spares in many parts of Britain against possible damage or loss. Beaverbrook ordered that these spares should be immediately assembled into airplanes. Critics complained that there would now be no spares for the planes, should they be shot down. But the argument was academic, and answered itself: if Britain had no planes, there would be no *need* for spares.

Between the wars, Beaverbrook had built up a powerful—and frequently imitated—newspaper chain largely by the power of his own prodigious personality and his ability to pick men of drive and ability. He now used the same technique in the Ministry. His great theme was improvisation for success and he kept three texts on display in his room. The first read: "Organization is the enemy of improvisation"; the second, "It is a long jump from knowing to doing"; the third, "Committees take the punch out of war."

"Beaverbrook's policy of speed and improvisation brought results at once," says General Hollis. "If Churchill was the master mind, then Beaverbrook was the master craftsman. Without his contribution in 1940 as Minister of Aircraft Production and later as Minister of Supply—when he increased the number of tanks being made from 82 a month at the time of Dunkirk to 598 a month in barely a year—there would have been no victory for Britain."

This policy was illustrated again when aluminum for plane construction became very scarce—despite his appeals to housewives to surrender unwanted aluminum pots and pans for a more glorious purpose. Britain had little aluminum, but plenty of wood; a *wooden* plane, the Mosquito, was built, and became one of the greatest of our wartime fighters. The Air Ministry refused to sanction its construction, so Beaverbrook on his own initiative gave an order for fifty to be built immediately. The Air Ministry complained that it had lost confidence in *him;* he retorted that he had never had *any* confidence in them!

Before his appointment some aircraft factories excused their poor production figures on the grounds that bottlenecks in the supply of bits and pieces were restricting their output. Beaverbrook made every aircraft manufacturer submit a list of these bottlenecks every night. He had a corps of dedicated men for the sole purpose of clearing them up.

"In some cases he found that aircraft manufacturers had really offered this excuse to cover their own inefficiency," writes Hollis. It shielded them no longer.

"So many complaints were made about Beaverbrook's high-handedness at the Ministry of Aircraft Production that he was called into the Committee Room at the House of Parliament before representatives of all the Parties, to attend an inquiry into the state of the British aircraft industry, and the large number of dismissals that occurred after he took over.

" 'What exactly *is* wrong with the aircraft industry?' someone asked him. Beaverbrook replied frankly: 'Everything is wrong with the Ministry of Aircraft Production and the aircraft industry—except production. That's just fine.' "

Mr. Churchill gave him complete and virtually dictatorial powers, and protected him from the anger of other less forceful Ministers who complained that he was interfering with what had hitherto been their concern. The Prime Minister's backing meant everything to him, for as he always admits, without this he would have found it impossible to do his job. Soon his Ministry became a showpiece. Neutral statesmen and leaders who were wavering between supporting Britain or the Axis toured his factories, and were so impressed that they went away reassured of a British victory.

Mr. Churchill used to carry with him a statement of the aircraft output for the preceding week. At any show of pessimism he would produce these figures which always helped to dispel the gloom.

Beaverbrook's only criterion was whether a man was efficient at producing the planes or the parts he had to produce. If he felt he was not, then out he went: no one had a second chance. Some people objected to this cavalier treatment. Nevertheless Beaverbrook remained. He was too valuable to lose, for when he became Minister for Aircraft Production, Britain had more pilots than airplanes. By the end of the year, the country had more planes than pilots. Beaverbrook therefore told the Air Ministry to stop complaining about the shortage of airplanes—and get on with their job of training more aircrews.

"For all Beaverbrook's tremendous achievement in producing airplanes, there was little to praise in the way he rode roughshod over everyone," says General Hollis. "He never carried an oil can. He did as he liked, when he liked. He once promoted an Air Commodore to Air Vice-Marshal—over the heads of fifty-five more senior Air Commodores. This sort of behavior did not make for happiness, but it was the way he worked, and the end justified the means. . . ."

Besides spurring on the British aircraft factories, Beaverbrook also bought many airplanes in America, but here difficulty lay in transporting them to Britain in time to be of service. Sometimes a month would elapse before a plane would arrive in Britain from America, and often the losses caused by German submarines were very high. Lord Beaverbrook therefore suggested that the planes should be *flown* from America. Again he clashed with the Air Ministry, who put up enormous opposition to this, explaining that airplanes of this type had never flown the Atlantic before; that the weather was wrong; and the whole project was doomed to failure. They prophesied that it could not be done.

But it was.

Of the first group of six planes to be flown over, all landed safely. Shortly afterwards, however, one plane was lost which was carrying a passenger, Sir Frederick Banting, who had helped to discover and develop insulin, and who was a close friend of Beaverbrook.

Official vindication of this policy of ferrying planes came after Beaverbrook left the Ministry of Aircraft Production. The Air Ministry at once seized the ferry service and from then on ran it themselves!

But although the results were inspiring they were obtained at the cost of much controversy behind the scenes, and especially between Beaverbrook and Ernest Bevin, who were alike enough in their rugged individualism to be often at loggerheads.

All through that summer—June, July, August and September— the aircraft factories worked tremendous hours, for as Churchill said in a broadcast on May 20th, "The hours of labor are nothing compared with the struggle for life, honor and freedom." Weekends, evenings, all were working hours, and as the planes and guns with which to resist invasion by air or sea poured out in ever-increasing numbers, so the bitterness grew between these two Ministers.

"Their quarrel turned initially on the use of manpower," says General Hollis. "Bevin maintained that the high rate of production of factories was falling because the men were tired through working seven days of the week for so long. Beaverbrook agreed that this might be so, but pointed out that Bevin was ignoring the fact of constant bombing on the factories, which were relatively unprotected.

"Bevin, who had grown up in the Trades Union movement, and who was a very great negotiator, wished to apply all the Trades Union rules and privileges to the use of labor in the factories. Beaverbrook disagreed. He felt that the moment when invasion was expected was not opportune for set working hours with half-days and week-ends off. He wanted to use the factories all-out to the limit, until the danger of invasion was past. Also, he seemed to delight in annoying Bevin, as a picador goads a bull."

Bevin replied by accusing him of breaking the Factory Acts— and even proposed to launch a prosecution against him, under the authority of these Acts.

"It was against this background of anger and disunity—and at a time when Hitler's plans to invade us were at their height—that the most fantastic letter I ever saw in all my career was produced in the Cabinet Room," General Hollis wrote later. It came from Sir Horace Wilson, head of the Civil Service since 1939, and was addressed to each senior member of the Civil Service in every office. It read:

> Treasury Chambers,
> Whitehall,
> S.W.ı.
> 26th July, 1940.

Dear ——

I have consulted the Prime Minister about the question of leave in Government offices. In view of the need for a period of recuperation in the case of large numbers of individuals before we enter on the coming winter, the Prime Minister directs that in each office, arrangements should be drawn up at once under which a period of leave (if not already taken recently) will be taken in every possible case during the next three months. Leave rosters should be arranged in such a way as to cause the minimum of interference with the discharge of public business, and all officers on leave will, of course, be liable to sudden recall should the course of events make this necessary. A fortnight's leave should be given in all possible cases, and Heads of Departments should, where necessary, insist on leave being taken as planned.

It is not intended that any public announcement should be made on this subject.

Yours very truly,

"This had an astonishing reaction in the factories and could have been critical," says General Hollis. "It directly threatened Britain's ability to produce more airplanes against the threat of invasion, for the Ministry of Aircraft Production employed many Civil Servants as Factory Inspectors to inspect the parts and the airplanes as they were made. When these Inspectors received this letter many naturally decided to follow its instructions.

"When the factory managers heard that the Inspectors were going on holiday they said, in effect, 'Well, there's not much use in producing planes that can't be passed for inspection, if our Inspectors are away. We might as well have a holiday, too.'

"The workers at the benches and lathes heard these views, and they decided what was fair for the masters was fair for the men. They also decided to take their holidays. The danger was that the factories would all shut down in a kind of national Wakes week on the eve of the German air and sea attacks. A nightmare situation threatened—and all because of this ridiculous letter."

The situation was desperate, but Beaverbrook was equal to it; crises in those days were his closest companions. As soon as he read the letter he immediately went to Downing Street to see Churchill in what he later admitted was "a gale of fury." Churchill at once sent for Wilson and the three men talked in the garden at No. 10. Wilson pointed out, quite reasonably, that Civil Servants had been working seven days a week for weeks on end. He did not think that they could do their best work under these conditions. Beaverbrook replied that if this letter prevailed then he would resign.

News of his anger later reached Bevin who announced that if leisure periods for the working people were not arranged then *he* would resign.

The issue between them was never resolved; the Battle of Britain saw to that. But Mr. Churchill was persuaded to rescind the order about leave, Beaverbrook still kept the aircraft factories working at full pressure, and the Civil Servants stayed at work. Sir Horace Wilson's circular did not prevail, but the personal enmity between Beaverbrook and Bevin continued, sustained and strengthened by it.

"This letter was the last important contribution I remember Sir Horace Wilson making," says General Hollis. "He had been Chamberlain's closest adviser during the years of appeasement, and as an almost forgotten figure of those days, he deserves some study. . . ."

Wilson, a tall, pale, stooping man with mild blue eyes, of whom it was said he had few intimate friends but some enemies, had entered the Civil Service as a Second Division clerk, by way of Bournemouth secondary school and the London School of Economics. In the Ministry of Labor after the First World War he came into some prominence on a Committee chosen by J. H. Thomas to solve unemployment problems. It solved little, but brought the hard-working Horace Wilson—whom Thomas called 'Orace—further preferment. He went to Ottawa as Chief Industrial Adviser with a delegation under Mr. Baldwin's leadership. There he worked so hard that Baldwin (who did not) was greatly impressed, and decided to make more use of him. In 1935 Wilson was seconded to the Treasury "for special service to the Prime Minister."

Mr. Chamberlain was also impressed by his achievements in settling labor disputes, for which he had a great reputation in Birmingham, Mr. Chamberlain's home city, and he believed he could use Wilson's technique to settle international disputes. Chamberlain's reasoning was simple: he longed for peace; Wilson had made a career out of making peace. Surely he could equally well apply his peace-making talents on the international scene? Together, these two men of peace and conciliation felt they could deal with Hitler as though he were a Trades Union leader in uniform.

Wilson and Chamberlain had much in common, not least their sincerity, and an objection to military matters. Wilson, always loyal and uncomplaining, would pad about the offices in Whitehall at Chamberlain's beck and call to such an extent that irreverent juniors nicknamed him "The Office Boy."

Together, Chamberlain and Wilson saved the peace for a time but, as Churchill said: "At Berchtesgarden one pound was demanded at pistol point. When it was given (at Godesberg) two pounds were demanded at pistol point. Finally (at Munich) the Dictator consented to take £1 17s. 6d. and the rest in promises of goodwill for the future . . ."

Now Sir Horace lives out his life on the South Coast, within sight of the Channel across which he flew on so many occasions with such high hopes. Of all the great figures involved in the miserable European political dealings of the thirties, he alone has kept silence on the negotiations in which he played so important a part.

"I wonder," says General Hollis, "whether now he speculates at all on how different the evening of his life might have been; what honors, awards and adulation would have been poured upon his quiet head *had* Hitler been just a Trades Union leader in uniform?

"Or indeed what terrible events might have overtaken this country—and probably himself—had his letter of July 26, 1940, been allowed to prevail?"

❖   ❖   ❖   ❖

"So Beaverbrook won the first round of his battle against giving holidays to the Civil Servants in 1940 when France had fallen and Britain was alone. Mr. Bevin resented this victory, however, and

in speeches around the country he began to draw attention to the
need for the workers to have holidays. Hostility between the two
Ministers became more marked," General Hollis wrote later.

"Their feud reached the point where Beaverbrook would oppose Bevin's point of view at Ministerial meetings, and Beaverbrook's dictatorial attitude would so anger him that he would
remove his false teeth and put them in his pocket in case he bit
his own tongue in his annoyance.

"Eventually, relations between them rose to such a pitch of hostility that Mr. Churchill summoned them both down to Chequers
for the night.

" 'These differences between you must be disposed of, dissipated and dispelled,' he told them both as though they were
schoolboys in the headmaster's study. That evening they were
more cordial, and by the time they went to bed, if not actually
friendly, they could at least bear each other's company in the
same room. Next morning, Lord Beaverbrook left first, and on the
way to London his car broke down. The roads were deserted, for
petrol was rationed and the first car to appear contained Mr.
Bevin, who kindly stopped and offered him a lift. Their new-found
spirit of goodwill did not survive the journey. Before they reached
London, they were in the middle of a further and even more
furious row!"

Bevin's public utterances became more and more critical of
Beaverbrook's proposals to work long hours. A week before Sir
Horace Wilson's letter, for instance, he declared that "the whole
of the Factory Acts have become demoralized. Appeals," he went
on, "perfectly understandable from new Ministers—arising from
their great exuberance—to work extraordinarily long hours had
resulted in many cases in young people working seventy to eighty
hours a week."

Mr. Bevin said he felt that it was his duty to stop "this sort
of thing," and an order had been introduced whereby the Factory
Acts would come into full use on August 1st.

"All the evidence goes to show that we have carried on with
these long hours too long and production is on the decline rather
than increasing," he added.

"Millions of men have been working twelve hours a day, seven days a week, for months," he declared quite truthfully, in a speech shortly afterwards. And while he admitted that production had reached record heights, he considered that, with the passing of the weeks, output had dropped; absenteeism in some plants reflected the strain of overwork. He said that his advisers, whom he did not name, had assured him that "production will not suffer" if hours were cut "by as much as twenty a week."

"The average hours of work should be reduced to a lower level," he said, "the ideal being the figure which will give, under existing conditions, the maximum output . . ."

He carried his dispute with Lord Beaverbrook into Parliament, where, on August 8th, to Socialist cheers, he answered a question about the high earnings of munition workers.

"I am not aware of the hours of work or output of these men," he said, "but I presume they are working according to the terms and conditions of collective agreements. If the question of the respective incomes of different citizens in this country is to be taken into account, it cannot be limited to workpeople."

These remarks by the Minister of Labor, clearly directed at one class of people and against another, had a very serious effect on workers in the aircraft factories.

Mr. Ernest Hives, now Lord Hives, who was then General Manager of Rolls Royce, and by reason of his experience and the works he controlled considered to be one of the most important men in the entire British aircraft industry, wrote to Lord Beaverbrook to suggest that the question of holidays in the immediate future for workers in the aircraft factories should be left to the discretion of individual managements. The fact that the Germans had been fairly quiet in the air for the past few weeks did not justify the giving of a general holiday, and since the Government's appeal for the working of a seven-day week, the general position had certainly not grown any better. Indeed, since then France had capitulated.

It was pointed out that statements from Ministers on the need for reducing hours of work made it very difficult for manufacturers to keep their production up to the required level. When Ministers suggested working shorter hours, the workers got the impression that the long hours asked for by the management and by Mr. Churchill were merely to ensure greater gain in money and profits for the companies.

"In fact," writes General Hollis, "these long hours were absolutely essential; and for our part, we worked far longer hours in 'The Hole in the Ground' than any aircraft factory worker at his bench. The hours were unpleasant but imperative. And, as events proved, victory in the air in 1940 was a close-run thing. Without long hours in the factories we would not have had anything like enough aircraft to win the Battle of Britain."

About this time, controversy also raged in the Government over the system of air-raid warnings, which were given whenever an enemy aircraft crossed the English coast. As a result, work in many factories stopped for hours and the men played cards in underground air-raid shelters although no German planes were within miles. The loss to production was enormous, and several times Mr. Churchill had asked for details of time lost through air-raid warnings—and discovered that among Government Departments most time was lost in the War Office.

"The question of changing the air-raid warning system was being discussed one day at a Defense Committee meeting consisting of Mr. Churchill, Lord Beaverbrook and Mr. Attlee," recalls General Hollis. "Sir John Anderson, the Home Secretary, was very strongly resisting the demand to abolish the air-raid warning, but he was on the point of being overcome.

"Beaverbrook and Attlee were in favor of changing the warning system because of the amount of work being disrupted at the factories. Mr. Churchill was about to give his vote, when Anderson's arguments were suddenly reinforced by the roar of bombs and guns. One of the heaviest raids of the war was on. Thus the argument of his opponents was silenced by the thunder of the cannonade. The air-raid warning system stayed!"

In December, 1940, another clash occurred between Bevin and Beaverbrook; this time on the subject of training in the aircraft factories. Bevin claimed that his Ministry should be responsible for this, and produced arguments to back up his proposal. Beaverbrook considered that the factories should be in charge of their own individual training of recruits. The quarrel raged between them, the advantage being first to one side and then to the other, but eventually Beaverbrook's view prevailed and the training of new men was left to the factories. The feud between the two Ministers thereupon reached even greater proportions.

"Their hostility grew to such an extent that it embarrassed Mr. Churchill, and caused a great deal of unhappiness in the Government. It seemed astonishing that, at such a time, two men of such stature and ability should be so eager to score points off each other," writes General Hollis. "I was especially grieved at this, because I admired both men very much."

Others took their disagreements less seriously.

Mr. Churchill intended to form a Committee of Public Safety to operate in the event of invasion, and announced that the members would be himself, Lord Beaverbrook and Ernest Bevin. A friend who knew the feelings that Bevin and Beaverbrook entertained for each other remarked: "Such a Committee would be *very* unsafe for Winston."

"Beaverbrook's ruthless, cut-throat, steam-roller approach to every problem made him feared as well as respected," recalls General Hollis. "You either got on with him or you did not; and in the latter case it was far better and safer to give him a wide berth. Nevertheless, he was a staunch and faithful friend to me, and immensely kind. I remember how on several occasions he took much trouble to send me new remedies for asthma, a complaint from which we both suffer.

"When he visited Marrakesh during Churchill's convalescence after his serious illness in 1943, which we will describe later, 'The Beaver,' as he was generally known, complained to the Prime Minister that I was not keeping him in touch with all the secret telegrams and cables which passed through my hands from Britain and America.

"Churchill reprimanded me strongly for this, and said that his Lord Privy Seal—as Lord Beaverbrook then was—should be shown *everything*.

" 'I presume, Sir, that when you say *everything*, I shall use my discretion as to what cables and papers shall be shown to Lord Beaverbrook, as is the practice with other Ministers?' I asked him.

"'*Exactly*,' replied Mr. Churchill. 'What on earth do you think I keep you for unless you use discretion?'

"Beaverbrook's friendship with Churchill was of very long standing, and, to my mind, stormy. They would fight and argue on Monday and Tuesday; part on Wednesday and Thursday, and then make it up again on Friday and Saturday. . . .

"Once, annoyed and frustrated to the limits of his endurance, Beaverbrook wrote a petulant letter to the Prime Minister, complaining about many things and especially about the urgent need to disperse the newly made aircraft about the countryside. The Air Ministry was against this, as they were against so much that he wished to do. Lord Beaverbrook therefore suggested that he should resign and let them get on with it themselves.

"Churchill received this letter at Chequers, and refused to take it seriously. He picked up the telephone and rang Beaverbrook.

"'Max,' he said, when his Lordship came on the line, 'I've news for you. I'm resigning, too.'"

"Beaverbrook stayed."

*   *   *   *

So 1940 passed, and resentment because leave remained cancelled, grew and festered. The Civil Servants were especially annoyed, and in a letter to Beaverbrook from their union dated St. George's Day, 1941, they claimed that "The maintenance of public morale in the present struggle depends upon adherence to the finer features of our British way of life, and the significance of this consideration must have escaped attention when the arbitrary decision was taken by the Cabinet without any reference to the official negotiating machinery. The Trades Union Movement has voluntarily relinquished many of its rights and privileges. A first-class crisis will however be created, of a highly dangerous nature so far as our war effort is concerned, if the essential principle of collective bargaining is flouted by the Government. . . ."

Such a letter showed how totally unrelated to the urgency and anguish of the times some people could still be, even at the gravest hour of British fortunes. But the methods Beaverbrook adopted to produce more planes worried the Army as well as the Unions. Everything that related to the air defenses—aircraft, anti-aircraft guns and equipment—had priority 1A as regards material and manpower; tanks and field artillery for the Army were relegated to priority 1B. This state of affairs was not popular with the Generals, nor was Beaverbrook in sympathy with their cautious thinking any more than they were in sympathy with him.

"In January, 1941, at a Commander-in-Chief's Conference, Sir Alan Brooke complained about the lack of arms in the country," writes General Hollis. "He declared that there was a shortage of rifles, ammunition, tracer ammunition, anti-tank guns, tanks, armored cars, and so on. Mr. Churchill was most annoyed at his complaint and told Sir John Dill that he thought Brooke most ungrateful to go on like that after everything that had been done for him."

On June 19, 1941, three days before Germany attacked Russia, Sir Alan Brooke made a note in his diary: "Attended 'Tank Parliament' run by P. M. at which I pressed for a better spare-part organization and for the necessity of maintaining some twenty per cent spare armored fighting vehicles per formation. This was not appreciated by the P. M. who likes to put the whole of his goods in the front window. This failure to provide adequate spare parts for tanks accounted for many of our failures and early difficulties in armored fighting in North Africa. . . ."[1]

What Sir Alan did not realize was that in aircraft, lorries, self-propelled guns and tanks—and in many other types of material—Britain's production between 1940 and 1942 was actually greater than Germany's during the same time.[2]

Meanwhile, a main concern of the Government was to sustain this production of planes and tanks—by no means easy to do—for despite the urgency of the demand, the traditional routine of memos, meetings and committees prevailed.

[1] *The Turn of the Tide.*
[2] *The United States Strategic Bombing Survey; the Effects of Strategic Bombing on the German War Economy.* Overall Economic Effects Division, Washington, D.C. Govt. Printing Office, 1945.

"What Mr. Churchill found so hard was to cut through the cocoons of red tape that existed seemingly to protect lack of enterprise," writes General Hollis. "The following account of the efforts made to protect the aircraft factories from bombing and an expected invasion shows the astonishing time it took for even a Minister of Beaverbrook's phosphoric energy—and all were not of his caliber—to get action on an absolutely vital matter.

"As the threat of invasion by parachutists grew throughout the early summer of 1940, workers at many aircraft factories urged that some plans should be made to defend their plants against such attacks, so that the flow of aircraft should not be disrupted for longer than was absolutely necessary. The production of airplanes *had* to be kept up, or else the war could be lost: the matter was as simple and urgent as that.

"But while the Generals were spending much time in siting traditional defenses—barbed wire coils, iron stakes and pillboxes —in the most vulnerable positions along the south and east coasts of England, little was being done to defend the factories where the tanks, guns, planes and ammunition were being produced. And Britain had such low reserves of these that a relatively small-scale attack on several well-chosen industrial towns could cripple the country's entire production.

"On May 25th, Lord Beaverbrook, as Minister of Aircraft Production, and well aware of this, wrote to the Secretary of State for Air, Sir Archibald Sinclair, drawing his attention to the need for additional balloon barrages to protect these aircraft factories from dive-bombing attacks. While awaiting a reply, the workmen organized themselves into as good a fighting force as they could (for they were gravely handicapped by a national lack of rifles and automatic weapons) and built concrete pill-boxes and strong-points. These might help to hold a land attack, but they could do nothing to save themselves from any aerial assault.

"On June 28th, Beaverbrook submitted a memorandum to the Government requesting immediate and adequate assistance so that the factory workers could be confident that their needs were realized, for both morale and production had already increased as a result of the few measures they had instituted themselves.

"On July 2nd, he submitted a further memorandum to the Government, asking for their authority to issue 16,500 rifles with ammunition to the aircraft factories. He wanted instructions to be given for the issuing of this material 'forthwith,' because the workers in the factories were becoming 'increasingly restless' under the threat of enemy aircraft landing on airfields near their works.

"Lord Beaverbrook wrote to Sinclair again on July 15th, and listed the totally inadequate defense arrangements at Filton, home of the Bristol Aeroplane Company: one company of soldiers, eight Bofors guns; 2 three-inch high angle guns; 6 Beaverettes[3] and 500 Home Guards, fully armed. To defend an area of 781 acres, with 27,000 workers, there was only one company of soldiers—*barely 120 men.*

"The Commander of the R.A.F. station at Filton, which adjoined the Bristol works, felt that at least a battalion was needed —and even this would not be too many men, because, in his view, the essential thing was to deal with an enemy *before* they could get into the works. Guns could cover the actual airfield, but those sides of the factory not on the airfield were very vulnerable to paratroops.

"On September 23rd, Beaverbrook, disturbed at what he called 'the meager character' of the defenses provided for the aircraft factories, airfields under Ministry of Aircraft Production control, as well as ferry pools and aircraft dispersed about the country, sought permission to form 'an armed force to be known as the Aircraft Defense Police.'

"He wanted to enlist up to 10,000 men, of fifty years and upwards, and his force would include men now serving with the Ferry Pools. This force would show the factory workers that they had not been forgotten, and as well as giving them confidence would be of very great value in the event of German parachute landings. They would be armed with rifles and some Beaverettes."

This request infuriated Sir Alan Brooke, who said he was already "desperately short" of tanks and other armored vehicles.

---

[3] Standard 14 h.p. cars with a sheet of armor plate in front and at the sides, but open on top.

"To make matters worse," he wrote in *The Turn of the Tide,* "Beaverbrook began to form an army of his own to protect aircraft factories in the event of invasion. He acquired a large proportion of armor plating for the production of small armored cars called 'Beaverettes' with which he equipped Home Guard personnel of factories for their protection. This was at a time when I was shouting for every armored vehicle I could lay my hands on with which to equip Regular forces. The whole conception was fantastic. How could individual factories have held out, and what part could they have played once the main battle for this country was lost?"

General Hollis comments: "This opinion gives a remarkable insight into General Brooke's attitude. Obviously, if the main battle for this country was lost then, for the time being, all would be lost. What Lord Beaverbrook wanted to ensure was that, despite German attack, his precious factories could still continue to pour out their planes. For without these planes 'the main battle' would have been lost in 1940—before it had properly begun."

Brooke triumphed, and although permission was at first given to Beaverbrook to form his own Police Force, it was later withdrawn.

On October 10, 1940, Beaverbrook appealed to Sinclair again for more balloon protection at Hawkers', Langley, and the Gloster Aircraft Company, the centers of Hurricane production. If these factories were destroyed, or captured by German paratroops, the production of Hurricanes would stop. He also sought more Bofors guns at Glosters and Langley to ward off an aerial attack, but nearly all the available guns were grouped on the coast for resisting attack—yet so far there were no attacks there to resist. On the other hand, the factories were under constant bombardment. Nine of the main ones had been bombed in the previous week: two in the week in which he wrote.

"Where the attack is, there let the guns abide," said Lord Beaverbrook. The Air Minister passed on his note to Sir Hugh Dowding, Commander-in-Chief, Fighter Command, who replied that he thought the situation was "generally satisfactory," in view of all the competing claims for protection. But he would "try to find some

guns" for Hatfield and some Bofors to supplement the balloon bar-
rage at Crewe.

"All through the summer and early autumn, the bombing of the
factories continued, while Beaverbrook begged for more protection," General Hollis wrote afterwards. "On August 15th, at Roch-
ester, Shorts lost more than three months' output of Stirlings from a
heavy attack. On September 4th, Vickers at Weybridge suffered
damage equivalent to the loss of 125 Wellington bombers. Three
weeks later, Supermarine, at Southampton, lost two out of three
plants; on the following day, September 25th, Bristol lost their
Rodney engine works, and several weeks' output of Beauforts and
Beaufighters, while on October 4th, De Havilland's lost a week's
output of Oxford aircraft. Then, in a letter, Sir Archibald Sinclair
explained that on Mr. Churchill's instructions thirty-six Bofors guns
were handed over to Home Forces against the advice of the Chiefs
of Staff. General Sir Alan Brooke was then Commander-in-Chief,
Home Forces.

"During October, the correspondence dealt with stationing
fighter squadrons near to the main factories. The Air Ministry did
not accept that this was the best method of defending them. On
October 26th, the matter was discussed by Government Ministers,
and the Air Minister, while still not accepting the policy, agreed
to base six Hurricanes 'as a special case' near Austins' factory at
Birmingham.

"It was only asked that ten factories should be defended—
Hawkers at Kingston and Langley: Glosters; Rolls Royce at
Derby, Crewe and Glasgow: Vickers at Brooklands, Castle Brom-
wich and Chester; and Bristol's at Filton. The machine tools at
all these centers were very valuable and would be irreplaceable
without a long and perhaps fatal delay. Fifty aircraft could protect them all; and at that time 1,000 planes were ready and idle
in the Storage Units.

"On November 4, 1940, Beaverbrook wrote to Churchill complaining that they had already lost many of their aircraft factories
in the South, and that the Midlands and the North would come
next. He appealed for smoke screens to protect them—as well as
for Air Force protection. Three weeks later, he told the Air Minister

that so severely had the aircraft industry suffered through bombing, and so disrupted had production been as a consequence, that
the Air Ministry must do 'everything possible' to defend Sheffield
and Birmingham. Should these two centers be bombed on the
scale of Coventry, then aircraft production could be irreparably
damaged.

"Throughout December 1950 and January 1941, he continued
to press the Air Minister for special protection for his aircraft
factories by day, and at the full moon. The Air Minister replied
that he 'was doing his best.'

"On January 28, 1941, Beaverbrook suggested to the Chief of
the Air Staff that a test pilot at each factory should be given a
fighter plane to protect the plant. Fighter Command considered
this, and on February 25 the C.A.S. replied that this scheme was
approved for nine factories 'on reasons of morale.' Then, on
March 29, Beaverbrook informed the Chief of the Air Staff that
Gloster and other fighters had not arrived. Finally, on March 31,
1941, the C.A.S. replied that details 'took time to resolve' and
invited a representative of the Ministry of Aircraft Production to
a meeting on April 5th, 'to relate needs of local air defense with
national requirements.'

"By then, of course, the danger of invasion either by air, or by
sea, was over; so was the bombing for a time. The meeting was
called ten months too late."

CHAPTER 5

This much is certain: that he that commands the sea is at great liberty, and may take as much and as little of the war as he will.

BACON, Essays: *Of Kingdom and Estates*

After the fall of France, it became clear that with the limited resources at Britain's disposal, the only means of returning to the offensive was by R.A.F. bombing sorties and raiding parties.

In 1932, a small organization had been set up under the control of the Director of Plans of the Admiralty, to study the technique and equipment required for amphibious warfare. This little organization was controlled by the Local Defense Section of Plans Division, the Director of which was Captain John Godfrey, and the Staff Officer, Major Hollis. The group operated at Eastney Royal Marine Barracks, Portsmouth, and because money was very tight, research was limited. Nevertheless, when the war broke out in 1939, this was a seed which could be fostered and made to flower. From such small beginnings began Combined Operations, which played a decisive part in the war. Indeed, this wartime integration of air, land and sea forces has influenced all subsequent strategy.

The idea of raiding parties landing on the French coast had two main advantages: first, they would oblige the Germans to disperse their forces, and secondly they would help to raise morale in this country. Mr. Churchill therefore appointed Lieutenant-General Sir Alan Bourne, Adjutant General of the Royal Marines, to the post of

Commander of Raiding Operation. Although the men General Bourne commanded were keen enough, their equipment was sparse indeed. At the outbreak of war, Britain possessed only six heavy landing-craft in home waters, and another three at Malta. Although ninety small craft were being built, they would not be ready until the following December. Thus Bourne's raiding parties had to sail to France as best they might in borrowed motor boats and air-sea rescue craft lent by the R.A.F.

"Bourne was an officer of the highest intellectual quality," writes General Hollis. "He had studied at both the Military and Naval Staff Colleges, and was a keen student of war. He was, perhaps, more of an academic strategist than an operational commander, but he was personally a man of great charm. Nevertheless, I formed the opinion that Bourne and Churchill would not last long in partnership. This feeling proved well founded when one evening at No. 10, Downing Street, he gave Churchill a dissertation on strategy. That was the end of Bourne as Commander of Raiding Operations. . . ."

On July 17th, Mr. Churchill sent the following message to General Ismay and Sir Edward Bridges: "I have appointed Admiral of the Fleet Sir Roger Keyes as Director of Combined Operations. He should take over the duties and resources now assigned to General Bourne. General Bourne should be informed that owing to the large scope now to be given to these operations, it is essential to have an officer of higher rank in charge, and that the change in no way reflects upon him or those associated with him. . . ."

"Combined Operations began in an atmosphere of controversy and acrimony," writes General Hollis. "They were hated by all three established Services, and came in for special loathing from the Admiralty, an attitude that stemmed from two sources.

"First, the Admiralty were traditionally jealous of what they imagined might become a rival concern. Secondly, they associated Combined Operations very closely with Admiral Sir Roger Keyes, who had fallen foul of the High Command for a reason which had nothing to do with his brilliant record of courage and achievement —simply because he was so much their senior. Admiral Sir Dudley Pound, for instance, the First Sea Lord, had been Keyes's Chief of

Staff when Keyes was Commander-in-Chief to the Mediterranean, and this juxtaposition of rank and authority suited neither of them."

Keyes, one of the bravest officers ever to serve in the Royal Navy, had won high honor at Zeebrugge on St. George's Day, 1918. Age had not dimmed his enthusiasm, and although at the outbreak of war he had not been to sea for twelve years, his vigor and aggressiveness were as strong as ever.

During the débâcle in Norway just two months before he became Director of Combined Operations, he dressed in full uniform as an Admiral of the Fleet to make a special journey to the House of Commons to explain how he had appealed in vain to be allowed to organize and lead a naval assault on Trondheim. When his request was turned down, he wrote passionately to Churchill: "St. Vincent was at his zenith as First Sea Lord when older than I am now, and hoisted his flag after that. I am younger than Howe was on the Glorious First of June. . . ."

"I have been unfortunate in the period of my birth," he said bitterly. "In the Gallipoli campaign I was considered too junior, and now I'm supposed to be too senior and out of date for my opinions to be seriously considered."

Thereafter, whenever Keyes appeared in the House in uniform it was traditional that a crisis was impending. Although sixty-eight years of age, he was anxious to repeat the far-off glories of that St. George's Day, a generation previously, and win a Victoria Cross leading his men into action.

By an irony of fate, his destiny was quite different. He did not fall in the hour of glory against the thunder of the guns like his heroes Wolfe, Nelson and Nicholson; he died in bed at home. And his son, Geoffrey Keyes, who shared his father's desperate dedication, was awarded the Victoria Cross posthumously in 1941 for his gallant attempt to kill or capture Rommel at his Headquarters in the Libyan desert.

But to return. Towards the end of August, 1940, Admiral Keyes moved his Combined Operations Headquarters from the Admiralty to Richmond Terrace; he wanted his men to be physically divorced from Admiralty association, and work apart from their influence, and this move would ensure that his organization could come to be regarded as a genuinely inter-Service establishment, and not an Admiralty off-shoot.

Sir Roger and his staff considered many brave operations in Richmond Terrace, most of which came to nothing. They prepared plans for installing General de Gaulle in Dakar; worked on "Brisk," which dealt with the capture of the Azores; and "Shrapnel," the code-name for a plan to capture the Canary Islands; but the one most associated with his memory in the Second World War was known as "Operation Workshop."

This plan caught the imagination of Mr. Churchill, who told General Ismay: "Reflection has made me feel the very high value of Workshop . . . the effect . . . if successful would be electrifying, and would greatly increase our strategic hold upon the Central Mediterranean."

The intention was to capture the island of Pantelleria, between Sicily and Tunis, in the Mediterranean, and 140 miles from Malta. This island was important to the enemy because it lay on their sea route to Tunis and Tripoli, and to Britain because it could help in the defense of Malta. On paper, the attack was simple; two or three troop-ships would follow behind a normal British convoy, and then, in Churchill's own words, "while the main body was engaging the enemy's attention, these would drop off in the darkness and storm the island by surprise."[1]

So enthusiastic and courageous was Keyes that he planned to lead this onslaught in person, disregarding his rank as Admiral of the Fleet. He was, indeed, so keen on this plan that it threatened to assume an importance quite out of all proportion to the facts.

"The Chiefs of Staff did not share his enthusiasm for the project," writes Hollis. "None of the earlier plans put up by Combined Operations had been notably successful, but since Keyes had the ear of the Prime Minister, they had to fall in with his wishes and examine all his propositions, including this plan for capturing Pantelleria. Indeed this gallant old Admiral continually bombarded them with new ideas and plans for attack. Soon they groaned when

[1] *The Grand Alliance.*

they saw his name on any new folder, for since they were already working from seven-thirty in the morning until perhaps one or two o'clock in the following dawn on their own plans, they did not take kindly to proposals which they considered from the start to be unsound.

"Since Keyes found it hard to visualize commanding more than a Commando Brigade of roughly five thousand men, any operation he put forward was therefore severely limited in scope because of its size. The Joint Planning Committee of the Chiefs of Staff were engaged in drafting operations involving ten or twenty times this number of men, and so they could not be expected to raise much enthusiasm for such small-scale raids.

"Further, although Sir Roger's staff at Combined Operations Headquarters were men of great enthusiasm, they were also in the main elderly; some were retired Naval Officers, who had rejoined the colors for the duration. Keen though they were, like their leader, many felt that their best years of thought and action were behind them. This knowledge did not lessen the disappointment Admiral Keyes felt when plan after plan was abandoned by officers almost young enough to be his sons, and gradually the frustration corroded even his iron enthusiasm, and provoked an irritation he was not slow in showing."

Such was the background to events when on an autumn evening in 1941 Mr. Churchill unexpectedly decided to dine at the "Other Club." This gave his staff the chance of a few hours' freedom, because they knew that he would be away from his office and his telephone from eight o'clock until perhaps midnight, and they welcomed this break as schoolboys might revel in an unlooked for half holiday.

Churchill, Lloyd George and the first Lord Birkenhead founded this dining club in 1911 to provide an opportunity for political opponents to meet and converse on friendly terms. One of the rules made it clear, however, that "nothing in the intercourse of the members shall be allowed to interfere with the full asperities of party politics."

Some met their wives and families for dinner; others caught up with their work or even went out to a show. Hollis spent the evening playing billiards and went to bed early in his room in "The Hole" which he used all through the war. He was unfortunate in that his home was in Sussex and he did not have a flat in London. General Ismay had a flat in Kensington and so could very occasionally spend a night there.

At one o'clock in the morning a Royal Marines orderly shook Hollis into reluctant wakefulness.

"The Prime Minister wants to see you, sir," he said. "At No. 10."

Hollis groaned; his hope of a quiet night was not to be realized. Slowly and wearily he began to put on his uniform, and walked round to Downing Street. He found Churchill alone in the Cabinet Room,[2] wearing his dressing-gown embroidered with Chinese dragons, sitting at ease in his big armchair with the heavy arms, drawing on a cigar and reading some papers.

"Sit down," he said, without looking up.

Hollis did so, and Mr. Churchill laid the papers on one side and looked at him for a moment through the haze of pale blue smoke. Then he began to speak.

"I have had reports that Sir Roger Keyes is said to be taking up too much time of the Chiefs of Staff," he began slowly. "He is a man of vigor and gallantry, but I'm told that they do not like his plans. I thought I would ask you what you think?"

"Do you expect me to tell you the truth, Prime Minister?" asked Hollis.

Mr. Churchill looked pained.

"I certainly did not ask you to come here at this hour to tell me anything else, Hollis," he said coldly. "I expect nothing *less* than the truth. Pray proceed."

"Very good, Sir. As I see it, Admiral Keyes is a very gallant officer but it is quite true that he *is* taking up far too much of the Chiefs' time. His plans aren't feasible, yet he is continually bombarding

---

[2] "The Cabinet Room at No. 10, although steeped in history, is not a particularly inspiring place for meetings. The walls are surrounded with bookcases, containing old records which never seem to be taken out of their shelves. The lighting is not very good, and the room feels either too hot or too cold. The old-fashioned windows let in a constant draught, or alternatively keep out the sun."—General Hollis.

them with new suggestions for landings, raids, and attacks on remote, unimportant places when they have more than enough to do
in coping with their own work. Then, when his plans are turned
down, as they invariably are, they all have to be reconsidered because he has your ear, Prime Minister, and he refuses to take 'No'
for an answer. This is reacting badly on the staff in the Service
Departments all down the line."

"This sounds serious. I see that you are a hard man, Hollis. You
take a very hard view."

"No, Sir. You asked for the truth, and that is the truth of the
situation as I see it."

"Hm."

Mr. Churchill sat in silence for a minute, drawing on his cigar,
and then he pressed a bell. An orderly appeared.

"Two whiskies and soda," he said.

The man brought them in and the Prime Minister and General
Hollis drank in silence. Then Mr. Churchill spoke.

"And what would you suggest that we do, Hollis?" he asked
with deceptive mildness.

Leslie Hollis took a deep breath.

"Since you *ask* me, Prime Minister, I'd suggest that you request
his resignation."

Mr. Churchill looked pained at this bald reply, and shook his
head slowly from side to side, disturbed at the suggestion.

"You *are* a very hard man," he said again, and then with a little
sigh pressed the bell for a second time.

"Send in the stenographer," he told the orderly. What General
Hollis had said confirmed his own views: Admiral Keyes, for whom
he had the warmest regard, was really too old for his job, but this
did not make any easier the task of breaking the news to his old
friend.

A shorthand-writer came into the room, and Mr. Churchill began
to dictate a letter to Sir Roger, removing him from his post. In a
few minutes it was brought back, typed and ready for him to sign.
He read it through and then laid it on the blotting pad on the
table, and indicated that the stenographer could withdraw.

Hollis knew how the Prime Minister's heart was divided, because he admired the gallantry and tenacity of the Admiral who still was full of fighting schemes at an age when others were in retirement.[3] Unless the Prime Minister signed it immediately, loyalty to his old friend might still make him change his mind.

"Would you sign it now, Prime Minister?" Hollis asked him.

Churchill pulled on his cigar again until the ash glowed orange. Slowly and reluctantly he removed the top from the gold pen which he used for signing letters, and wrote his name. They sat together in silence while the ink dried.

Hollis stood up.

"I'll take it with me," he said.

For a moment he thought that Churchill was going to disagree, and then the Prime Minister nodded and pushed it across the table to him. Hollis put it into an envelope, and into his pocket.

About four hours later that same morning the Prime Minister was on the phone to him.

"You didn't despatch that letter, I hope?" he began. "I feel that we have been too hard, much too hard. I don't want it to go."

"I'm sorry, Sir," replied Hollis, "But it has already gone. It will be on the Admiral's desk this morning."

So Admiral Keyes departed from the active scene, and Lord Louis Mountbatten succeeded him as Director of Combined Operations, a job he did not want.

Mountbatten was the antithesis of Keyes. He was young—forty-one that June—of noble birth and Royal relations, married to a very rich wife, and known to be ambitious, and a lover of the modern and unorthodox. He also possessed in full measure the rare and enviable independence, and the utter indifference to criticism or calamity which comes from great wealth. On the morning Mountbatten was appointed Director of Combined Operations, Keyes telephoned him from his home outside London.

"Well, Dicky," he began rather sadly, "do you want me to come in to turn over to you?"

[3] "When Keyes was raised to the peerage in 1943, he chose his supporters aggressively. Dexter: a sailor of the Royal Navy in working rig, proper; Sinister: a Royal Marine equipped for trench raiding, proper. One need seek no further for the story of a brave and patriotic life."—General Hollis.

"No, sir," replied Mountbatten. "I'll come out to your house and you can brief me then."

Mountbatten was acutely conscious that on the last time they had met, Keyes had been a full Admiral, while he had only been a two-striper, and he did not look forward to the interview before him. He found Keyes dejected; for the first time the Admiral looked his age.

"Dicky," he said sadly, "the trouble is that the British have lost the will to fight. There's no spirit of attack any more. The Chiefs of Staff are the greatest cowards I've ever met."

He rambled on, full of an old man's annoyance at what he considered was the lack of enthusiasm for his schemes.

Mountbatten, for his part, was equally unenthusiastic about taking over Combined Operations. After commanding the *Kelly*, which had been sunk, he had just been offered command of the newest aircraft carrier of the day, H.M.S. *Illustrious*, and this appeared to be more worthwhile than drafting plans that would probably never be used. In fact, he had been in Pearl Harbor with the American fleet in October, 1941, when the signal arrived that brought him home; he was to report immediately to Mr. Churchill at Chequers. He returned by air, a hazardous and wearisome journey in those days, involving many delays and refuelling stops, and as soon as he reached England, he met the Prime Minister. He found him wearing his blue siren suit, and in a particularly belligerent and Churchillian mood.

"Hmm, why have you been so long?" he began testily as Mountbatten came into the room.

This question surprised Mountbatten, who replied rather tartly: "I was so far away, Prime Minister, that the only delay in my trip occurred when I wondered which way round the world I should come!"

Mr. Churchill grunted, and pierced the end of a new cigar.

He motioned Mountbatten to a chair and began to explain the reason for his urgent summons home. He wanted him to take command of Combined Operations. He saw no answering light of enthusiasm to this suggestion and asked him quickly: "Don't you *want* the job?"

"No, Prime Minister, I don't," replied Mountbatten frankly. "I've just been offered a new command—the *Illustrious*—and I don't want an office job. I'd rather go back to sea."

"Hmm, you like a life of glory," said Mr. Churchill musingly. "But you've already been sunk in the *Kelly*. And if you go back to sea, you'll probably be sunk again. *That's* not glory."

He then went on to explain what was in his mind. The Chiefs of Staff were all older than Mountbatten, and continued reverses of fortune to our arms in many theaters of war had taught them caution. As a result, they were thinking defensively. Some held that a German invasion of this country was still not out of the question, and so problems of defense were taking the place of methods of attack. As head of Combined Operations, Mountbatten would have nothing to do with defense.

"You will continue Commando raids, for they are important for the morale of this country and of our allies," said Churchill. "But your primary object will be to prepare for the great invasion, for unless we return to the Continent and beat the Germans on land we shall never win the war.

"All the other headquarters in this country are thinking defensively. Your job will be to think *offensively*—to restore the offensive spirit, to devise the technique and find the appliances and the landing-craft that will be needed. You will set up training centers where the three Services can be trained as one; and you will organize bases from which the great organization can be launched."

Such was the brief that Lord Louis accepted with some reluctance from the Prime Minister at Chequers on a rainy morning in October 1941.

"Considering that at this time there seemed no likelihood of America coming into the war of her own volition; considering that France had fallen, Italy was against us, and the fate of Russia was entirely in the balance, this indeed was in the Churchillian conception of waging war—that the best means of defending yourself is to attack your enemy," Mountbatten remarked to Hollis when they discussed the interview afterwards. Churchill had explained the size that Combined Operations would reach; but for a long time thereafter Mountbatten's detractors, never lacking, abused him for gathering a big organization around him, and indulging in what they called empire building.

For the first six months as Director of Combined Operations, Mountbatten was a Commodore 1st Class with no real staff status, and as such he could only attend the Chiefs of Staff Committee meetings sitting below the line, which meant that he could not submit a Paper unasked.

The Chiefs of Staff naturally resented his presence as such a junior officer and suspected (rightly) that Mr. Churchill was behind it.

"Up till then they had thought of themselves as a three-pronged fork," says General Hollis. "They did not want a fourth prong."

Churchill sensed this latent hostility and he promoted Mountbatten to sit on the Chiefs of Staff Committee with the rank of Lieutenant-General, Air Marshal, and Vice-Admiral.[4]

"Now you're a *full* member," he said, beaming, when he told him the news. "You can attend *every* meeting."

"Must I?" asked Mountbatten. "I really haven't got the time."

This reply astonished Mr. Churchill, who removed his cigar from his mouth and looked at the young man long and earnestly, wondering whether he had heard him correctly.

"These three Chiefs of Staff direct the whole conduct of the war," he reminded him severely. Mountbatten remained apparently unimpressed.

[4] On March 18, 1942, the Chiefs of Staff received a memorandum by General Ismay, paragraphs of which read:

"(3) The title of the appointment of 'Adviser on Combined Operations' has been altered to 'Chief of Combined Operations.' The appointment will in future carry with it the rank of Vice-Admiral in the Navy, Lieutenant-General in the Army and Air Marshal in the Royal Air Force.

"(4) The Chief of Combined Operations will attend meetings of the Chiefs of Staff as a full member whenever major issues are in question and also, as heretofore, when his own Combined Operations, or any special matters in which he is concerned, are under consideration."

"From what I can see, they seem more anxious to discuss priority on air travel," he retorted.

"Then you need not attend the meetings if you don't want to," said Mr. Churchill graciously; and so it was agreed.

Thereafter, relations between the Chiefs of Staff and Mountbatten improved and eventually became noted for their cordiality. In Canada after the Quebec conference, for instance, when a fishing trip was proposed, Mountbatten's name happened to be left off the list of guests, and Sir Alan Brooke at once rectified this error. "We *must* have Dicky with us," he said. And now they had him with them at their meetings and deliberations all the time.

"News of this promotion, and the legend of his independence, his Royal relations and the easy way in which he wore authority and responsibility carried across the Atlantic," General Hollis wrote later.

This became abundantly clear in April 1942, when Eisenhower paid his first visit to Great Britain, as a Lieutenant-Colonel made up hurriedly to Major-General, and sent over by General Marshall to see what could be done to help the Allied cause. He attended a Chiefs of Staff meeting—only the fourth at which Mountbatten had been present as a full member—and, of course, the two men had never met.

"In a brief and soldierly speech Eisenhower said that the Americans had not much material of war as yet and their forces were still small, but they wished to join us in the great invasion of Europe. Sir Alan Brooke, realizing that now the Americans were in the war with far more men and equipment than we possessed, they would obviously demand some say in the choice of commander for this invasion—if, indeed, he were even British—asked Eisenhower who they had in mind for this post.

"Eisenhower replied: 'In America I have heard much of a man who has been intensively studying amphibious operations for many months. I understand that his position is Chief of Combined Operations, and I think his name is Admiral Mountbatten.

" 'Anyone will be better than none; such an operation cannot be carried out under committee command. But I have heard that Admiral Mountbatten is vigorous, intelligent and courageous, and if the operation is to be staged initially with British forces pre-dominating I assume he could do the job.'

"Brooke held up his hand.

" 'Before you go on,' he said drily, 'I'd better introduce you.'[5]

"This greatly embarrassed Lord Louis who did not particularly want to be picked out at that moment.

"He was further embarrassed when General Marshall arrived and attended another Chiefs of Staff meeting. So were the Chiefs of Staff—but for a different reason. They all wanted to be friendly to Marshall, who was head of the American Armed Forces. . . ."

"We would be very honored, General," said Sir Alan Brooke, "If you would care to visit our War Office. Naturally, we'll do everything we can to show you whatever you want to see."

"Thank you very much," replied Marshall graciously, "I would indeed be pleased to visit the British War Office, and see how you do things over here."

Sir Charles Portal, the Chief of the Air Staff, felt that he should not be outdone when invitations were being given.

"Since the American Air Force is under the command of the Army," he said, "You might care to see our Air Ministry. We'd all be very pleased to see you any time you have a free moment. We've one or two things there that might interest you."

General Marshall again expressed his pleasure at this invitation and Sir Dudley Pound added that he would also be honored if the General would care to visit the Admiralty.

"You are all very kind, gentlemen," said Marshall, looking round at them. "But the only invitation I've not yet had is the one I'd really like the best—a visit to Admiral Mountbatten's Combined Operations Headquarters."

All eyes at once turned to Lord Mountbatten.

"When would you like to visit us, sir?" he asked.

"This afternoon," replied Marshall promptly.

It was then about one-thirty, and so after a brief lunch they visited his offices, and Mountbatten showed him what there was

[5] General Hollis: Also recalled by Eisenhower in his book, *Crusade in Europe*.

to see—mostly models of landing-craft and other ships, for the real landing-craft were still in process of being built.[6]

Towards the end of the brief visit, Marshall, who was accompanied by Colonel Wedemeyer—later to work with Mountbatten in S.E.A.C.—asked bluntly: "How can I get into this game as soon as possible?"

"Cable Washington this afternoon," Mountbatten told him, "And double all the orders you've already given for landing-craft."

"Right," said Marshall, and told Wedemeyer to send that signal. "Now, have you got anything else?" he asked Mountbatten.

"Yes, we've got a new type of landing-craft."

Marshall at once appeared interested, and Lord Louis explained how Combined Operations had learned at some cost in men and material that, when sailing at night without lights, it was not possible to handle more than about twenty landing-craft in any assault in one area. Since the landing-craft then in use could only carry thirty men each, this meant that any assault on any particular point was necessarily limited to 600 men, rather less than a battalion. For the eventual cross-Channel landing in France, it had been decided to increase the size of each vessel, and make large landing-craft—L.C.I.(L)—each of which could transport two hundred and fifty men. This meant that 5,000 could land at one time, roughly the equivalent of a Brigade, which would increase the size of the assault nine times.

When General Marshall heard this proposal he was immediately enthusiastic.

"My goodness!" he exclaimed, "This is worth the whole trip, for the numbers of men we'll need for the invasion of France will be enormous."

Mountbatten sketched on the back of an envelope a plan of the type of landing-craft he visualized, so that Marshall could see for himself how they would look.

---

[6] Landing-craft were so short that Churchill declared petulantly: ". . . The destinies of two great Empires . . . seemed to be tied up in some damned thing called L.S.T.s whose engines themselves have to be tickled on . . . by L.S.T. engine experts of whom there was a great shortage." *European Theater of Operations—Cross Channel Operations,* United States War Department.

"We've got to have them big enough to come across the Atlantic under their own steam with their own crews," Mountbatten pointed out, and Marshall agreed.

"How many would you like?" he asked.

"Let's say three hundred," replied Mountbatten, doing a quick piece of mental arithmetic.

"That will mean 150 for you and 150 for us, then," Marshall replied, and at once dispatched a further signal to Washington ordering the immediate construction of three hundred landing-craft of this size.

Since Mountbatten was young and relatively inexperienced in office routine, and also because he was tired and overworked, he neglected to make a note of this transaction in a proper and official fashion to their Lordships at the Admiralty.

Thus, when these landing-craft were delivered from America in a few months' time, the Admiralty found, with considerable concern and petulance, that Mountbatten had increased the size of the Royal Navy by no less than 150 ships—and without a word to anyone.

*   *   *   *

As an essential preliminary to future combined operations Colonel Sam Bassett's Inter-Services Topographical Department was asked for details of various beaches where landings were proposed and figures regarding the rise and fall of tides and other information of importance of the planners. These details were not all available, and so once more Colonel Bassett and his staff went round the travel agencies, and asked for pre-war brochures of Continental holiday resorts, but very little information of value was discovered. Bassett therefore suggested that a B.B.C. broadcast should be made appealing to listeners to send in any snaps they might have taken on holidays abroad. The appeal would be for world-wide pictures so that it would not be possible for enemy intelligence agents to deduce where the next landings might be.

A short time before this, the B.B.C. had already broadcast an appeal from the Ministry of Economic Warfare, which controlled various secret organizations, for listeners to send in any Continental telephone directories they might have, and, as a result, 8,000 had been received. It was thus expected that perhaps, at the outside, 10,000 people might send in holiday snapshots, and the Admiralty made contracts accordingly with firms who specialized in copying photographs. In fact, the response to the appeal astonished every one connected with it.

The broadcast was made on a Sunday evening. By Monday afternoon, 30,000 photographs had been received. This response alarmed the Admiralty; they wondered who would pay for them, and whether they should cancel the whole thing. Their alarm knew no bounds when something like 9,000,000 photographs arrived, but they were reassured that new estimates would be made to cope with such numbers.

Bassett recruited a temporary staff of girls from Labor Exchanges until W.R.N.S. could be posted to his department, to collate and file the copies made from these photographs, and he issued them with gazetteers so that they could check the various place names. As he watched them work, he noticed that one girl sat poring for nearly an hour over a picture of a small tent surrounded by sand, and at last he asked what was puzzling her.

"Well," she explained, "This picture is called "Bivouac in the Desert." But I've looked through all the B's in the gazetteer, and there's no town called Bivouac listed. . . ."

Sometimes, however, work went to waste. Just before the war, for instance, a man had spent six months in Madagascar collecting material on that island "in case it should prove useful."

After the fall of Malaya and Burma, when it became imperative to secure Madagascar—then occupied by the Vichy French—against a possible Japanese invasion, his exploits were remembered, and Bassett assured the planners of the Madagascar landings that detailed information on beaches and roads and railways was already in the Admiralty files and would be available for them on the following morning. They were naturally delighted at this, and the meeting adjourned.

Bassett walked over to the Admiralty, understandably pleased at the prospect of being able to place so much valuable information before his superiors so speedily. He went into the department concerned and spoke to the clerk in charge.

"I'd like these files on Madagascar," he said, handing him a sheet of paper that contained their numbers and code mark. The man disappeared into the back recesses, and was away for an hour or more, but Bassett felt that he was no doubt taking such a long time because he had so many different files to collect.

At last, the clerk returned.

"We've no files with these numbers here," he said.

"But you *must* have. It's imperative you find them," replied Bassett with some heat.

The man disappeared and again returned with more news.

"No one will *ever* find them," he announced dramatically. "We've had a big clear out here since the war, you know. We got rid of a lot of that old stuff. These files have been given away for salvage!"

The shock of this news robbed Bassett of any effective reply: he just nodded and left the building, wondering how he was going to provide the necessary information by the following morning, as he had promised.

He returned to his office and telephoned to the Oxford college where his staff filed all names and addresses of people who had recently arrived from foreign lands, and asked for details of anyone who had lived recently in Madagascar. They replied that they knew of a high cleric who had spent many years there, and who had now retired to a remote part of Scotland. Bassett asked for his telephone number, and, after the frustrating delays endemic to trunk calls during the war, he finally got through to him.

"This is Colonel Bassett speaking from London," he explained. "We are preparing some details about Madagascar. I wonder if you could help us?"

"I will not be a party to *any* warlike operations," replied the cleric primly. "If your inquiry has anything to do with the war at all, I will bid you good-day."

Bassett took a deep breath.

"As a matter of fact, sir," he said carefully, "Most things concern the war one way or another. We are, in fact, preparing a number of details for an expedition to Madagascar. Among other things they will study the—ah—the orchids and butterflies. We wondered if we could count on your help, and if we can I will be delighted to forward you a travel warrant immediately so that you can come and talk with us."

The cleric was pleased to accept.

Late that night, he was sitting in Oxford, a glass of port in his hand, discussing Madagascar memories. Bassett arranged for various officers to interview him, and gradually they prised from him details of the roads and terrain on the island without his realizing that he was being interviewed for any warlike purpose; nor did he ever know how valuable his contribution was to the successful invasion of Madagascar which followed shortly afterwards.

"Probably the triumph of Sam Bassett's Department concerned the bombing of the Moehne and Eder Dams in 1943," writes General Hollis. "Barnes Wallis, the distinguished scientist, had invented a special bomb that would literally bounce on the water at the base of the dam, and what the Air Staff had to know was the exact hour of the twenty-four that the two dams would be full of water, because the weight of this water was needed to crack the concrete after the bomb exploded.

"We referred this problem to Sam Bassett, and I remember thinking at the time that it seemed almost impossible to solve, for we were sending no reconnaisance planes within 150 miles of the dams lest the Germans should suspect a raid and increase their anti-aircraft defense.

"Bassett took it in his stride. He found several photographs of the dams that had been sent in as a result of our broadcast appeal, for in peace-time they had been something of a tourist attraction, and the Germans were rightly very proud of them.

"Some of these photographs showed the dams full and with shrubs in bloom at one side. Bassett immediately contacted a friend in Kew Gardens who had made a study of German flowers, and he examined an enlargement of the picture under a powerful magnifying glass, and announced that this particular shrub only bloomed for one week in the year. Bassett already knew that the photographs were taken in 1939, and this information gave him the actual week. He and his staff, with the aid of other recent air photographs taken of similar shrubs outside the 150 mile radius, and studying the angle of shadows in the pictures, calculated at what hour of the day they had been taken. This done, he knew that at three o'clock in an afternoon of the first week in June, 1939, the dams were full. He could not work out the exact day of the week, but the information he did have was sufficient for his team to calculate the hour at which the dams would be full during certain nights in May 1943—four years afterwards.

"So accurate were their calculations that the "Dam Buster" planes arrived with fifteen minutes to spare, and as a result breached both dams successfully."

The official German report on the results of these raids called it "a dark picture of destruction." Altogether 124 factories within an area of 50 miles were destroyed or severely damaged by the flood-waters from these two gigantic dams, 25 bridges were ruined, 21 seriously weakened, and the equivalent loss of production of 100,000 workers for many months. This result owed much to the painstaking thoroughness of Sam Bassett and his willingness to examine any project, and to follow the slenderest clue.

In this he resembled Mountbatten, but whereas Bassett in the early days ran his Department on a very small allowance, Mountbatten had the benefit of being able to spend incalculable sums of public money on projects that took his fancy.

One of these—and probably the most criticized of all—began when a scientist on his staff, Mr. G. Pyke, discovered that if woodpulp or old newspaper and certain other ingredients were mixed with water, and frozen, the resulting amalgam was as strong as concrete and very slow to melt, even in sea water.

When it did begin to melt, the edges became furred and provided their own insulation, so that the center of the block still stayed cold. Such a discovery seemed to have some use, and Mountbatten, ever interested in new ideas, suggested making a floating airfield of it, about 200 feet long by 300 feet wide, which would be large enough to be used by the largest four-engined bombers of the day. Round the edge, twelve electric motors would be fitted, either outboard, or in nacelles with aircraft propellers, to drive this strange craft through the water at between seven to ten knots. A built-in refrigeration plant would ensure that even in the warm waters of the Gulf Stream this floating airfield did not melt away.

"The whole idea seemed ridiculous," writes Hollis, "but we had heard of even stranger devices that had worked and this was given various tests."

Such floating islands would be virtually indestructible, for all above-water damage by bombing or shell fire would be no worse than comparable attacks on concrete, and under-water holes could be filled with liquid Pykrete which could then be frozen solid again. It was estimated that between fifty and seventy torpedoes would be needed to put them out of action, for they would displace two million tons, and could sail far into the Atlantic.

There they could be used as a mid-ocean refuelling base, or they were proposed for use in mid-Channel because Fighter Command claimed that the range of planes at their disposal would not allow them to cross France from England and return. It was also said that the Americans would find them useful in the Pacific.

This fantastic proposal was given the code-name of "Habakkuk" by Mr. Churchill, from a Bible text:

> Behold ye among the heathen, and regard, and wonder marvellously: for I will work a work in your days, which ye will not believe, though it be told you.
>
> Habakkuk, Chapter I, verse 5

Mountbatten was so enthusiastic about this extraordinary project that he took a cube of Pykrete to the Quebec Conference to demonstrate to the Americans what a great discovery it was. His audience seemed at first as skeptical as the British had been earlier on, and to prove what a great advantage Pykrete had over ice, Mountbatten set up a block of each on the table, and without any further preamble drew his revolver from his holster.

"I'll now demonstrate the qualities of these two blocks in a way which will indicate beyond any doubt the advantages of Pykrete," he announced, and before anyone else could speak, he fired a shot into the cube of ice, which splintered like glass. Mountbatten then aimed at the Pykrete and fired again. The mixture was as hard as a rock, and the bullet ricocheted round the room. Hollis dived under the table and bumped his head against Sir Alan Brooke, who was in the same place. From this undignified position, Brooke called out: "Dicky, for goodness sake stop firing that thing!" Then there was silence, and the two men crawled out rather shamefacedly, while Mountbatten, smoking revolver still in his hand, beamed amiably round at everybody.

Before anyone could speak there was a tremendous hammering on the door, and in rushed Hollis's secretary, Captain Beer. The sentry posted outside, hearing the noise of firing, had roused him with terrible news.

"Captain Beer, sir!" he explained breathlessly. "Come quickly or you'll be too late! The Chiefs of Staff have started to shoot each other!"

"This story of the iceberg airfields has been used to discredit Mountbatten as being a man willing to foster foolish ideas," writes General Hollis. "But, in fact, at Quebec, the idea of floating a harbor across the Channel—as we did with Mulberry—or laying the pipeline under the Channel, met with far more criticism. Only when these schemes were successful did the iceberg airfield come in for contempt. I must confess I thought the whole thing rather far-fetched and Sir Alan Brooke was even more skeptical of the whole idea."[7]

"Habakkuk" was never proceeded with because the Portuguese had second thoughts about letting the Allies use the Azores; Fighter Command had second thoughts about the range of their aircraft, and America had so many conventional aircraft carriers on order, and quickly became so completely in control of the

---

[7] "One of Dicky Mountbatten's bright ideas," he wrote. ". . . Heaven knows how much money went down the sink over this project." *Notes on my Life,* quoted in *Turn of the Tide* by Sir Arthur Bryant.

Japanese submarine menace, that unsinkable floating airfields were no longer needed in the Pacific.

The Mulberry harbors were essential for landing stores in France, but criticism of them remained until their worth was proved. On "D" Day, minus one, for instance, Admiral Sir Bertram Ramsay, Naval Commander of the Expeditionary Force, stood on the bridge of his flagship and surveyed the impressive scene around him. As far as his binoculars could reach, the English Channel was full of landing-craft, assault vessels, naval ships of every size, type and kind. He turned to a friend of Hollis standing by him and remarked on this vast array of warlike vessels all sailing with a common aim.

"Isn't this an astonishing sight?" he said. "It is the greatest armada that has ever put to sea in all the history of naval warfare. We must give Dicky Mountbatten *some* credit if we're successful, even if he has introduced the seeds of his own destruction in wishing on us those crazy ideas of Mulberry and Pluto, that are bound to ruin the assault. . . ."

❋   ❋   ❋   ❋

There remains a footnote to the stormy start of Combined Operations which underlines the clash of personalities and of Services.

Some weeks after Mr. Churchill had promoted Mountbatten to Vice-Admiral, and he had also been commissioned as a Lieutenant-General and Air Marshal, the Law Officers of the Crown discovered that it was not necessary for an officer to hold a commission in all three Services in order to command them; it was sufficient that the officer concerned should be given an *appointment* to command his rival Services.

Thus, when Field-Marshal Alexander was later appointed Commander-in-Chief in Italy he was not made an Admiral and an Air Marshal at the same time, but was given an appointment to command the Navy and Air Force at that level. Lord Louis Mountbatten's position of holding the King's commission in all three armed services was therefore unique.

After the war, however, when Winston Churchill was no longer Prime Minister, Lord Portal, as Chief of the Air Staff, and Lord Alanbrooke, the C.I.G.S., wrote to Mountbatten about his rank in the Royal Air Force and the Army. They pointed out that since the war was over and he would no doubt wish to return to his own career in the Navy, or else return to civilian life, they felt that it would be inappropriate for him to hold such ranks in the Air Force and Army, and they suggested that it would be fitting if he resigned from them.

King George VI was therefore approached. He was furious at the suggestion, and is said to have replied: "You can't take away the King's Commission save for misconduct."

Thus Admiral of the Fleet Lord Louis Mountbatten still remains General Mountbatten *and* Air Marshal Mountbatten.

"This attitude of the orthodox commanders hurt Mountbatten more deeply than he liked to admit, for he had held the rank from 1942," writes General Hollis. "But it was typical of the attitude of the other three Services to Combined Operations during the war. The three Service members of the Chiefs of Staff Committee did not like to admit that an outside organization such as Combined Operations, responsible only to the Prime Minister and not to them, could have such an important part to play."

CHAPTER 6

The only hope of safety was in boldness.
(Unam in audacia spem salutis.)
TACITUS, *History,* Bk. iv., sec. 49

The climacteric year of the war was 1942, the third year—just as 1917 had been the third and crucial year of the First World War.

During the early months of 1942, the flood of German conquest reached high water mark in Europe and Africa, while Japan triumphed in the Far East. Yet, at the year's end, the situation was almost completely and unbelievably reversed—and for three reasons. First, America was in the war; second, Russia was putting up a quite unexpected resistance; and lastly, the new factories of war in Britain and America were pouring out their weapons and vehicles in quantity.

The Prime Minister was among the few who believed that the Russians would hold out, but General Sir Alan Brooke and many other Generals took a very gloomy view of prospects on the Eastern Front. General Hollis, however, expected that the Russians would at least hold out long enough to force a winter campaign on Hitler "which," says Hollis, "I personally felt sure would seal Hitler's doom—as indeed it did.

"The Prime Minister's object, therefore, was to help the Russians by all possible material means, while they were still in the fight. Many felt that should Stalin not be supplied with sufficient material to conduct his defense, and should he not be appeased by various political concessions, then he might well conclude a separate peace with Germany—as Lenin had done in 1917. It was also fondly thought by many Americans and some British leaders that if the Western Allies treated Russia favorably, Communist hostility to them would die and Russia would become a friend and ally after the war. Time has shown both these beliefs to have been false, but in 1942 they appeared very reasonable.

"Britain and the United States were therefore making the most strenuous and increasing efforts to sustain the Russian armies: for the six months ending December 1942, they guaranteed an increase of 50 per cent in their monthly quotas, and a further equal increase for the first six months of 1943, with the promise that, if more could be done, it would be. But Britain's war industry was almost at a manpower level, her factories were under regular enemy fire, and she could not promise to do more than she had done already. The United States was believed to be prepared to accept a larger responsibility for 1943, though in some respects her immediate contribution was less than Britain's, and at Britain's expense, through the diversion of supplies which were originally intended for this country.

"Thus, by the autumn of 1942, the Germans were halted at Stalingrad; and by Christmas, Stalin's counter-offensive had been successfully launched. In October, Rommel was within reach of Alexandria, but by the end of the year he had been driven out of Egypt, and was under fierce and victorious attack from the Eighth Army."

Elsewhere the news was equally encouraging. The Anglo-American landing subdued Algeria, and from the Pacific came heartening news of Japanese defeats in the Coral Sea and Midway. These spectacular American victories, General Hollis considers, were two of the most decisive battles of the Second World War, and spelt the doom of Japanese superiority in the Far East. "The way was then clear for the huge United States Marine Corps to land on the Japanese-occupied islands with control of the sea beyond them."

In the eleventh month of the year the victory at El Alamein, and the North African landings, gave the initiative to the Allies. By next spring, the Germans were out of Africa altogether, and in the following July, Allied landings in Sicily were to bring nearer the invasion of Southern Europe. But not till June 6, 1944—nearly *two years* after the tide of events began to turn in our favor —was this decisive stage of the offensive begun, and a so-called "Second Front" opened in Europe.

This long delay was the cause of much bitterness and disagreement on many levels of command, and of a deep controversy that still remains unresolved. Before 1942, it had been possible for Britain to lose the war on many occasions in many parts of the world: in France during the spring of 1940, over the skies of Kent, in North Africa in September, in the Far East in December, 1941, and in the long-drawn-out battle with German U-boats in the Atlantic[1] all through the year.

After 1942—and especially after the Battle of Alamein—the issue was decided; all that remained was to agree on the quickest means of finishing the job. As Churchill said, before then we had, broadly speaking, nothing but defeats; afterwards, we had nothing but victories. It was with the object of accelerating these victories that some of the bitterest disputes and discussions of the war took place in "The Hole in the Ground"—discussions that were continued at No. 10, at Chequers, and on the trans-Atlantic telephone to President Roosevelt, as well as at various international conferences, in London, Quebec, Casablanca, Cairo and Teheran.

The issue that split first of all the British Cabinet, and then threatened to divide the Allies, was outwardly simple: how to help Russia to the best advantage. This problem resolved itself into two schools of thought. One, urged by Churchill and the majority of the Cabinet, was that all possible American and British stores —tanks, guns, airplanes, ammunition and raw materials—should be diverted to Russia, by way of convoys to Archangel and Murmansk. The second view, put forward by America, and vociferously backed by Beaverbrook, was that in addition, a "Second Front" should at once be mounted in Northern Europe against an

[1] In the North Atlantic, 2,232 ships with a tonnage of 11,899,732 were sunk, 43.3 per cent of all British, Allied and neutral merchant shipping lost during the war.

enemy who, they reasoned, would be able to offer less resistance because of his enormous battle-front against Russia, which extended from the Baltic to the Black Sea.

As a background to this argument the belief spread throughout the country, fostered by British Communists and other non-combatants of the Left, that all possible aid was not being given to Russia because of Conservative elements in the Government and on the boards of factories. Lord Beaverbrook, countering this entirely wrong but widely-held belief in a speech to 1,500 workers in the Albert Hall, Manchester, on November 8, 1941, was told afterwards by a representative of St. Helens Trades Council that "there was the suspicion in the minds of thousands of workers that not all those in high places want to help the Soviet Union 100 per cent."

The man from St. Helens was quite right, but not in the way he would have imagined. For it was not Conservative M.P.'s but Labor members who were violently against the policy of Mr. Churchill and the defenders of Free Enterprise of giving Russia all the aid that could be afforded. These critics objected to the emphasis laid on helping Russia—sharing the view of the Generals, who believed that Russian resistance would collapse under the tremendous attack from Germany. The man from St. Helens, and others like him, would have been astonished to know that by October 1, 1941, the British Government had already sent 440 airplanes to Russia—airplanes which, had they been dispatched to the Far East instead, might have spared Britain her defeats in Malaya and Burma, and the political and economic repercussions of those shattering humiliations that still rumble round the world.

The mood of the time was one of belligerence, well summed up by Churchill in his address to the Canadian Parliament in a snow-covered Ottawa on December 30, 1941, after his visit to Washington. The most stirringly effective passage was his reference to Pétain's remark to the French Cabinet after the fall of France that, if Churchill thought England could fight on alone, "In three weeks England will have her neck wrung like a chicken."

"Some chicken!" commented Churchill. "Some neck."

This produced a tremendous roar of applause from the Members, "the most terrific cheer I have ever heard on either side of the Atlantic," says General Hollis. After the meeting Churchill asked him why that particular phrase had caused such violent enthusiasm: when he used the word "neck," he had not realized that it had another meaning, which Hollis explained.

The phrase took a powerful hold on the national imagination that inspired a popular song which expressed this spirit of aggression—a pugnacity that also helped to father a feeling of guilt that Britain, who from the spring of 1940 to the summer of 1941 had fought alone on land fronts as far apart as France and Africa, and of course continually at sea and in the air, was now in some way dragging her feet.

Anything that smacked of defensive thinking, of the Maginot mentality or even of reasonable prudence and caution suddenly became anathema to the British public, and especially to those who were not likely to take part in any attack themselves. As Hannen Swaffer wrote in *The People* on April 26, 1942: "You would scarcely believe that nearly two years after Dunkirk—the Commons is still discussing what, in case of invasion, the citizens are to do . . ." This feeling expressed itself in many ways, from chalking such slogans as "Second Front Now" and "Russia bleeds while Britain blancoes" on factory walls to holding mass meetings demanding an immediate landing in Europe.

The agitation for a Second Front was unquestionably the war's biggest political and military issue—and almost certainly the most popular one. All over the country it was supported with passion and enthusiasm—although later on much of this enthusiasm was quenched by the Dieppe raid, with its heavy casualties, which became recognized as a rehearsal for further landings in Europe—and which some still hold was designed to have this dampening effect on public emotions.

Many of those who advocated an early Second Front had no idea what preparation such an operation required, nor of the complicated considerations involved. They assumed vaguely that troops could cross the Channel easily in boats, land in France and carry the day. They were unaware of the requirements for tank landing-craft, and for vessels of all kinds to ferry the men and machines, equipment and arms over the Channel. As one General remarked to Hollis: "To hear them talk you'd think we could walk across the water like Jesus Christ!"

All this agitation for action was not unhealthy, although what disgusted many people—and among them, Ernest Bevin—was the strange, almost feverish eagerness with which so many Britons were willing to aid Russia to victory in preference to helping their own country. The desire for a "Second Front" was also strong in America, and Churchill agreed with Roosevelt, after the Washington Conference in December, 1941, that "a major operation against the enemy must be made in 1942."

*   *   *   *

The seeds of victory had actually been sown in the previous year, when Hitler, against the advice of his military and civilian experts, attacked Russia, and in so doing lost all chance of victory —and also saved Britain from invasion.

Hitler laid his plans for attacking Russia more than six months before he was able to carry them out. On December 18, 1940, in his twenty-first directive of the war, with the code name "Barbarosa," he decided how Russia should be invaded. The core of this argument was that he would crush Russia in "a quick campaign" before the end of the war against Britain. He felt that Britain had come to some secret arrangement to receive aid from Russia—by all the rules of war and logic, Britain should have surrendered long ago—and both he and Stalin had expected her to sue for peace. By attacking Russia, Hitler also hoped to capture raw materials which he was otherwise forced to pay for under the German-Soviet agreement.

A month previously, on November 12, 1940, Hitler had ordered plans for a campaign against Russia to be continued, regardless of any consequences that might arise from the forthcoming conferences between the German and Russian Foreign Ministers. Ribbentrop had invited Molotov to Berlin, possibly to lull Soviet suspicions regarding a German attack, or maybe to try and divert Russian influence and interest from Europe towards India and Persia, where they could be more harmful to Britain.

He told Molotov bluntly that "the entry of the United States into the war was of no consequence at all to Germany. Germany and Italy would never again allow an Anglo-Saxon to land on the European continent. . . . Any attempt at a landing . . . on the European continent by England . . . backed by America was doomed to complete failure at the start." He explained that the English did not yet understand this "because the country was led by a political and military *dilettante* by the name of Churchill, who throughout his previous career had completely failed at all decisive moments, and who would fail again this time."

Hitler's advisers were against attacking Russia, for they felt that, while such an attack would no doubt eventually be victorious, there were not enough economic reasons for making it. Colonel-General Jodl, head of the O.K.W.,[2] was one of those who advised most strongly against it. The fact that he was subsequently hanged does not alter the fact that he gave Hitler some very sound advice. And as late as April 28, 1941, Weizsacker, the head of the German Foreign Office, strongly advised Ribbentrop against making such an attack.[3]

> If every Russian city reduced to ashes were as valuable to us as a sunken British warship (he wrote), I should advocate the German-Russian war for this summer; but I believe that we should be victors over Russia only in a military sense, and should, on the other hand, lose in an economic sense.
>
> It might perhaps be considered an alluring prospect to give the Communist system its death-blow, and it might also be said that it was inherent in the logic of things to muster the Eurasian continent against Anglo-Saxondom, and its following. But the sole decisive factor is whether this project will hasten the fall of England.
>
> We must distinguish between the two possibilities:
>
> (a) England is close to collapse. If we accept this assumption we shall encourage England by taking on a new opponent. Russia is no potential ally of the English. England can expect nothing good from Russia. Hope in Russia is not post-

[2] Oberkommando der Wehrmacht (Armed Forces Supreme Command).
[3] *The Grand Alliance.*

poning England's collapse. With Russia we do not destroy any
English hopes.

(*b*) If we do not believe in the imminent collapse of England, then the thought might suggest itself that by the use of
force we must feed ourselves from Soviet territory. I take it as
a matter of course that we shall advance victoriously to Moscow and beyond that. I doubt very much, however, whether
we shall be able to turn to account what we have won in the
face of the well-known passive resistance of the Slavs. I do
not see in the Russian state any effective opposition capable
of succeeding the Communist system and uniting with us and
being of service to us. We should therefore probably have to
reckon with a continuation of the Stalin system in Eastern
Russia and in Siberia and with a renewed outbreak of hostilities in the spring of 1942. The window to the Pacific Ocean
would remain shut.

No matter. Hitler had guessed right too often before to be
swayed by such views. Also—since his experts did not doubt that
the Russian invasion would be a military success—he hoped that
with Russia defeated "as soon as possible," Japan would be relieved of any specter of a Russian attack on her, and could then
embarrass America in the Far East.

Once Hitler had given orders for the attack to be made, the
build-up of men and material against Russia went ahead with all
speed. In December 1940, the Germans had only thirty-four divisions on their Eastern front. By May 1941, they had eighty-
seven, but of these twenty-five were in the Balkans, fifteen of them
engaged in the invasion of Yugoslavia and Greece. The attack on
Russia was therefore postponed until these could be regrouped
more favorably for an operation which would mean supply lines
of enormous length, and, although no one doubted its eventual
success, to begin such a vast engagement without every available
division would be criminal folly.

Now from the Führerbunker in Berlin to the more homely, less
ostentatious "Hole in the Ground" in London. To those in authority in Whitehall who guessed what was afoot, this was a time of
desperate worry but, says General Hollis, "there was no sign of
panic or dissension."

On January 8, 1941, the Defense Committee realized the imminence of a German attack on Greece by way of Bulgaria, and decided that Greece should be supported with all the means available. These were, in fact, not many, for Britain already had her forces strung out round the world, and any troops intended for Greece would have to be removed from some other place. Also, the Greeks were unwilling to accept British help until such help could come on a scale large enough to be decisive; their own army was almost without communications, and so wretchedly equipped that it would be little better than a liability. To fight Italians with such an army was one thing; to face Germans, another, and the Greeks did not wish to precipitate a German invasion of their country.[4]

The controversy about the British aid to Greece will probably continue to be argued for as long as debate continues on the Second Front. General Hollis always regarded Churchill as completely right in sending troops to her aid, for this helped to delay the German attack on Russia by valuable weeks,[5] since they had to divert troops to crush the unexpectedly strong Greek resistance.

"Of course," says Hollis, "the Generals were against this diversion at a time when our fortunes were in a very precarious state. But they did not seem to realize that this was only one move in a very long game."

Sir Alan Brooke was strongly against sparing troops for Greece. Fearful of a German invasion of Britain, he did not want to send any troops at all out of the country, feeling they would be better

---

[4] "It is hard to picture a more ridiculous situation in war than that of the German Military Attaché (in Athens) standing on the quay and counting the British troops. . . ." (Major-General Playfair and others, *"The Mediterranean and the Middle East,"* Vol. II, London, 1956.)

[5] The German General Blumentritt considered that "the Balkan incident postponed the opening of the (Russian) campaign by five and a half weeks." General Westphal put the delay at "a good six weeks." (Guenther von Blumentritt and others, *"The Fatal Decisions,"* London, 1956.)

Sir Winston Churchill says that "a delay of five weeks (from May 15th to June 22nd) was imposed upon the supreme operation as a result of our resistance in the Balkans, and especially of the Yugoslav revolution. . . . It is reasonable to suppose that Moscow was saved thereby." (*The Grand Alliance.*)

used at home. He wrote of the departure of the Foreign Secretary, Mr. Eden, and the C.I.G.S., Sir John Dill, in February 1941, on "a journey that was destined to take them to Greece and Dill to Yugoslavia, and one that influenced our operations in Greece and Crete, as one of the very few occasions on which I doubted Dill's advice and judgment, and I am not in a position to form any definite opinion as I was not familiar with all the facts.

"I have, however, always considered from the very start that our participation in the operations in Greece was a definite strategic blunder. Our hands were more than full at that time in the Middle East, and Greece could only result in the most dangerous dispersal of force . . ."[6]

General Kennedy, the Director of Military Operations, agreed with this view. So did General Sir John Dill, who feared "a bad mistake had been made in Greece."[7]

Sir John Dill, as we have said, was a man of extreme sensitivity, and in 1941 after a year of disasters to British arms, he was so tired mentally that sometimes he could not concentrate on the business in hand at the Chiefs of Staff meetings, and would sit asking totally irrelevant questions. In his reaction to the grave situation, Dill stood in contrast to the other Chiefs of Staff. Admiral of the Fleet Sir Dudley Pound, for instance, who all this time had to contend with the seriousness of the war at sea, was imperturbable; Air Marshal Sir Charles Portal too, seemed well on top of the job, and never showed any outward sign of disturbance although he was acutely aware of the urgency of the situation.

It must also be remembered, says General Hollis, that Intelligence sources had already reported the German troop movements that presaged their attack on Russia. And as early as January 10, 1941, the Chiefs of Staff had warned the Commanders-in-Chief in Cairo that a German attack on Greece was likely within three weeks, and would in all probability come by way of Bulgaria. In Cairo it was thought, quite wrongly, that German concentrations in Roumania were merely "a war of nerves cleverly operated by

6 "Notes on my Life," quoted by Sir Arthur Bryant, *The Turn of the Tide.*
7 Kennedy, *The Business of War.*

the Germans" in the hope that we would disperse our forces and so stop advancing in Libya. Wavell went so far as to suggest that the Chiefs of Staff should "consider most urgently whether the enemy move is not bluff."

Mr. Churchill had read the Intelligence reports himself, however, and believed they could not be dismissed as bluff. He therefore ignored this suggestion and put what troops he could into Greece: the British First Armored Brigade, the 6th and 7th Australian Divisions, and the New Zealand Division, with the Polish Brigade. They began moving on March 5th, with orders to join the three Greek divisions already there, and some other battalions from Thrace, on a front that stretched up to the borders of Yugoslavia. Although within the next six months Britain would send 440 airplanes to Russia, the British contingent that went to help Greece had only 80 operational aircraft. When the Germans invaded Greece and Yugoslavia simultaneously on April 16th with fifteen divisions—four of them armored—these few British airplanes were outnumbered by more than ten to one.

Within a week the Germans were in Belgrade, and the Greek General Papagos tactfully suggested that the British should withdraw from Greece. Bad weather throughout the first week of the Greek campaign had kept many of the German aircraft out of the skies, but by the middle of the month the weather cleared and the Luftwaffe fighters were up in force. On April 24th Greece surrendered, and the British were faced with a repetition, though happily on a smaller scale, of the retreat at Dunkirk. About 80 per cent of the forces involved were successfully brought out to fight again. Militarily, the British and Dominion intervention in Greece was a failure. Politically, and historically, it is shown to be the opposite.[8] The views of the Generals with regard to sending men

[8] Oddly, Germany's equally swift occupation of Norway in 1940 did not afterwards seem to be as valuable as she had hoped, though the airfields and harbors were useful for attacking British convoys to Russia. In subduing Norway Germany lost one eight-inch cruiser, two light cruisers, ten destroyers and eight submarines. Recording these losses Dr. Stefan T. Possony ("*United States Naval Institute Proceedings*," July 1946) noted: "A fleet had been sacrificed to gain a base, but the base had little value without the fleet

and tanks might appear justified if Greece had been the last round of the last battle of the war, but it was not.

"Sir Alan Brooke, Commander-in-Chief of the Home Forces, stoutly resisted any further depletion of his command," says Sir John Kennedy.[9] ". . . He hoped we would not 'raid his orchard' any more to reinforce the Middle East. Churchill, in the meantime, was constantly urging the despatch of more tanks to Wavell . . . We know now that he was right."

When Greece fell, Mr. Eden, with great vigor, urged that a hundred tanks should be sent to Egypt to reinforce the armies there: Kennedy and Dill were against it. ". . . But next day, Mr. Churchill returned to London and, after a talk with the tank experts, gave orders for sixty-seven more tanks to be loaded in the convoy. Events proved that he was utterly and completely right."

The same events also proved that the Generals were utterly and completely wrong. It was fortunate indeed for this country that their counsels of caution were overruled, but then, as Churchill has pointed out,[10] "Generals are often prone, if they have the chance, to choose a set-piece battle, when all is ready at their own selected moment, rather than to wear down the enemy by continued unspectacular fighting. They naturally prefer certainty to hazard. They forget that war never stops, but burns on from day to day, with ever-changing results, not only in one theater, but in all."

"Churchill," writes General Hollis, "took the view, agreeing with Clausewitz, that 'the subordination of the political point of view to the military would be contrary to common sense, for policy has declared the war; it is the intelligent faculty, war only the instrument, and not the reverse. The subordination of the military point of view to the political is, therefore, the only thing which is possible. . . .'

"I remember the moment when he came to this grave decision, which was one of the major turning-points of the war, a hinge of victory. The odds against sending tanks and guns to North Africa were tremendous. He might easily be sending a very large part

[9] *The Business of War.*
[10] *The Grand Alliance.*

of our meager armaments to the bottom of the sea, and even if they reached Africa safely and Britain should be invaded meanwhile, these same tanks and guns might have made the difference between victory and defeat. But on the other hand, if the Germans won in North Africa, then all was lost; Churchill knew the risk *had* to be taken.

"He gathered up all the reports and papers and took them into his room, and studied them on his own, and then came to the decision on his own.

" 'Pray God,' he said, 'it's the right decision.' "

Thus, out of what appeared to be yet another example of British bungling and withdrawal, the German invasion was now delayed for at least five weeks—some German generals put the time as even longer—which meant that Hitler would be unable to finish his campaign in Russia before the winter set in, and would thus be forced into winter operations.

The delay inflicted upon the Germans by Churchill meant as he well knew, that the greatest Russian generals of all—Generals January and February—would throw in their forces against the invaders. Hitler would not be able to defeat Russia before the summer ended, but would see his armies freeze and break, as Napoleon had seen the flower of his forces wither in the fearful Russian winter nearly 130 years previously.

The militarily unsuccessful Greek action had a further political success in that it stirred American opinion in favor of Britain, who although hard pressed herself, still appeared in her traditional role of champion to a smaller country under grievous attack. Roosevelt cabled warmly to Churchill: "You have done not only heroic but very useful work in Greece, and the territorial loss is more than compensated for by the necessity for an enormous German concentration and resulting enormous German losses in men and material. . . ."

Shortly before the Germans invaded Greece, reports from agents in Yugoslavia had reached "The Hole in the Ground" that three out of five Panzer divisions that had come south towards Greece and Yugoslavia *had returned north to Cracow*. No less than sixty trains of armor were on the move *away* from the expected scene of operations. As early as April 3rd Churchill decided this could only mean that a German attack on Russia was imminent, although the Russians seemed entirely unaware of their danger.

He had last sent a direct message to Stalin on June 25, 1940, when Sir Stafford Cripps had been appointed Ambassador to Moscow, but he decided to warn Stalin immediately and personally of the danger while there was still time for Russia to take steps against it. Mr. Churchill therefore sent a message to Sir Stafford:[11]

Following from me to M. Stalin, *provided that it can be personally delivered by you:* I have sure information from a trusted agent that when the Germans thought they had got Yugoslavia in the net—that is to say, after March 20—they began to move three out of the five Panzer divisions from Roumania to Southern Poland. The moment they heard of the Serbian revolution this movement was countermanded. Your Excellency will readily appreciate the significance of these facts.

Unfortunately, His Excellency was not given the chance to appreciate their significance while he had still time to regroup his forces to face the threat from the West, for Cripps, replying to Mr. Churchill on April 12th, explained that just before he received the telegram he had written a personal letter to Vyshinsky, then Vice-Commissar for Foreign Affairs. In this note he had urged Russia to a more vigorous co-operation with countries opposed to the Axis in the Balkans, lest she should miss the last chance of defending her own frontiers. He did not wish, therefore, to present Churchill's message to Stalin as he felt that, coming so soon after his own, it would be "not merely ineffectual, but a serious tactical mistake." Stalin, then, did not receive Mr. Churchill's message for nearly three more weeks—on April 22nd. Even so he had two months to prepare for the impending attack, but he did little with this time.

On May 31st, the Chiefs of Staff cabled to the Middle East

11 *The Grand Alliance.*

commanders in Cairo: "The Germans are now concentrating large army and air forces against the Russians. Under this threat they will probably demand concessions most injurious to us. . . . If the Russians refuse, the Germans will march. . . ."

One day before the German attack on the Soviet Union, on June 21st, Hitler wrote to Mussolini:[12] "The elimination of Russia means . . . a tremendous relief for Japan in East Asia, and thereby the possibility of a much stronger threat to American activities through Japanese intervention . . . Since I struggled through to this decision, I again feel spiritually free. The partnership with the Soviet Union . . . was . . . often very irksome to me, for in some way or other it seemed to me to be a break with my whole origin, my concepts, and my former obligations. I am happy now to be relieved of those mental agonies. . . ."

On the evening of Friday, June 20th, Churchill drove down to spend the weekend at Chequers. His car was fitted with a bell which could be operated by his chauffeur through a foot pedal, and when the policemen, who often rode ahead of his car on motorcycles, were not on duty, he sometimes used this to warn policemen controlling the traffic of his approach. Those who travelled with him never knew when he wanted the bell rung. In some moods, he would urge the chauffeur through the speaking-tube: "Ring the bell! ring the bell!" But if he were tired or worried, sitting back with a black bandage over his eyes to rest them from the light he would instead be stung into sudden annoyance by the clamor of the bell, and exclaim testily: "Stop ringing that bell! You'll have us charged with bad behavior."

On this journey to Chequers, the bell was silent and so was Churchill. He had much to think about; he believed that the German attack would be launched within the next few days, and should this happen he had tentatively arranged to broadcast on the following day. Only the previous Sunday he had cabled to President Roosevelt in America that "a vast German onslaught on Russia was imminent." Roosevelt's reply had been to send across the American Ambassador to Britain, John G. Winant, in a

[12] *Nazi-Soviet Relations*, 1939-41.

bomber. So urgent was the journey that although one engine of the bomber failed some miles over the Atlantic, Winant continued on three. He and his wife were staying at Chequers for the week end, and as soon as Churchill arrived he told the Prime Minister that should Russia be attacked, the President would immediately support any announcement he might make welcoming her as an ally.

There was still no news of attack on Saturday, however, and Churchill postponed his broadcast for another day. Strolling on the croquet lawn in the warm dusk after dinner on Saturday evening, Mr. Churchill and his private secretary Jock Colville, were discussing the probability of the attack, when Colville asked whether for Mr. Churchill, the arch-anti-Communist, "being ready to help Russia was not bowing down in the House of Rimmon?"

"Not at all," Churchill immediately replied. "I have only one purpose, the destruction of Hitler, and my life is much simplified thereby. If Hitler invaded Hell I would at least make a favorable reference to the Devil in the House of Commons."[13]

On Sunday morning, when he awoke at his usual hour[14]—eight o'clock—he was handed a message with the news that he had so long awaited. The Prime Minister made no comment when he received it, but simply told his Private Secretary: "Tell the B.B.C. that I will broadcast at nine tonight."

In fact, so complicated was the script he wrote for his talk, and so determined was he to strike exactly the right note, with every phrase Churchillian and splendid, that the speech was only ready twenty minutes before he went on the air. Meanwhile, Sir John Dill, who informed General Kennedy "that he regarded the Russians as so foul that he hated the idea of any close association with them,"[15] arrived with details of the invasion, which was taking place on an immense front, and against comparatively little opposition. The initial news was grim; hundreds of Soviet air-

[13] *The Grand Alliance.*

[14] Actually, news of the German attack had arrived at Chequers at four o'clock in the morning, but Mr. Churchill had issued strict instructions that he was never to be awakened before eight, "save for the invasion of England." News of the invasion of Russia was therefore delayed until that hour.

[15] *The Business of War.*

planes had been caught on the ground, and destroyed before they could take the air.

Churchill immediately sent for two men whose opinion he valued, to hear their views on the best means of helping the Russians. The first was Sir Stafford Cripps, who had arrived in England from Moscow only a few days previously. The second was Lord Beaverbrook, then Minister of Supply, who was in bed when the message was delivered to him. He at once rose, dressed and drove over to Chequers.

These two men were as unlike in appearance as in outlook. Cripps, tall, thin, pale and ascetic, seemed to look disapprovingly at those who did not live their lives on the same cold, passionless level as his own. Beaverbrook, part pirate and part poet, was shorter in build, with quick, darting eyes, and a manner accustomed to obedience; his occasionally harsh Canadian accent concealed a quick, impetuous kindness and a prodigal generosity when his heart was touched.

Cripps, who wore his rigid, almost puritanical, Socialist views and unquestioned, unquestioning idealism like a steel brace, might have been expected to welcome the opportunity of helping Russia, the spiritual home of the Left. Beaverbrook, the apostle of initiative and success, a millionaire at thirty, whose newspapers carried into millions of homes his own personal amalgam of Calvinism and Canadian enterprise every day, might have been forgiven for being less eager to help Communist Russia.

In fact, it was the other way about.

Sir Stafford, who earlier had thought that Germany would not attack Russia despite irrefutable evidence from various sources that such a move was impending, now declared that before the mechanized forces of the Führer the Russians would rapidly collapse.

"The Germans will go through Russia like a hot knife through butter," was how he put it. Like the Generals, he predicted a Russian defeat, and was therefore against aligning himself with them. ("A brilliant, sincere man, but a goose politically," was General Hollis's opinion of Sir Stafford on this occasion.)

Beaverbrook argued from the opposite side. He had no love

for the Russian system of politics,[16] but he felt that Churchill should align himself with the Russians forthwith, and proceeded to produce unanswerable arguments for such a move. As they lunched together, he declared that everything possible should be done to help them, for an ally with such enormous manpower and so great a potential in production would be invaluable to the British cause. Churchill, caught between the Scylla of a cautious Cripps and the Charybdis of an audacious Beaverbrook, made a bold decision: to announce that evening, when he spoke on the radio, all-out aid to the Russians.

"Lesser leaders would have delayed until further news came in from the front," says General Hollis; "until other advice could be given; until events themselves might give a lead, for Churchill had for years been hostile to Russia, and had indeed been responsible for the British intervention in the Russian Revolution at Archangel in 1918. But now that the moment had come for an instant decision, he did not waver. Only a very great man could have acted thus, and so swiftly."

John G. Winant, the American Ambassador, who never gave decisive advice if he could help it, and who generally spoke in such a low voice that people could hardly hear what advice he did give, left the table to telephone Roosevelt and explain what was afoot. After lunch, Churchill drafted out his speech with Winant in support, and Cripps by then had acquiesced in the Premier's decision. Millions who listened in that night were moved by Churchill's broadcast words.

"I have to declare the decision of His Majesty's Government—and I feel sure it is a decision in which the great Dominions will in due course, concur—for we must speak out now at once, without a day's delay," he said. "I have to make the declaration, but can you doubt what our policy will be? We have but one aim, and one single, irrevocable purpose. We are resolved to destroy Hitler and every vestige of the Nazi regime. From this, nothing will turn us—nothing. We will never parley, we

[16] "I am no Communist; I am a Capitalist. I do not favor a sharing of wealth, I only want a sharing of opportunity." Lord Beaverbrook, speech in House of Lords, February 23, 1943.

will never negotiate with Hitler or any of his gang. We shall fight him by land, we shall fight him by sea, we shall fight him in the air, until, with God's help, we have rid the earth of his shadow and liberated its people from his yoke. Any man or state who fights on against Nazidom will have our aid. Any man or state who marches with Hitler is our foe. . . . That is our policy and that is our declaration. It follows therefore that we shall give whatever help we can to Russia and the Russian people. We shall appeal to all our friends and allies in every part of the world to take the same course and pursue it, as we shall, faithfully and steadfastly to the end . . .

"This is no class war, but a war in which the whole British Empire and Commonwealth of Nations is engaged, without distinction of race, creed or party. . . .

". . . The Russian danger is therefore our danger, and the danger of the United States, just as the cause of any Russian fighting for his hearth and home is the cause of free men and free peoples in every quarter of the globe. Let us learn the lessons already taught by such cruel experience. Let us redouble our exertions, and strike with united strength while life and power remain . . ."

Russia had men enough and to spare, but, as had been proved in France, Greece and the Balkans, men against machines were of little value. Because Russia was short of tanks and guns, and because so many of her fighter airplanes had been destroyed, Churchill decided that the first priority, and the best way of sustaining her resistance, was to provide her with the raw materials of war, of which in those days she had little enough.

In September, therefore, Lord Beaverbrook as Minister of Supply, with General Ismay and some others, set off to Moscow with a list of war material that was already on its way to Russia by way of the most perilous supply route of all, through the frozen Arctic seas, north of Norway, where every convoy met fearful and relentless opposition from German aircraft and submarines, based chiefly on that country.

Beaverbrook's party travelled as far as Archangel in H.M.S. *London,* and then flew to Moscow in a Russian aircraft, a journey that took nearly eight hours. As they flew, Russian anti-aircraft batteries, apparently unable to distinguish one of their own airplanes from an enemy—although no Germans were within hundreds of miles—opened fire on them. The pilot waggled the wings as a recognition signal, and then, when the firing still continued, brought down his heavy aircraft almost to the tops of the forests of fir trees so that the anti-aircraft batteries could not hold it in their sights. When they arrived in the capital and explained what had happened, they were solemnly assured that the Colonel in charge of the battery had himself been shot for his efforts.

The British Government were so anxious to help Russia that they denuded their own armies of weapons and stores for which in many cases they had already been waiting two years and more.

Between October 1941 and June 1942, inclusive, for example, Britain promised to deliver no less than 1,800 fighters, in addition to the 440 already promised. The British forces would also send 2,250 tanks, aiming at a target of 250 every month; and as well as naval assistance, which had already been agreed, 1,000 twenty-five pounder guns with 1,000,000 shells were on their way, plus 7,000 Bren guns, 2,250 two-pounder high-velocity guns (which were fitted to the tanks), and a further 500 two-pounder guns to be used as anti-tank weapons. Britain was also going to turn over 23,000 Tommy-guns, already ordered by her from America, so that they could go direct to Russia, and 20,000 British-made Sten guns.

Britain further promised to send enormous quantities of raw materials, such as tin from Burma and rubber from Malaya, which she was herself only receiving by way of long and dangerous convoys, and which had already been earmarked for her own war effort.

There would thus be 72,000 tons of rubber for Russia plus 25,000 tons of electrolytic copper, and 5,000 tons of aluminum, with 2,000 tons a month thereafter until June. The Russian armies would also be supplied with 3,000,000 pairs of boots, and 250,000 greatcoats.

Mr. Churchill had empowered Lord Beaverbrook to offer British troops to Stalin in the Caucasus, but when Beaverbrook gave him this news, Stalin shook his head.

"There's no war in the Caucasus," he pointed out.

"Well, we'll send troops to Archangel," suggested Lord Beaverbrook.

"That proposal at least has the advantage that Churchill knows the way there—and the way back again," retorted Stalin drily, for British troops had been in Archangel in 1918, during the abortive British intervention against the Bolsheviks.

The differences in temperament and outlook between Sir Stafford Cripps and Lord Beaverbrook were further exemplified during these discussions in Moscow. Cripps was in favor of what Beaverbrook called a "League of Nations" manner of conducting the conference. He wanted Britain, America, and Russia—for though the United States was not then in the war, an American Mission under Averell Harriman was visiting Moscow simultaneously, and acting in concert with Beaverbrook—to give each other a complete disclosure of war information, followed by a "general share-out" of material. This concept would also include the disclosure of places of campaign for the coming year. In other words, Cripps wanted negotiation to take the place of utilization. Russia's aim was much simpler—she wanted to go on fighting the Germans offensively or defensively along the whole front—and Beaverbrook was determined to do all he could to help her implement this intention.

Cripps also pressed for the trading of goods against information, and further attempted to introduce into what was intended as a single-minded conference such issues as supplies for China and for the Polish Army. Beaverbrook and Harriman, more interested in helping Russia to fight back, refused to be caught up in such side issues. Beaverbrook, with the born journalist's eye for noting details of behavior that could illumine the whole character of a man, found that he and Stalin shared the same views about the waste of time in committees and discussions. Both were men of action, and to illustrate his point Stalin told him a story of a visit he had paid to a commissar in a village, who seemingly preferred talk to action.

STALIN:	How are you getting on with the sowing?
COMMISSAR:	With the sowing, Comrade Stalin? We have mobilized ourselves.
STALIN:	Well, and what then?
COMMISSAR:	We have put the question squarely.
STALIN:	And what next?
COMMISSAR:	There is a turn, Comrade Stalin; soon there will be a turn.
STALIN:	But still?
COMMISSAR:	We can say there is an indication of some Progress.
STALIN:	But for all that, how are you getting on with the sowing?
COMMISSAR:	So far, Comrade Stalin, *we have not yet begun to sow!*[17]

Stalin, a short man, with close-cropped gray hair, wearing a khaki jacket buttoned up to the neck, with neither badges of rank nor decoration, and his trousers tucked into long, soft leather boots, worked with Lord Beaverbrook from dusk till dawn for several nights. He appeared abstemious, and would only take a drink after their discussions were finished, and then he would sip the wine sparingly.

The "Big Three" leaders could all hold their liquor. Churchill would take a drink at lunch-time, and perhaps have a glass of whisky in the late afternoon. At dinner he might drink as much as half a bottle of wine or champagne. He also had a liking for brandy. Stalin would indulge in a drinking "session" which would put the strongest drinker to a sharp test. Roosevelt delighted in preparing cocktails before dinner which were not appreciated by those with tender stomachs, for he made them from Argentine vermouth. "It always seemed to me that his zest was for mixing cocktails rather than for drinking them," says Lord Beaverbrook. "Once this task was over, then to dinner with not a drop to drink, not a sign of anything at all but a glass of ice-cold water which one tried to warm up by delay and procrastination."

[17] *Don't Trust to Luck,* by Lord Beaverbrook.

One evening, when news from the Russian front was very grave, he gave a great dinner-party for three hundred guests to the British delegation, and Lord Beaverbrook sat in the place of honor on his right hand. Stalin waited until all were gathered in the room, and then he appeared with his lieutenants, Mikoyan and Voroshilov, both taller than he and wearing more resplendent uniforms. Stalin first toasted Great Britain and then America— although America was still technically neutral—and talked a great deal, especially during the Russian speeches being made by his subordinates.

He had his personal bottle of wine at his place, and over the top of this he placed a tumbler which, he explained, was "to keep the vitality in the wine." Some of the British delegation thought that it served a more useful purpose in keeping any poison out. Stalin would pour his own drink from the bottle into a very small glass, and his food was served by a special waiter.

As the meal progressed Stalin, casting about for conversation, told Beaverbrook how much he had been impressed by meeting George Bernard Shaw during the latter's visit to Russia before the war. Shaw's reputation as a writer and philosopher was unusually high at that time, and when he came into Stalin's room he brought Lady Astor with him. Stalin asked her how Churchill was getting on in England, and Lady Astor replied: "Winston Churchill's done. You will never hear more of him."

Stalin could not agree.

"When England goes to war, England will send for the old war horse," he told her.

"Did Lady Astor ask you any questions?" Beaverbrook inquired.

"Yes," replied Stalin after a moment's thought. "She asked me whether I ever read the Bible."

Soon after Lord Beaverbrook's return from Russia he began to campaign for more aid to be sent there. He had been impressed by the way the Russians were holding out against the Germans, and in a letter to a friend he summarized his opinions thus: "There is today only one military problem—how to help Russia. Yet on that issue the Chiefs of Staff content themselves with saying that nothing can be done. They point out the difficulties but make no suggestions for overcoming them . . . For the Continent is still considered by our Generals to be out of bounds for British troops. We must strike before it is too late."[18]

Friction with the Russians soon appeared, however, when Churchill, who had agreed with Stalin (September 6, 1941) that he would put pressure on the Finns, even to declaring war, if they showed signs of going beyond their old frontiers,[19] was reluctant to go so far, as during the next months the Russians were constantly pressing him to do. Lord Beaverbrook took Stalin's side and also urged the Prime Minister to declare war, whatever the consequences might be.

The Socialist Ministers, and Ernest Bevin in particular, were strongly in opposition to this. Bevin, who in 1945 was to claim unctuously that, should the Socialists win the General Election, "Left would speak to Left," was not at all anxious at this stage to speak to the Left in Russia, nor were many of his Labor colleagues in office. Mutual distrust of Socialists and Communists was very great, and with cause.

A sharp message from Stalin on the British "failure" to declare war on the Finns also stung Churchill to anger, and he was all for composing a very acid reply to the Russian Ambassador, until Beaverbrook urged him to tone it down.

On October 19th, Beaverbrook presented a memorandum which stated in frank terms his views on helping Russia. He pointed out that, since the start of the German invasion, British military leaders had been "consistently averse" to taking any offensive action to assist the Russians. The successful Anglo-Russian occupation of the Persian oilfields in the previous August, which had brought German influence in the country to an end, had been merely a

[18] *Sherwood, Roosevelt and Hopkins.*

[19] I.e. those obtaining before the Treaty of Moscow in 1940, when they were forced to cede Eastern Karelia to Russia. "It is difficult to see what value the Finns were to either side, but Stalin feared that since he was fully occupied with the Germans they might take back, not only this territory, but also other land which had been in dispute for years. The point is not really important, but it does show how very hard pressed Stalin was at this time, and how desperate for assistance."—General Hollis.

small preventive operation, in which the British used barely a quarter as many troops as the Russians. The only other British operations up to then had been bomber and fighter sweeps over Western Germany and France which, he said, had done nothing to help Russia, nor had they been of much use to Britain, because they had cost her many of her best aircrews.

British strategy so far, in his opinion, was still based on a long-term view of the war that ignored the urgencies and opportunities of the moment, and there had been no attempt to reassess the position, now radically changed by the entry of Russia into the war on their side. The Russian resistance had swept away the old conception of a long war, and long-term strategy; also, it had probably denuded Western Europe of German troops, and had prevented the Axis from taking the offensive on any new fronts. More, it had stirred up a restless, well-nigh revolutionary situation in enemy-occupied countries, yet the British armies were virtually confined to Britain, thanks to the views of the British Generals, and so in Eastern Europe the Germans moved without hindrance. Further, any sign of revolt against them there was deplored by the British Generals as being premature, because they were not ready to take advantage of it.

While Britain was thus losing opportunities, said Beaverbrook, she was also creating new perils. For should the Russians—deprived of British support—collapse, there would be nothing to hold back Hitler from a concentrated attack on the West.

Churchill, discussing this paper next day, said that he had not taken it as an attack requiring detailed reply. Yes, retorted Beaverbrook, it *was* an attack, and it clearly stated where he differed from his colleagues on the Russian issue. He wanted to take advantage of what he called "the rising temper in the country" to help Russia; others did not. He wanted, to this end, a tremendous effort to increase production; others did not. He wanted to fulfill the agreement he had made in Moscow, in every particular; others did not. Most of all, he wanted the Army to support Russia; but the Chiefs of Staff disagreed.

Mr. Churchill said he was sorry to hear of these criticisms of the Chiefs of Staff, which he must, "as a matter of course," take as a personal criticism of himself. What, then, did Lord Beaverbrook suggest as an alternative plan?

"The attack on Trondheim in northern Norway," replied Beaverbrook immediately.

The possibility of a landing in Norway had been under consideration that autumn, when the Prime Minister had suggested to General Ismay and the Chiefs of Staff that, unless some entirely unexpected development elsewhere interfered—such as invasion—the liberation of Norway should be attempted at the earliest possible moment.

Beaverbrook had also carried with him to Moscow—in the general directive the Prime Minister and he had drawn up—a clear guarantee that "we have every intention of intervening on land next spring" (i.e. 1942), and, among possibilities, specified a suggestion that "an expedition into Norway would raise a serious revolt, and might, if it succeeded, win the Swedish Government, with its good Army, to our cause." The directive added that this possibility was being studied, and that it was not proposed to ask for Russian military aid in this matter as "their intervention would antagonize Sweden beyond all hope."[20] This would be an entirely British enterprise, taking the form of capturing the port and airdrome of Trondheim, which Admiral Keyes had so dearly wished to capture in 1940.

Mr. Churchill agreed that he was in favor of carrying out this operation, but it could not take effect until December; by then he expected the Russian crisis to have been resolved, one way or the other.

Lord Beaverbrook pointed out that a Norwegian operation would involve the Germans directly, and would thus be of direct value to Russia. The Prime Minister replied that even if, by December, the Germans were still fighting in Russia, a Norwegian landing would not divert any of their forces: they might reinforce their front with troops from Finland or the Low Countries, but certainly not with any engaged on the vital Eastern Front. Besides, he said, British troops would not be able to seize the

20 *The Grand Alliance.*

enemy's airdromes within "a reasonable time," and so gain control of the air, because the coast of Norway was beyond the range of our fighters.

The Prime Minister, originally enthusiastic on the subject of a Norwegian landing, had been persuaded against it by Brooke and the other Generals, who were still consumed by fear of a German invasion of Britain. The Battle of Britain was the death-blow to "Sea-Lion," the German plan for invading Britain; and Germany's invasion of Russia destroyed the likelihood of any further attempt at invading England, but Brooke still felt that such an event *was* possible, and even probable.

Whenever troops were withdrawn from Britain for other theaters of war, like the Middle East, he became increasingly worried and annoyed. Churchill, more concerned with attack than defense, was skeptical of the continuing danger of a German invasion.

"He would not acknowledge," wrote Brooke in February 1941, "that an invasion of this country on that scale was possible in the face of partial sea-control and local air-control." And when Brooke explained his own counter-measures for defense and the details of the German plans, after an exercise, Churchill "considered that the umpires had exaggerated the German threat of invasion. He even implied that this had been done in order to influence him into considering the threat greater than it really was."[21]

General Kennedy, writing sixteen years later, observes:[22] "It seems odd now that we were still regarding a German invasion of England as possible. Our view in April 1941 was that it was a real, though diminishing danger. It must be remembered that the Germans had not yet attacked Russia; comparatively few of their troops were engaged in active operations, and they had some two hundred divisions available for new enterprises."

"Brooke and Kennedy were not alone in their fears," writes General Hollis, "for on May 6, 1941 Sir John Dill, the C.I.G.S., presented Mr. Churchill and the Chiefs of Staff, General Ismay

[21] *The Turn of the Tide.*
[22] *The Business of War.*

and me with a paper entitled: 'The relation of the Middle East to the security of the U.K.,' in which he said frankly that in his opinion there was not enough armor in the country both to defend it against invasion and at the same time to carry out offensive action in the Middle East. Dill ended: 'I believe that we have gone to the limit, if not beyond it, in respect of the security of Great Britain, with which the defense of Ireland and the seizure of the Atlantic islands are inextricably bound up. In my view it would be unjustifiable, during the next three months, to risk sending away from this country more than an adequate maintenance reserve for the tanks already in, or on the way to the Middle East. Even this, at a wastage of 10 per cent per month, will involve the monthly dispatch of about fifty tanks.' "

This communication incensed the Prime Minister, for, "unlike his C.I.G.S., or the United States Chiefs of Staff, Churchill had not the slightest intention of abandoning the Eastern Mediterranean to strengthen still further his British home base for defensive or other reasons."[23]

Even after Hitler had attacked Russia, Brooke still feared the possibility of invasion, for, like many of his brother Generals, he did not really think the Russians could hold out against Hitler's divisions. If they failed, he reasoned, what was there to prevent the invasion of Britain? Before the assault on Russia, however, Brooke held that "wherever the next thrust may be on the Continent it is certain that the process of attempted strangulation will continue . . . And if these attempts are sufficiently successful, eventually invasion will be attempted."[24]

He was irked by the irresponsibility of those who thought that holiday-makers might be allowed to visit the East coast where, of course, if there was going to be an invasion the danger would be enormous. On top of this he considered the fact that sixty or so cruiser tanks were being withdrawn from the country for the Middle East "an appalling blow."[25] Months later he wrote: "An-

[23] *Winston Churchill and the Second Front.*
[24] *Diary,* March 13, 1941.
[25] *Diary,* April 21, 1941.

other extraction of armored forces from this country this evening in the shape of a brigade from the Sixth Armored Division. When will the War Office learn not to break up armored formations which it has taken months to build up?"[26]

"Even when others, including the Germans, were looking Eastward, Brooke was still racking his brains over the proper cover of all points in this country against the threat from the air, whether, to ensure against that, he should 'further denude the beaches'; whether in that case he was only laying the country bare to invasion by sea. Had they enough air support? How long would the Fleet take to assemble for defense? Could they hold back enemy tanks in Kent? Indeed, so anxious was Sir Alan about the possibility of invasion that he wished to stage an Exercise on a large scale in London against the possibility, which he regarded as a highly dangerous one, of enemy airborne landings in the parks. But on the grounds that the threat was not so ominous, and that such an exercise would cause needless alarm among the public, the Cabinet refused his suggestion."—So General Hollis later summed up the situation.

In the first months of the German invasion of Russia, when the campaign appeared to be going disastrously for the Red Army, as if indeed the Germans were going through the country "like a hot knife through butter," Churchill was sympathetic to the popular demand for diversionary action by the inactive British Army in Britain, and in September 1941, when Lord Beaverbrook was in Moscow, he was considering what Brooke dismissed as "a mad scheme." This was a proposal by the Joint Planning Staff for a diversionary attack in the Cherbourg peninsula, where the enemy was vulnerable, which could relieve pressure on the Russians. The idea, which had the American General Marshall's support, was abandoned because it was argued on the British side that such a narrow strip could not form a practicable base for a major offensive, nor would it divert German forces, but would be easily cut off by those already in France.

It was then that Churchill, still anxious to take the offensive, turned his attention to Norway, where a landing would not only

[26] *Diary*, October 27, 1941.

divert German troops from Russia but would lessen the dangers
to our Murmansk convoys which took the Norway route.

At midnight on October 3rd, the War Office sent a special
messenger to Brooke with orders to investigate the possibilities of
an attack on Trondheim, and to prepare a plan within the next
few days. This news did not greatly please the General, who was
very busy on his most ambitious anti-invasion exercise so far—
Operation Bumper, comprising "the Armored Divisions, nine Infantry Divisions, and two Army Brigades." He was controlling
this personally from Oxford, while General Alexander commanded
the forces defending Britain against the so-called German army
which was supposed to have landed in East Anglia. Brooke was
kept busy interviewing the Press, establishing his Control Center,
travelling by car and air "to find out situation," and "rushing
round by air from 8 A.M. to 7 P.M. and conference till midnight
after dinner."

"Manœuvres going very well and day most interesting," he wrote
in his diary, and, later. "They have been a great success. I am
delighted with the way Armored Divisions have come on, but
very disappointed at the way Higher Commanders are handling
them . . ."[27]

At the end of these week-long, absorbing activities, he was
called upon to produce a plan for the Norwegian operation, of
which he thoroughly disapproved, on the grounds that they could
not supply adequate air support, and would "fall into the same
pitfall as we did before." The discussions continued for hours, for
days, and the more he thought about it, Brooke, exhausted by
his week of maneuvers and lack of sleep, and eager to concentrate
again on the final phase of "Bumper," became more and more
convinced that the Trondheim project was "folly to attempt."

He did not like the assignment. He had resisted the Greek
expedition, and he still thought that any operations to help Russian resistance were a waste of time and manpower. He had only
a week to produce the plan, "ready to the last button," though
the Chiefs of Staff Committee had already turned down such a

[27] Quoted in *The Turn of the Tide.*

plan because of inadequate air support. Brooke therefore demanded that the Commander-in-Chief, Home Fleet, the Air Officers Commanding Fighter and Bomber Commands, the Minister of War Transport, and several others should be placed at his disposal. They were, at once.

For the next few days he found himself dividing his time between conferences on Trondheim and conferences on "Bumper," journeys, and a visit to Chequers.[28]

"Sometimes," says General Hollis, "we wondered which was the more important—winning the war and fighting Germans, or playing soldiers on Salisbury Plain. I remember one officer saying to me at this time, more in sorrow than in anger: 'The Generals dislike war—it interferes with training!' Churchill would say, 'I sometimes think some of my Generals don't *want* to fight the Germans.'"

Brooke did not like the "final shape" of the Trondheim proposal and admitted he "would have liked to recast the whole thing. But," he added, "my conclusion would still remain the same —that the operation is impracticable."[29]

The Prime Minister did not like its final shape, either. He told General Brooke aggressively that he had expected a detailed plan for the operation, but had been given "a masterly treatise on all the difficulties." The meeting at Downing Street, with Eden, Attlee, the Chiefs of Staff and others, was a prolonged and stormy one.

Mr. Churchill, his chin angrily set forward, cross-questioned Brooke for nearly two hours on what Brooke thought were the minor points of his plan; he would not follow Brooke's repeated lead back to the lack of air support for the operation: "You state that you will be confronted by frosts and thaws—how can you account for such a statement? . . . You state that it will take you

[28] This was exhausting. "The last fortnight has been a hard one with the large Exercise and the Prime Minister's task on top of it to examine 'Trondheim Operation,'" he wrote in his diary on October 10th. "The Exercise was of the greatest value and a landmark in the higher training of that year . . ." —*Notes on my Life*, IV, 300, quoted by Sir Arthur Bryant.

[29] *Diary.*

some twenty-four hours to cover the ground between A. and B. How can you account for so long being taken?"—and so on. Brooke explained the necessity to allow time for overcoming resistance, and such operations as the removal of road-blocks, while everyone else in the room listened to the cross-examination, and the Prime Minister punctuated his own questions from time to time with sarcastic comments.

Sir Alan Brooke always spoke very quickly, rattling his words off in short staccato sentences so that, as Hollis puts it, "he sounded like a Gatling gun." Churchill would propose some form of action, at which General Brooke would shake his head in vigorous disapproval.

"No, no, Prime Minister. I cannot agree with that"—and he would propose some counter-suggestion of his own. Mr. Churchill, who had heard his reply perfectly well, would then turn to General Ismay and cup a hand to his ear.

"I cannot hear what he says," he would observe, as though General Brooke were not even present. Ismay would then repeat Brooke's comments more slowly and in a louder voice. Churchill would nod, as if the words were just reaching him for the first time. Then, if he did not wish to enter into an immediate argument, he would suddenly change the subject completely and discuss other matters. Otherwise, he would still affect not to hear the opposing point of view, and it had to be repeated in an even louder voice for a second time.

"Oh," Churchill would say disconcertingly, *"Oh!* So *that's* what he says. *Oh!* I see."

Finally, at the end of the meeting, General Hollis recalls, "As the other members of the War Cabinet or Staff began to gather up their papers to leave, Mr. Churchill would unexpectedly return to the point with which General Brooke had disagreed, presenting his view from a different angle, and by surprise and determination would often carry the day."

At last, after much argument over the capture of Trondheim, Brooke declared that the success of the plan clearly depended on whether the First Sea Lord would provide adequate Fleet cover for the landings.

Admiral Pound, who had apparently dropped off to sleep during the discussion (he was already ill, and one of the symptoms of the brain tumor that finally caused his death was a form of seeming drowsiness), became alert at once when the Navy was mentioned. He put forward the difficulties of affording Fleet protection, and the Prime Minister was reluctantly persuaded that the plan ought to be abandoned.

A fortnight later, no less generous of his hospitality after their heated meeting, Churchill invited Brooke down to Chequers where he spent an hour listening to Brooke's account of "Exercise Bumper," and then, as was his way, continued a private discussion far into the night (stopping at one point for sandwiches) on his hopes for the African and Mediterranean campaigns, and next on the defense of Britain against invasion. He reassured Brooke, who was still anxious about his defense forces, that he would have 4,000 tanks available in the country by the spring of 1942.

Since the spring, relations between the Prime Minister and the C.I.G.S., Sir John Dill, had fast been deteriorating. Dill was not only a sick man himself; he was overburdened with anxiety for a wife slowly dying of a paralytic stroke, and was so unhappy that even in the little free time allowed him he would visit troop formations rather than be left alone with his own thoughts. Now, on November 13, 1941, Dill told Brooke with great sadness that his appointment as C.I.G.S. would very shortly end, and that he hoped that Brooke would succeed him.

That same evening, only three weeks after his last visit to Chequers, Brooke was invited there again for the week-end, and after dinner on the night of his arrival the Prime Minister told him of Dill's impending supersession—and offered him the post of C.I.G.S.

General Brooke, who was not ashamed to admit that as soon as he was left alone after this offer, he knelt down to pray for guidance, foresaw at this time "only one shaft of light" in the uniformly black prospect: America's possible entry into the war. He still believed that invasion was a likelihood, while the problems of a possible Russian defeat on top of the difficulties of the Middle East campaign seemed overwhelming.

Largely because of Brooke's antagonism, the Norwegian project was dropped, and now disagreement between Beaverbrook and the Prime Minister continued throughout the winter. There was still the question of the Polish frontiers, which Stalin wanted to move so that Russia obtained with official recognition the line she had reached in 1939. He could not extract from the British Government any promise to support this claim at the peace conference at the end of the war. Beaverbrook was strongly in opposition to Churchill and others in urging that they should accede to Stalin's wishes. And when, the following January (1942), after Mr. Churchill had returned from Washington, the matter came up for discussion and the Prime Minister insisted on deferring it, Lord Beaverbrook seized this opportunity to claim that, since no decision had been taken, his newspapers should be allowed to campaign in Stalin's favor.

Ernest Bevin resented this idea; Winston Churchill denounced it. Beaverbrook then presented a paper to the Cabinet supporting a recognition of Stalin's claims, but Churchill refused to permit a general discussion of the question, and Attlee even threatened to leave the Government rather than accede to the threat of Russian domination over the Baltic States.

Then there was the question of the troops and aircraft which it was proposed to send to the Caucasus. Lord Beaverbrook observed that he had brought up this matter in Moscow, when Stalin had replied that there was no war in the Caucasus, but that there was a war in the Ukraine.[30] Yet the British had now told the Russians that they were preparing such a diversionary move. There was, however, disagreement among the Chiefs of Staff about the actual performance; the Air Ministry wanted to substitute a different type of airplane for those promised to Russia; the C.I.G.S. said that no spares could be released to be sent with the tanks.

[30] This was a favorite *riposte* of Stalin's. On receiving a highly-colored message from President Roosevelt at Christmas, 1942, followed by an offer of an American bombing force in the event of a Japanese attack on Russia, Stalin somewhat acidly replied that they would prefer an air force on the Soviet-German front rather than one where there happened to be no war—General Hollis.

Lord Beaverbrook, most vigorously putting forward the view that "Moscow will not fall," still wished to aid Russia by all possible means. Since his Ministry was in charge of tank production, which before his appointment had been flagging in output, he announced a "Tanks to Russia" week, when all tanks produced would go direct to Russia. This provoked a storm of protest from Ernest Bevin, who considered it both an insult to British workers, and demeaning, that they should be asked to work harder and with greater enthusiasm to help Russia than to help their own country. Lord Beaverbrook replied that, demeaning or not, he was only interested in seeing that he got more tanks. He got them.

But his chief target, at which he unceasingly fired his arrows, was the need for an early Second Front, to help Russia; and indirectly, ourselves.

The term Second Front was, to be exact, a misnomer, for it implied—as the Communists intended it to imply—that the only place where any fighting was taking place was on the Russian front. They were always ready to forget that the British had been fighting since 1939, first with the aid of France, and after May 1940, alone, on several fronts including the vital struggle at sea and in the air. In the event, the term "Second Front" came to mean the operation for the full-scale assault on Hitler's "Festung Europa."

"To begin at the end of the story," says General Hollis, "it is certain that historians for many years to come will argue whether an assault on the Continent in 1942 or 1943, with such resources as were then available, would have reduced the German pressure on the sorely-tried Russians, and would have caused an earlier ending to the war, with such consequences as a relief from the V-1 and V-2 weapons on England, a considerable reduction in the casualties, and possibly an entirely different outcome to the shape of post-war Europe.

"In my view the answer to this is a simple one. If an assault could have been made in either 1942 or 1943 *in sufficient strength* to secure and hold a beach-head on the heavily defended coast of France, with a subsequent rapid and adequate build-up before the arrival of German reinforcements to the threatened points, followed by a successful campaign and the destruction of the German armies, then, *and only then,* would the gamble have been worth taking.

"But who could be sure that this would be the outcome? What would have happened if the conditions I have outlined had not been fulfilled, and we had suffered a bloody repulse and been thrown back into the sea?

"The relief then to the Russians would have been negligible; the blow to the Western Allies would have been devastating. The war would have been prolonged indefinitely, and indeed might well have been lost. These are the questions which cannot be answered by any rule of thumb. So many imponderables were involved. The Russian attitude was quite simple. As predominantly land animals, they had little if any experience of the mounting and launching of a large-scale seaborne expedition against a heavily defended coast-line. Nevertheless, at the Teheran Conference Marshal Stalin asked us why it was that the British and Americans could not assemble some resolute soldiers, put them into boats, proceed across the English Channel, and attack the Germans wherever they were to be found. Perhaps the British and Americans did not like fighting Germans? To him, it was all as simple as that.

"There was also a large body of intelligent opinion which felt strongly that if the war was to be brought to a rapid conclusion, it was essential to relieve the hard-pressed Russians and to cause Hitler to do what he had always dreaded doing, namely, to fight on two fronts. As I have mentioned already, this theory was a perfectly sound one—*if we could be certain of success.*

"The American view differed somewhat from ours. At that time they were also relatively inexperienced in the many problems of a large-scale amphibious landing. They had, however, since their entry into the war in 1941, assembled together with remarkable speed a large number of men and a vast quantity of equipment. They aimed to use these resources at the most vital point in the shortest possible time. The American public demanded swift and resolute action. Thus the American High Command were constantly pressing for an early cross-Channel operation.[31]

"We had learned our lessons in making landings the hard way. The disastrous Gallipoli campaign of the First World War, so nearly a success, was still a fresh memory. We had the bitter experience of the Norway campaign, of Dieppe, of the evacuation from Crete, of Dakar; all amphibious exercises, which, in their differing ways, gave us much food for thought.

"I remember once when General Marshall persisted in arguing for an immediate invasion of France, Lord Cherwell, 'the Prof.,' turned to him and said: 'It's no use—you are arguing against the casualties on the Somme.' "

"The British Empire lost one million men dead—the pick of a generation—in that war, most of them in France. Churchill was determined that this fearful slaughter should not be approached in the Second World War.

"Further, to launch a successful large-scale assault on the coast of France required complete command of the air, as well as of the sea. Conditions of weather, tide, moon and a variety of other problems had to be evaluated, and solutions found, before the expedition could be certain of success. Perhaps this would be regarded as an unduly cautious outlook, but the consequences of failure could not be entertained. And remember that in June 1944, in spite of the vast resources of the Anglo-American expedition, with its Mulberry harbors, Pluto, and other ingenious aids, the struggle for supremacy was still extremely tough.

"To sum up: In my view, the adoption of the Mediterranean strategy prior to 'Overlord'—the 1944 invasion of Normandy—was correct. It brought large American forces into action at an early date, and experiences learnt in the battles of North Africa, Sicily and Italy were invaluable in 'Overlord.' Moreover, this strategy ensured the elimination of Italy and the pinning down of many

[31] General Marshall admitted to Professor S. E. Morison, the American historian, in 1957 that "the great lesson he learned in 1942 was this: in wartime the politicians have to do *something* important every year. Thus they could not simply use 1942 to build up 1943 or 1944; they could not face the obloquy of fighting another 'phony war.' "—*Strategy and Compromise*, Little, Brown and Co.

German divisions which could have been used on the Russian front. After all, even Stalin was heard to invoke God's blessing on our Mediterranean operations—although his piety was a matter of dubiety. . . ."

Beaverbrook disagreed with this view: he had all the New World's eagerness for action. His newspapers carried lengthy accounts of their principal shareholder's speeches and views on the subject, so that their readers were kept fully informed. The *Sunday Express* of November 9, 1941, reported a speech he made in Manchester when he warned a large audience that to earn victory over the Germans—"who had the most immense assembly of guns in the world . . . all pointed in the end at Britain," strong action was necessary.

"We have not yet got steam up," warned Lord Beaverbrook. He gave short shrift to those who believed Russia would fall, and expressed his own confidence in the Red Armies' "courage, resolution and devotion." He described the promises he and Harriman had made in September to Stalin for the supply of airplanes and tanks; the required quota for October had, he stated, been fulfilled, and the earnestly refuted stories that "the British Government is not doing everything expected of it." It was his own responsibility, he said, "and, please God, with your support I will not fail. I will see that they go forward in November and every month thereafter."

Beaverbrook also expressed in this speech his admiration for Stalin as well as for the other Russians. "Stalin is a great man. I could feel the pulsating power of the man . . . I put my faith in the man's leadership, and I believe in the Russian resistance."

With this enthusiasm he not only argued that the Russians were an inspiring example to the British, but that their own resistance ought to be helped to the utmost by the British; since we were not sending troops and air squadrons to the front in South Russia, he wished to increase the flow of tanks.

In December, however, he met with opposition on this point from the Service Ministers, and an actual proposal to reduce the number of tanks for Russia. He offered to produce 500 tanks and 500 aircraft over and above those promised, if he were given per-

mission to develop means of increasing output from the production lines. The proposal was rejected. When, in December 1941,
Lord Beaverbrook accompanied Churchill to Washington, deliver-
ies fell off at once, and on his return it was only with the greatest
difficulty that he was able to restore the situation so that later he
could announce the fulfillment of all British obligations to Russia
up to January 31, 1942. Even so, delivery of some raw materials
remained unsatisfactory.

Then, in January, the War Office decided to cut down the tanks
promised under protocol for the next two months by 283, promising that the deficiency would be made good later. The commitments to India, Australia and New Zealand made it impossible to
honor the agreement. Lord Beaverbrook then called a meeting
at the War Office and put over a plan by which these tanks could
be supplied without interfering with the Russian program.
Nothing was allowed to stand in the way of the output. The Russians were short of aluminum? Beaverbrook called on housewives to give up their pots and pans. There was a chronic shortage of metal? Beaverbrook had railings torn from town parks and
gardens, and they were melted down.

In the House of Lords he spoke of the need of a Second Front,
urging that it should be mounted with all speed. Apart from helping Russia with practical aid the best help, he argued, was to
draw off German troops from that front by making another front—
a Second Front in Europe. But he had no real support on the matter, and furthermore, as the Prime Minister was against opening
a Second Front at this time, Beaverbrook's campaigning embarrassed Mr. Churchill, which, as one of his oldest friends, he
had no wish to do.

To Mr. Churchill it seemed as though Lord Beaverbrook was
campaigning against him, and he was often obliged to make compromise. At a Press conference with foreign correspondents, for
instance, the Prime Minister was asked what he thought about the
Second Front agitation—the public outcry, the chalking up of
slogans on factory walls. He replied diplomatically that he regarded it all as "most useful."

Despite their different views on the best way to win the war, their personal feelings for each other remained unchanged. Beaverbrook has always stressed that without the complete confidence, friendship and backing of Churchill he could never have been successful, first as Minister of Aircraft Production and then as Minister of Supply, for Churchill supported him against all critics.

Beaverbrook, for his part, frequently showed his affection for Mr. Churchill. In his speech at Manchester in November, for instance, he said: "I was an aluminum hoarder, and when I saw what the Russians had asked for I spoke to Mr. Churchill about it. I told him I did not know if I could give them all of it, but Churchill said, '*Give it.*' When I told Stalin that, he was pleased. But I told him that it was Churchill who had done it. *He* had the vision. *He* had the long-sightedness. Stalin chuckled and said, 'The old war-horse Churchill . . . is our symbol of victory.' "

But by the end of February 1942, friction between Beaverbrook and the Government on the issue of an early Second Front had become so acute that he resigned—although this was not the published reason for his resignation.

Churchill had agreed to the creation of a new Ministry, the Ministry of Production, which was to be given to him, but although this was eventually settled, Beaverbrook still sent in his resignation. His health had been much undermined by asthma and he had been working at full pressure for a long time. On February 26th he wrote to Churchill:

> Everything that has been done by me has been due to your holding me up . . . I owe my reputation to you . . . And my courage was sustained by you . . . In leaving, then, I send this letter of gratitude and devotion to the leader of the nation, the savior of our people, and the symbol of resistance in the free world.[32]

On the last day on which Lord Beaverbrook was a member of the Government he offered a paper to the Prime Minister in the following terms:

> I ask for a decision from my colleagues on the Russian request for a recognition by us of their 1941 frontiers, subject to

[32] Churchill, *The Hinge of Fate.*

the agreement on Poland reached by Stalin and General Si-korski.

It is now impossible for the British Government to refuse the Russian claims. When the Prime Minister gave his pledge of help to Russia on June 22, 1941, he said: "The Russian people are defending their native soil. Russian soldiers are standing on the threshold of their native land."

How can it be argued now that territory occupied then by the Russians—Lithuania, Latvia and Estonia—is not the native soil of the Russians, the threshold of their native land?

The British Government will not be fulfilling the Prime Min-ister's pledge of June 22, 1941, unless it concedes the rightful frontier claims put forward by the Russians.

Once Beaverbrook was on his own he could devote himself to the campaign for such a landing with all his enormous vigor. He went to America, where Roosevelt, eager for an early landing in France, and not aware of all the complications, readily listened to his views. On St. George's Day, 1942, Lord Beaverbrook ad-dressed a vast meeting in New York. The tough, uncompromising Admiral King was on the platform with him—not because he sup-ported a Second Front, for he was only interested in fighting the Japanese in the Pacific, but simply because the President had asked him to be there.

Lord Beaverbrook said: "In the midst of disaster, Stalin ordered an attack. Attack everywhere, violently, on every sector of the front. I believe in the Russian system, which holds to the faith that the best form of defense is attack. And I believe that Britain should adopt it by setting up somewhere along the two thousand miles of coast-line now held by the Germans a Second Front in Western Europe." The answer to the question why he was so in-sistent on aid for Russia was, he said, "the knowledge that Russia may settle the war for us in 1942. If the Russians are defeated and driven out of the war, never will such a chance come to us again." But the Russians were showing a remarkable example in War. "Communism under Stalin has produced the best generals in this war."

Afterwards Beaverbrook admitted privately that he was "a little ashamed" of saying such things, but in the heat of the hour his loudly cheered words found an echo in many hearts. When this speech was reported in the English papers, Mr. Churchill telephoned to him in America and pointed out that such utterances and activity were making things very difficult for him. He added that he would be grateful if Beaverbrook would return to London, for it seemed to him that he had been making speeches criticizing both the Prime Minister's handling of the war and his policy. Fortunately Lord Beaverbrook had made a recording of his speech in New York, and when he met Mr. Churchill again he played this back to him to show that he was mistaken, and that the newspaper reports had edited his views and not given a fair impression of his speech. Churchill then telegraphed President Roosevelt, to ask whether he would find Beaverbrook acceptable as the next British Ambassador to America. Roosevelt replied that he would, but the proposal came to nothing for Beaverbrook was not prepared to go so far away from the heart of events.

The Second Front issue had become so controversial, says General Hollis—and it remained the most vehemently debated issue of the whole war—that in the end Beaverbrook was forced to choose between dropping his agitation (which he felt was very important to the shortening of the war), and further embarrassing the Prime Minister with his campaign. His loyalty to Churchill swayed the balance; when he again took his seat in the House of Lords, he was asked whether this meant that after all there would be a Second Front. Beaverbrook did not reply; he just nodded.

About this time, another argument on the Second Front gained strength. It was expounded by Major-General J. F. C. Fuller, in the *Sunday Pictorial*, April 19, 1940:

> I have always been against such an operation, and for the simple reason that should I be right in supposing that if two hundred thousand motorized boys plus one hundred and fifty thousand armored men can keep the Germans out of these islands, then a similar number of German motorized boys and armored men should be able to keep us out of France.
>
> Yet there is this difference.
>
> We are not being attacked by several million Russians, whereas the Germans are. What this spring and summer are go-

ing to bring forth no man can say; nevertheless that fact holds good until Germany is crushed or Russia collapses.

In any case, the manpower drain of both parties will be enormous, and, as Germany's manpower goes down, indirectly ours goes up.

If there is to be an invasion of France, then it is on this fact that we must build.

While Lord Beaverbrook was the main propagandist for a Second Front, supported by a strange and unwanted group of Leftist allies whose pacifism had only been shaken by Russia's entry into the war; and while General Brooke opposed this Second Front with equal single-mindedness, Mr. Churchill found himself, not for the first time in his career, faced with a political problem that lesser men would have found insuperable.

He did not wish to launch a Second Front at this time because of the lack of men, ships and material and had to hold a balance between the public opinion that supported him, and that which did not. This was a most delicate political situation, for he knew more about the dangers from the inside than did the Americans, who never wavered in their demands for an early invasion, but who also never put forward a workable plan to make this successful.

He earnestly believed that, with Russia in the war, with our own war production figures growing, and our own armed forces increasing in training and experience, the only chance of *losing* the war would result from premature engagement in a so-called Second Front. Yet on the one side he was being bombarded by politicians and writers—both British and American—who badgered him to launch a European landing forthwith, regardless of the fact that Britain did not possess the vessels to carry the troops to France. On the other was Stalin, who as early as July 18, 1941, had written to Churchill asking for a Second Front in Europe.

"It seems to me," he wrote, "that the military situation of the Soviet Union, as well as of Great Britain, would be considerably improved if there could be established a front against Hitler in the West—Northern France—and in the North—the Arctic.

"A front in Northern France could not only divert Hitler's forces from the East, but at the same time could make it impossible for Hitler to invade Great Britain. The establishment of the front just mentioned would be popular with the British Army, as well as with the whole population of Southern England."

In the same letter Stalin, while conceding the difficulties attendant upon this new campaign, went on to stress that this was the psychological moment to attack in the West, while Hitler's forces were diverted Eastwards. The Arctic operation, he thought, could be mounted using naval and air units only, and Stalin would guarantee Soviet participation. On second thoughts, however, he wrote that he "would welcome it if Great Britain could transfer to this theater of war one light division or more of the Norwegian volunteers, who could be used in Northern Norway to organize rebellion against the Germans."

This from an ally who had been engaged for the past eight months in contemplating "the possible partition" of Britain's Empire "between Stalin and Hitler,"[33] but who now was determined to wring the last ounce of aid from her! On July 20th Churchill replied to this insistent demand in realistic terms:

Anything sensible and effective that we can do will be done. I beg you however to realize limitations imposed upon us by our resources and geographical position. From the first day of the German attack upon Russia we have examined possibilities of attacking Occupied France and the Low Countries. The Chiefs of Staff do not see any way of doing anything on a scale likely to be the slightest use to you. The Germans have forty divisions in France alone, and the whole coast has been fortified with German diligence for more than a year, and bristles with cannon, wire, pill boxes, and beach mines. The only part where we could have even temporary air superiority and air fighter protection is from Dunkirk to Boulogne. This is one mass of fortifications, with scores of heavy guns commanding the sea approaches, many of which can fire right across the Straits. There is less than five hours' darkness, and even then the whole area is illuminated by searchlights. To attempt a landing in

33 *The Grand Alliance.*

force would be to encounter a bloody repulse, and petty raids would only lead to fiascos doing far more harm than good to both of us. It would be all over without their having to move, or before they could move a single unit from your front.

You must remember that we have been fighting alone for more than a year, and that, though our resources are growing, and will grow fast from now on, we are at the utmost strain both at home and in the Middle East by land and air, and also that the Battle of the Atlantic, on which our life depends, and the movement of all our convoys in the teeth of the U-Boat and Focke-Wulf blockade, strains our naval resources, great though they be, to the utmost limit.

It is therefore to the North we must look for any speedy help we can give. The Naval Staff have been preparing for three weeks past an operation by seaborne aircraft upon German shipping in the north of Norway and Finland, hoping thereby to destroy enemy power of transporting troops by sea to attack your Arctic flank. We have asked your Staffs to keep a certain area clear of Russian vessels between July 28th and August 2nd, when we shall hope to strike. Secondly, we are sending forthwith some cruisers and destroyers to Spitzbergen, whence they will be able to raid enemy shipping in concert with your naval forces. Thirdly, we are sending a flotilla of submarines to intercept German traffic on the Arctic coast, although owing to perpetual daylight this service is particularly dangerous. Fourthly, we are sending a minelayer with various supplies to Archangel.

This is the most we can do at the moment. I wish it were more . . .[34]

A week later Churchill sent an outline of his own plans for the next two years: "After providing for the security of essential bases," he wrote, "it is necessary to plan on the largest scale the forces needed for victory."

He continued to stress the need for a softening-up process to precede the final major attack; the intensification of the propaganda campaign; the development of area bombardment from the air, which would, he hoped, help to "produce an internal convulsion or collapse." He further developed the theme that was to

[34] *The Grand Alliance.*

recur in his utterances during the next few years; the essential need to produce adequate landing-craft in sufficient numbers before any "Second Front" attack could be launched. Trumbull Higgins maintains that this landing-craft shortage "so often to be represented as a cause for Mr. Churchill's strategy, was actually in large measure a reflection of it." Certainly, in 1941, to allies unversed in amphibious operations, it offered an unanswerable argument.

Meanwhile, the differences of opinion between Mr. Churchill and his new C.I.G.S. continued, on the same grounds as before. Brooke wished to conserve what resources Britain had for a major effort at some future and unspecified date. Churchill, while equally keen on an ultimate major campaign, preferred to implement his promises to Russia by a series of minor but immediate enterprises: the Cherbourg landing, the Norwegian operation, and a landing in French North Africa—all ventures demanding ships which, as Brooke pointed out, Britain simply did not have. By March, 1942, the French offensive—as ever the subject of clamor—was still under debate.

"I had to go round to see the Prime Minister at 10:30 P.M." Brooke wrote in his diary towards the end of March, "and was kept up till 1 A.M. discussing possibilities of some form of offensive in North France to assist Russia. The universal cry to start a Western Front is going to be hard to compete with, and yet what can we do with some ten divisions against German masses? Unfortunately, the country fails to realize the situation we are in."[35]

Regarding the Norway landing, plans for which had so interfered with his invasion exercise, Brooke was even more scathing.

"Why he wanted to go back, and what he was going to do there . . . we never found out. The only reason he ever gave was that Hitler had unrolled the map of Europe starting with Norway, and he could start rolling it up again with Norway . . . Heaven knows what we should have done in Norway had we landed there!"[36]

There was also the continued question of aid to Russia; and

[35] *Diary,* March 30, 1942.
[36] *Notes on my Life.*

almost daily meetings of the War Cabinet and the Defense Committee were called to discuss what offers could be made.

"Some members were in favor of offering tanks," writes Sir Arthur Bryant, "others aircraft, others two divisions from the Middle East to hold the Caucasus in the event of a German breakthrough." This last proposal pin-pointed Hitler's main interest in Russia, for from the Caucasian oil-fields came more than 80 per cent of Russia's petroleum output.

But any such diversions would mean denuding the forces in Libya at a critical phase in the campaign; while General Brooke, still apprehensive over a possible German invasion,[37] was loath to spare anything from Home Defense, urging that even the transfer of three hundred tanks to Russia would seriously weaken his forces in Britain. And if Russia were defeated, as he felt she would be, these defenses would have been depleted in vain.

A post-war American survey has shown that British production figures of "aircraft, trucks, tanks, self-propelled guns, and various other types of material" exceeded those for Germany over the period 1940-1942.[38] This information was unfortunately not available in London at the time; otherwise the war then might well have followed a different course.

But even Brooke and his sympathizers admitted, as Sir Arthur Bryant puts it, that Churchill "by his perpetual readiness to attack, even at the most depressing times . . . not only kept up the courage and faith of the British people, but distracted and confused the enemy."[39] And the Norwegian project, so disturbing and so futile to Brooke, also induced Hitler to order the *Scharnhorst* and the *Gneisenau* back from Brest—in their wild dash through the Straits—to help protect Norway against invasion.

"If the British go about things properly," Hitler wrote to his

[37] Serrano Suñer, the Spanish Foreign Minister, returning from talks with Hitler via Dunkirk, in September 1940, observed that the Germans were not taking "Sea-Lion" seriously. This disappointment certainly influenced his master to seek over-generous terms in return for Spanish participation in the war—Higgins.

[38] *The United States Strategic Bombing Survey, the Effects of Strategic Bombing on the German War Economy*, 1945.

[39] *The Turn of the Tide.*

Naval Commanders-in-Chief, "they will attack Northern Norway at several points . . . take Narvik if possible, and thus exert pressure on Sweden and Finland. This might be decisive for the war. The German Fleet must therefore use all its forces for the defense of Norway."[40]

The Russian winter was taking its toll of the Third Reich. More than a million casualties—most of them from frostbite—had been sustained on the Russian front in what Goebbels called "this long, hard, cruel winter"; and whatever he might say in the *Voelkischer Beobachter,* he could confess privately in his own diary that it was "nothing short of a miracle that we stood it. Sometimes, the Führer said he feared it simply would not be possible to survive. . . ."

[40] Hinsley, *Hitler's Strategy,* 195-198; Ciano's Diary, February 7, 1942, makes the same point.

CHAPTER 7

Achilles, though invulnerable, never went
to battle but completely armed.
LORD CHESTERFIELD, Letters,
January 15, 1753

The first plan for the Anglo-American invasion of Northern France
—"Operation Round-Up"—was also the first venture of Major-Gen-
eral Eisenhower as head of the War Plans Department in Wash-
ington. It was produced for President Roosevelt's consideration in
April 1942, by his Secretary for War, Henry Stimson, and his
Chief of Staff, General Marshall.

"Neither of these gentlemen had a very profound strategical
background," writes General Hollis, "although they were both
masters in the art of procurement. Their plan therefore seemed
almost childish in its simplicity. They earnestly believed that once
they had established their beach-head on the coast of France they
could go right on regardless. Nor did our unfortunate earlier experiences in France, and in Greece and Norway, convince them
that this would not be as easy as they imagined."

The Stimson-Marshall plan aimed to divert units of the German Army from the East, and so relieve the pressure on the Soviet
Union, by tackling the Germans frontally, instead of "falling into
the most deadly error of the Axis, that of fighting private and
separate wars against their preferred and widely separated
enemies."[1] The plan envisaged a Channel crossing at the narrow-

[1] Trumbull Higgins, *Winston Churchill and the Second Front.*

est point between Le Havre and Boulogne, the establishment of beach heads, with a subsequent break-through to seize the Oise-St. Quentin Line, and thence on to Antwerp.

April 1, 1943, "All Fools' Day," was the earliest possible date for such an attack, as the essential forces—and the necessary 7,-000 landing-craft in particular—could not be assembled before then. Thirty American and eighteen British divisions would take part, of which nine (six American and three British) would be armored. A supporting fighter force of 5,800 aircraft would be needed. It was proposed to use at least six divisions for the landing, and to supplement them at a rate of 100,000 men a week.

"In one sense," writes General Hollis, "the fifteen months between April, 1942, when the Americans first discussed an early landing in Europe, and July, 1943, when Sicily was invaded, were wasted. We were just not building enough landing-craft. This was caused by the changing priority needs in ship-building. The Americans geared their production to destroyer escort and carriers in view of the mounting casualties caused by the U-boats from the Atlantic and elsewhere. Enormous though their production potential was, they just could not supply these vessels *and* landing-craft on the same high priority."

Meanwhile some other diversionary attack was needed to alleviate the immediate pressure on Russia, so an altogether lighter operation, code-named "Sledgehammer," was projected for the autumn of 1942. A "glorified Commando raid," as Higgins calls it, this was to be concentrated on Brest and Cherbourg, and would be mounted chiefly by British forces, with only three-and-a-half American divisions in support. The object here was to make a lodgement to be held until the main "Round-Up" attack was launched.

Marshall and Stimson disapproved most strongly of Churchill's "diversion," and favored a single-all-out attack, Stimson going so far as to refer to the Prime Minister's proposals for a landing in French North Africa as "the wildest kind of dispersion debauch." Marshall wrote in a memorandum to Mr. Roosevelt, "Successful attack in this area will afford the maximum support to the Russian front. . . . The bulk of the combat forces of the United

States, United Kingdom and Russia can be applied simultaneously only against Germany, and then only if we attack in time. We cannot concentrate against Japan. . . ."[2]

"So far," writes General Hollis, "the Americans had concentrated on Japan, making great use of carrier-based aircraft and bombers, as well as large numbers of troops for garrisoning islands, although at a secret Staff conference between American and British officers of all three services in Washington, during February and March 1941—nine months before America was in the war—it had been decided that if and when America became involved, her main military weight would be thrown into the European theater. Even if Japan declared war on her and she had to fight in the Pacific, she would still remember that the essence was to beat Hitler first. Three reasons lay behind this.

"First Germany was more dangerous than Japan, and it was feared that she might produce some unanswerable weapon in time —as she did with the V-1 and V-2 guided missiles. Secondly, she already controlled all the west coast of Europe, save Spain and Portugal, and so threatened sea communications between the Continent and the Americas. Thirdly, Britain had already been fighting Germany for two years, and could be helped immediately this way. The only nation fighting Japan at that time was China, and she was a very long way off.

"However, Admiral King, although he shared with Lord Beaverbrook an unswerving belief in all-out action against the enemy, envisaged all-out action against the Japanese in the Pacific, and had acted accordingly. America thus was faced with the same bottleneck that confronted Mr. Churchill—lack of troops and lack of shipping. The U-boat war was taking a heavy toll, as were the persistent demands of King and General MacArthur; consequently the potential American contribution to the cross-Channel invasion they advocated was as yet small, although at the 'Arcadia' Conference in Washington in December, 1941, Churchill and Roosevelt had agreed that 'the United States

[2] Strategical Planning for Coalition Warfare, 1941-1942, 185; *White House Papers II*, 524-5.

should adopt the strategic defensive in the Pacific, and devote its major offensive across the Atlantic.' "

Both Roosevelt and his Chiefs of Staff accepted Eisenhower's invasion scheme, but Admiral King was only persuaded to surrender his Navy's requirements in favor of the European Second Front by the argument that, if the additional ships were made available, Britain might be cajoled into supporting "Round-up" (the code name for the Second Front in France, later changed to "Overlord")—and then, with the Germans defeated, all the Allied strength could be unleashed in concert upon Japan. He did so with reluctance, for King, already sixty-four, furiously Anglophobe, and a naval commander who liked "a taut ship" rather than "a happy ship," was proud of his deserved reputation for hardness. After being given command of the Pacific Fleet in 1941 he told a friend; "When they get into trouble they always send for the sons of bitches!" This adequately summed up his reputation at that time.

Nor was King under any illusion about the length of the war: "The plain fact is we haven't the tools," he said. "It can't be done with what we have to work with." An equally plain fact was that he was determined to use what tools he had in the Pacific and not in the European theater.

When Roosevelt called Admiral King to the White House and described his task, King retorted, "That's a big slice of bread you're giving me, and damn little butter."

Later, Roosevelt asked him how the "butter"—in the shape of new ships—was coming along.

"The butter's fine," replied King. "But you keep giving me more bread!"

It therefore remained to persuade the British that the attack in France was now feasible; and to wear down the obdurate British protests that a shortage of landing-craft was an insuperable obstacle, as Churchill had stressed in his earlier letter to Stalin. Harry Hopkins and General Marshall were accordingly sent to London, their arrival being heralded by a personal letter from the President to the Prime Minister, stating emphatically that the plan "has my heart and mind in it," and maintaining that the popular clamor for a Second Front was a wise desire. Churchill welcomed the aggressive spirit of the Americans, but was more skeptical of the "Round-up" plan.

"Neither we nor our professional advisers," he commented, "could devise any practical plan for crossing the Channel with a large Anglo-American army and landing in France before the late summer of 1943"—five months later than the earliest date quoted by the Americans. "Sledgehammer" he was prepared to consider: in fact, he and his colleagues would give serious consideration to any diversionary project that might be possible.

According to Harry Hopkins, Churchill told the Americans that he personally favored the plan, but that his Chiefs of Staff were opposed to undertaking anything too suddenly. To the President, Churchill wrote that, in principle, he and the Chiefs of Staff were "in entire agreement" with what he termed "a masterly document," which was now under detailed discussion, and added: "If, as our experts believe, we can carry the whole plan through successfully, it will be one of the grand events in all the history of war."

The President did not understand all that an invasion involved: he regarded it as imperative to invade before the Russians were overwhelmed, and went so far as to cable to Stalin that "a very important military proposal" to relieve the Russian front was under discussion.

The Chiefs of Staff, however, were not impressed. They expected to be offered a plan of revolutionary originality—instead, they were served up with no more and no less than an invasion of France that September.

"The Americans opened with a very simple approach," General Hollis recalls. "I remember their spokesman, Colonel J. E. Hull, saying as though he were propounding some new theory, 'If we can keep Russia in the war, then we have the opportunity of defeating Germany next spring. To achieve the defeat of Germany we must get ashore on the Continent and fight them.' Then he looked around and wondered why we British still sat silent. We were with him all the way. The only question in our minds was *how* to get ashore.

"True, we had ships—of a kind—to carry the million men across the Channel at the cost of other commitments. But it is one thing to ferry a million men over a narrow sea and quite another to put them ashore, with all the equipment and vehicles of a modern army, under fire from bombs, guns, mines and other vessels. This we tried to point out as patiently as we could. . . ."

Brooke was not impressed by Marshall, any more than by his plan. He thought him "pleasant, and easy to deal with," but "not a great man." Marshall's reaction to Brooke was that he was "probably a good soldier, but without Dill's brain." The plan itself, to the ever-cautious C.I.G.S., was "just fantastic."[3] Marshall, in his eyes, had only just touched on the implications of an invasion of France, and he did not see how the Americans could destroy thirty or more divisions with their tanks. He noted also that American participation in the preliminary "Sledgehammer" operation was now limited to two-and-a-half divisions—"no very great contribution."

One argument after another against a landing was put up by the British, and always the Americans obstinately refused to see that, with the flimsy reserves available, an invasion was not only unpractical but doomed to failure. Believing that, in war as in geometry, the shortest distance between two points is a straight line, they were determined to cross the Channel.

The main British objections to a landing in France were simple and, to them, insuperable. First, with the fighters available, air protection was only possible over a small area between Dunkirk and the River Somme—and no major ports lay within this area. Worse, the beaches were flat and sandy, and in April, 1942, landing craft capable of landing on such beaches were only in the process of building.

As a minor difficulty, the considerable discrepancies of the tides were also mentioned. At Dunkirk, the difference between high and low spring tides was seventeen feet; at Calais, twenty-two; at Brest, twenty-four; at Boulogne twenty-eight; at Dieppe, twenty-nine feet.

[3] *The Turn of the Tide.*

Landings elsewhere were then suggested, and finally with reluctance the Americans accepted a North African plan. Here expediency triumphed—for the United States Government still
smarted from the blows inflicted by the Japanese on land and sea,
and "Remember Pearl Harbor" was no idle slogan. Public opinion
demanded action somewhere; if that somewhere had to be North
Africa, this was at least preferable to a passive policy.

Admiral Pound—whose views had already torpedoed the original Norwegian project—explained that the Royal Navy just could
not guarantee the safe passage of troops across the Channel.
This news received unexpected support from Admiral King, who
said: "It is pointless to argue against the knowledge of the British
Navy, who know the English Channel better than any of us."
King, of course, still hoped that the European plans might be
scrapped in favor of an all-out offensive in the Pacific, and was
delighted to gain support from an unexpected quarter.

However, after several days of continuous discussion and conference with the Chiefs of Staff Committee, at Chequers and at
Downing Street, at "a momentous meeting" of the Defense Committee at midnight on April 14th the proposals were accepted,
in principle, "for offensive action in Europe, in 1942, perhaps,
and in 1943 for certain."[4]

According to the record made at that meeting by General Ismay, Churchill accepted the plan unhesitatingly, but with the
broad reservation that he could not face the loss of 600,000 men,
and would not contemplate denuding India, and leaving the Middle East and the Antipodes defenseless. He was not prepared at
this stage to sacrifice everything else to a Second Front.

"Churchill, to his eternal credit," says General Hollis, "was determined that this war should not repeat the incredible folly of
1914-18, when tens of thousands would die in a single action, and
for no tangible result. The shadow of that lost generation, one
million men of the British empire who had died so needlessly,
continually darkened our counsels."

Speaking for the Chiefs of Staff, Sir Alan Brooke expressed entire agreement with the 1943 project, but he reminded the Ameri-

[4] General Brooke's diary, April 14, 1942; *The Turn of the Tide.*

cans at the same time that, if the Japanese were not halted, and prevented from joining forces with the Germans—that is, if they gained control of the Indian Ocean—there would be a grave threat to the Middle East and a loss of oil supplies, as well as free German access to the Black Sea, and a successful interchange of raw materials between Germany and Japan.

Mr. Churchill, sanguine and confident as ever at the end of the meeting, looked forward to the success of the joint Anglo-American venture. It was agreed that the American Army and Air Force in Britain should be built up at once, in order to carry out the American plan. But, in effect, the British Chiefs of Staff had not committed themselves to *any* specific operation. They had merely agreed to "start preparing plans," in conjunction with the United States, for an invasion of Europe, whenever it became a practical proposition, and to welcome in the meantime the maximum concentration of American military and air strength in England. Brooke, however, was still pessimistic. "We were," he considered, "hanging on by our eyelids."

"Britain had only sufficient landing craft to handle 4,000 men at a time, and could muster only ten fully trained and equipped divisions for the landing, while even by the autumn the Americans could only contribute another two," says General Hollis. "Worse, General Ian (now Sir Ian) Jacob said that it was impossible to increase the construction of landing-craft in Britain without interfering with the building of merchant ships." In Brooke's view this puny force would not detach any German division from Russia.

The following day he discussed the plan in detail with Marshall. "In many respects," he confided to his diary, "he is a very dangerous man whilst being a very charming one." The American General seemed to have no plans beyond the actual landing, and Brooke complained that he could not extract from him whether he proposed to advance west, south or east. The plan looked still weaker in the face of the insistent demand for troops and shipping from Admiral King in the Pacific and General MacArthur in Australia. The British Chiefs of Staff were hard put to it to explain to the Americans that the beach-head itself was the least of their troubles; their forces would be smaller than the Germans, and the transport of reinforcements by sea would of necessity be slower and more hazardous than the passage of enemy troops across France. Further, the Allied troops had no battle experience: and the shortage of sea transport would be an insurmountable handicap as long as the Axis controlled the Mediterranean.

The Generals, who still visualized an imminent Russian collapse, felt that Germany would concentrate her troops in France. It was all very well for the uninformed public, Brooke and his sympathizers argued, to demand a new front in the West, but the chances of success hung on a chain of unknown factors, while the chances of disaster were great, and dependent on a mass of well-established facts. In North Africa, however, where the ingredients of catastrophe were less apparent, a landing stood a good chance of success.

Further, the clearance of Axis forces from the Mediterranean —the consequence of a landing in French North Africa—would alleviate the intolerable burden upon Allied shipping. The losses for the first half of 1942—four-and-a-half million tons—nearly equalled the *total* tonnage lost in 1941. In June, a ship was going to the bottom of the sea every four hours—825,310 tons were sunk during the month. In July, Mr. Churchill cabled to President Roosevelt that Allied shipping losses in the preceding seven days were "close on four hundred thousand tons" for this one week . . . unexampled in either this war or the last.[5]

The Prime Minister's attitude, then, to the preliminary French venture was one of balancing the chance of "Sledgehammer"—the limited attack on Cherbourg or Brest—with his other pet projects: "Gymnast" (later to be known as "Torch"), the attack on Algeria, and "Jupiter," his plan for Northern Norway. He thought North Africa a better bet than the "more difficult, less attractive, less immediately helpful or ultimately fruitful" Cherbourg bridgehead, a rash enterprise while the Germans were so powerful and while the Allies were still lacking in striking force. Higgins quotes Gen-

[5] Chester Wilmot, *The Struggle for Europe.*

eral Speidel, the German area Commander, in *We Defend Normandy*, as saying that his defenses were "a propaganda wall," but as viewed in perspective, "Sledgehammer" compared unfavorably with "Gymnast."

At the end of May, Churchill informed the President that he was sending Lord Louis Mountbatten, his Chief of Combined Operations, to Washington to put before him the problems of mounting "Sledgehammer," and that his staffs were studying "Jupiter." The American Chiefs took this as a warning that the British were obsessed with the idea of "diversions." Mountbatten, in emphasizing the pivotal shortage of landing-craft, strengthened their mistrust. King, resolutely anti-British as ever, was strongly suspicious of any scheme we put forward that involved American aid. He absolutely refused to move any of his Navy from the Pacific to help with any landing that might be made in France.

"If the Army want ships to carry them to France," he announced dogmatically, "they can man them themselves, but *my* Navy aren't going to man them."

"All right," retorted Marshall, "we *will* man them ourselves." As a consequence of King's attitude, he formed an amphibious regiment, which wore the Combined Operations badge of an eagle, an anchor and a tommy gun in yellow instead of the British red.

After the meeting, which ended in some acrimony over King's refusal to admit any problem but his own, Mountbatten asked if he could see him privately for a few minutes. When Mountbatten went into his office King asked truculently: "Well, what can I do for you?"

"Nothing at all," Mountbatten replied calmly. "Instead, I want to do something for you."

Admiral King looked surprised.

"Go on," he said in a puzzled voice.

"I want to stop your Navy making a fool of itself," said Mountbatten quietly. "Do you mean to tell me that you seriously think that the great landings to liberate Europe must be mounted by the Royal Navy with men of the American army hastily trained to man the ships that your Navy can't run? Why, Admiral King, you are abrogating the right of the sailor. You're making fools of yourselves."

Admiral King was silent for a moment, deep in thought. Then he made up his mind.

"There's something in what you say," he agreed. "In fact, you're right. I'll reverse the decision. What shall I do afterwards?"

"I suggest you send an American Admiral to England so that he can study what we are trying to do, and we'll train him in Combined Operations."

Admiral King nodded.

"Now let me ask *you* something," he said with a grin. "What are you doing for lunch tomorrow?"

When Mountbatten returned on the following day to keep the appointment, he found an American Admiral in a rather scruffy uniform reading a newspaper in King's office. He was introduced as Admiral Kent Hewitt, who came to England to ensure that the Combined Operations technique of the British and American Navies was the same.

        ✾   ✾   ✾   ✾

Although the British might be short of landing-craft, they had plenty of unusual ideas, and against the background of acrimonious discussion at the highest level General Hollis also had his hands full with the various secret agencies over which he exercised co-ordination. As soon as he had finished recording the minutes of the discussions of the Chiefs of Staff Committee, and of the Prime Minister and the American delegates, he would return to his own office in "The Hole in the Ground" to receive the directors of these strange and almost unknown groups which carried on their secret activities, for the essential co-ordination between whom he was responsible.

They specialized in such activities as propaganda, the work of secret agents, sabotage in Germany and occupied countries, and "deception," which meant that the enemy would be led to believe a landing would take place along a certain coast when, in fact, it was planned for many miles away, perhaps even in a different country.

One of the most important of these organizations was P.W.E. —the Political Warfare Executive, under Robert (now Sir Robert) Bruce Lockhart, a pre-war diplomat and author of distinction. P.W.E. had two sides. One dealt with millions of leaflets that were dropped over Europe during the war to harass the enemy and give news of the Allied successes and also the publication of a German newspaper which was dropped by air regularly over the German lines after the invasion, the first newspaper ever to be delivered to an enemy in wartime by such a means.

The other dealt with the forging of ration cards to drop over Germany in an attempt to disrupt their rationing system, and controlled secret radio stations which were manned by "free" Germans, Czechs and Poles, and others.

Germany in return used 140 Jewish slaves to forge £3,000,000 worth of pound notes to drop over Britain in the hope of ruining our currency system. This was known as Operation Bernhard, after the man in charge, Bernhard Kruger, who acted on instructions from Walter Schellenberg, head of the Foreign Intelligence Service. Some notes were dropped but the forgeries were discovered; the scheme had little success.

To prevent any overlapping of the various agencies, and because it was not always wise for one agency to know who controlled another, Hollis used to arrange for the P.W.E. representative to see him at his office in "The Hole in the Ground" at three o'clock in the afternoon; the Special Operations Executive man to come at half-past three; and the other representatives of secret groups to call at four.

Throughout the war various means were employed—particularly in the desert, and before any major landings such as "Torch," the assault on North Africa, and "Overlord," the Normandy landings —to make the enemy think that that attack was coming in a different place and at a different time.

Elaborate feints were carried out to conceal the nature of the North African campaign; troops issued with tropical kit were led to believe that their destination would be Suez, while the Canadians were actually to receive Arctic kit.

False targets were bombed for nights on end, although no

landing was contemplated near them. Then special groups of men would go ashore from submarines in rubber boats and deliberately leave traces behind them: a frogman's rubber "foot," a British army belt, or an empty cigarette packet. These ruses were also used in the more publicized deceptions, such as Operation Mince- meat—when the body of an officer was carried by submarine to the coast of Spain, and then released to float ashore with false letters and instructions in his brief case. This led the Germans into believing that we were going to land in Greece and so di- verted their attention from the impending Sicilian invasion.

Later on an actor, Clifton James, impersonated General Mont- gomery, flying to Gibraltar and staying with the Governor shortly before D-Day, and then on to North Africa, so that the Germans would be confused, and left wondering whether any landing at all was contemplated in Northern France. The Allies wanted the Germans to think that an invasion was possible in the Mediter- ranean. Both these deceptions have been the subject of books, *The Man Who Never Was* by Ewen Montagu, *I Was Monty's Double,* by E. Clifton James.

Altogether, by various such deceptions, 450,000 German troops were kept pinned down in Europe *after* the Normandy landings. And the German troops already in the South of France were not withdrawn and sent north for ten days following this landing. Had they been available earlier, then the invasion of Northern France would have been infinitely more difficult, and the casualties far greater.

In the desert campaigns, deception was also successfully car- ried out, taking advantage of the dust storms which lowered visi- bility, and could make anything over a hundred yards very difficult to establish clearly. In the early days, when we were short of tanks, dummy tanks were rigged up out of canvas and wood or metal frames, from a distance appearing quite realistic. From such crude beginnings sprang an organization that built hundreds of rubber tanks which could be inflated by a small pumping engine, but when deflated were packed fifty to a lorry and sent where they were most needed. At El Alamein and at the battle of Sidi Rezegh a whole brigade of dummy tanks was used.

They would be set out on a flank, and the enemy, supposing that they were real, would deploy a similar number of their own tanks, which blazed away harmlessly at the dummies. The lorry that carried these dummies about the desert was also equipped with long chains and strips of metal which it towed behind in the sand to create dust clouds, which would confuse the enemy and persuade them that it was being made by tanks on the move. In a sense, of course, it was.

On occasions these dummy tanks would be drawn up in order in their "park" for the night, and an old tractor fitted with tank tracks would drive in between them and all around them to mark the sands of the desert with tracks, and so convince any German observation plane—which might be deliberately let through—that the tanks were real.

Great ingenuity had to be used with these dummies, because no brigade of real tanks would remain in the same position from early morning until night. Thus, after a dawn air reconnaissance by the enemy, the rubber tanks were hastily towed to different positions; some even had maintenance crews to "work" on them.

The Germans used rather different means to produce the same effect. They mounted old airplane engines with propellers in the backs of lorries. The sandstorms generated by these tremendous blasts of air gave the impression that numbers of tanks were on the move, when, in fact, only one lorry was in action.

As the war went on, and continued to be fought more and more in the air, any concentration of gliders that appeared on an aerial photograph caused the deepest concern and alarm. At a time when Britain was not over-stocked with real gliders, therefore, she had at least a thousand dummies which were used to great effect in North Africa and elsewhere. These would be drawn up in formation on the ground, and an enemy observation plane allowed to photograph them. They had several peculiar snags, however, not the least being the fact that their wings were very long, and since they were only made of thin rubber filled with air, and very weak, they had to be supported by struts at each end or else they would bend.

An R.A.F. reconnaissance pilot flying above the dummy gliders reported that these struts threw shadows on the ground which would almost certainly be reproduced in any enemy aerial photograph. To try and conceal these shadows, trucks were parked and rough tents erected so that they would cast a longer shadow, and so hide the struts. This did not prove a very satisfactory means of concealment, however, and the whole project seemed in danger of failure until someone suggested putting a sandbag at the bottom of each strut and making no attempt to hide them. The enemy were led to think that these were placed, as they often were in the desert, to hold the gliders down against a sudden storm. Maintenance parties were put to work on the gliders, and petrol lorries were drawn up to fuel non-existent towing planes.

✻ ✻ ✻ ✻

The fruition of many of these ideas was still to come in this summer of 1942 when the threat to Russia was grave. In June, after the Red Army had failed in a counter-offensive, the Germans attacked Sebastopol. Stalin again began to press for Western arms and a Second Front. On July 23rd he wrote, in a "rough and surly answer to Churchill, that he felt that the question of creating a Second Front "is not being treated with the seriousness it deserves," a point that had already been brought home in May by his Foreign Minister, Molotov, when he passed through London *en route* for New York. A Treaty of Alliance between Britain and Russia was formally signed, and Molotov, fortified by President Roosevelt's recent assurances of an impending Second Front, urged action on the Prime Minister and the Foreign Secretary, who were careful not to commit themselves.

Bitter experience had shown that landing in the teeth of enemy air superiority was not a sound military proposition, and Churchill pointed out that, thanks to German command of the air, British sea power alone could not guarantee a successful operation. British fighter production being indissolubly wedded to the Spitfire, which was essentially an interceptor aircraft, long-range fighters were not available, and so the area in which such an invasion could be launched was limited to the strongly fortified Pas de Calais. This was the only part of the coast which fighter cover based on Kentish airfields could reach and still be able to return home in one journey.

An attack on the Pas de Calais would succeed in drawing off German fighters, and thus the limiting of the operation to this area, rather than to Brest or Cherbourg, might achieve the objective of relieving the Russians without fatal long-term consequences to the Allies.

Small raiding operations on the French coast had been going on since July, 1940, as we have seen. However fruitless these raids may have been from a military view-point, they served an excellent propaganda purpose in raising morale at home. Later sorties, such as the destruction of the dock gates at St. Nazaire, brilliantly executed by Mountbatten's Combined Operations Command, had been more than mere morale-boosters, and these spurred on the already aggressive Prime Minister in the face of Brooke's attempts to restrain him.

Barely a fortnight before Molotov's arrival in London, the C.I.G.S. had secured the abandonment of a plan for the Brigade of Guards to raid Alderney. Churchill, however, only discarded this scheme in favor of a Combined Operations raid on Dieppe which would furnish valuable experience in landing on open beaches. According to Brooke, at a luncheon with Mountbatten the Prime Minister was so carried away that, in the C.IG.S.'s view, he was overlooking all the unpleasant realities that obstructed the plan. But, faced with Brooke's arguments about the inadequacy of landing-craft and troops, even for this limited operation, the Prime Minister became less optimistic. He was no idle lobbyist for the Second Front, and Molotov failed to to win the specific promises he had sought.

Molotov was told frankly of the weaknesses of an invasion plan. Air superiority, Churchill said, was imperative, and, this could be ensured only within range of the English fighter bases, where the German squadrons marshalled from France and the Low Countries could be engaged in battle, and whittled down.

"The virtual destruction of the enemy's air-power on the Continent" could be encompassed after ten days of continuous air-battles. By selecting a strategic point for the beach-head, German air superiority could be circumvented, but nothing could be done on the spot to compensate for the shortage of landing-craft. Churchill went on to warn Molotov that, with the small forces he could command at present, he could not promise that many German divisions would be diverted from the Eastern front, but that he could expect to force the Germans to withdraw some of their air squadrons from Russia.

To Molotov's request that the Western Allies should aim to draw off not less than forty divisions from Russia, Churchill replied that they were holding down—in Libya, Norway, France and the Low Countries—a total of forty-four divisions, but that, far from being content with that modest quantity, the Allies were eager to increase it.

"Clearly," he observed, "it would not further either the Russian cause or that of the Allies as a whole if, for the sake of action at any price, we embarked on some operation which ended in disaster, and gave the enemy an opportunity for glorification at our discomfiture."

He ended by reaffirming his faith in an ultimate Russian victory, and reassured Molotov that in the event, contrary to expectation, of a Russian defeat, her Western Allies would fight on inexorably.

    ❀   ❀   ❀   ❀

"While the differences between Russia and the West were being thus discreetly concealed," General Hollis wrote later, "the Prime Minister and his C.I.G.S. were heading for a new disagreement. It had become clear to Churchill and his colleagues, early in 1942, that General Auchinleck, then in command in North Africa, had taken up a defensive position near Tobruk, and was in danger of losing the initiative. Auchinleck wanted a set battle in the summer—an operation wasteful of lives, which would also give the Russians a valid pretext on which to base their allegations of Western inertia. Bound up with the situation in the desert was the fate of Malta, now under heavy bombardment from the Luftwaffe; and on the survival of Malta depended our hold on the Mediterranean. Unless Benghazi and the airfields of Cyrenaica could be retaken, there was small chance of sending the island the supplies without which she would starve. All through the spring German air attacks continued unallayed, and convoy after convoy was wiped out.

"Many plans for saving ships were put forward. One of the most ingenious made use of the fact that every time a British convoy was due for Malta, British submarines left their depot ship in the Mediterranean on patrol, to try to sink German surface raiders. News of their departure was very hard to keep secret, since German reconnaissance planes would see a submarine lying surfaced off the depot ship one morning, and when by the evening she was gone, it was tantamount to announcing the arrival of a convoy. It was suggested that a dummy rubber submarine should be constructed and sunk alongside the depot ship, underneath a real submarine. When the real submarine left, water would be pumped out of the dummy which then surfaced. From the air, it would appear that the original submarine was still alongside.

"This seemed a reasonable proposal, and the officer in charge of the plan was instructed to make a dummy submarine, to try out the success of the scheme. A team of experts in the manufacture of rubber tanks therefore assembled in an inlet off the Red Sea, with pictures and plans of submarines and began to construct an enormous rubber shell complete with periscope and conning-tower.

"A short time later, a British airplane returning from Alexandria reported the arrival of an unknown submarine in the Red Sea. No other patrol had spotted this, and so a corvette set out and also reported that an unidentified submarine had surfaced in an inlet. The crew appeared to be on shore. This news was of the utmost seriousness, and at once the Red Sea, more than a thousand miles long, was closed from end to end. Shipping was ordered to make for port, and an air strike of heavy bombers ordered immediately to attack this strange submarine before she could escape.

"Thus it came about early one morning, when the deception team were working against time with their sheets of rubber and great drums of solution and complicated frameworks of tubes and wire, that the sky was suddenly darkened by a British bomber squadron racing towards them. There was no doubt that they were about to be obliterated, for they had neither time nor place to hide. Their only hope of safety lay in convincing the bombers of their nationality. They tore off their shirts—some even ripped off their trousers—and waved them, frantically leaping up and down in a desperate attempt to prove their nationality. Fortunately, the bomber crews were not satisfied that these oddly dressed or naked men *were* Germans, and returned to base without bombing them.

"The Admiral in charge of the Red Sea, who, by an oversight, had not been informed of the scheme, was understandably furious. In the event, the plan was not adopted. But it was some time before the subject could be discussed in safety in Royal Navy company."

❖   ❖   ❖   ❖

In March, when Churchill found that he could not induce Auchinleck to take the offensive, he was only just prevented by Brooke from sending the General "a bad wire—in which he poured abuse on him for not attacking sooner . . . Thank heavens we were able to stop the wire and re-word it."

This was not the only occasion when Brooke toned down the wording of the Prime Minister's messages to Auchinleck. A week later Mr. Churchill was infuriated because Auchinleck refused his request to return to London for a personal consultation. Churchill now spoke, as he had done before, of relieving him, and again Brooke felt impelled to vet his cables to Cairo. The C.I.G.S. continually protected Auchinleck, writing to assure him that he still enjoyed some support at home.

Early in May Auchinleck added fuel to the fire by sending a telegram reaffirming his defensive policy, and announcing that he proposed sending large reinforcements to India. A furious Churchill summoned Brooke, and told him he would recall Auchinleck and replace him with General Alexander.

Brooke, ever the vivid commentator, noted in his diary: "He was a wonderful sight in bed, with large cigar in his mouth, hair somewhat ruffled, bed littered with papers and messages, and alongside of the bed one of those large cuspidors to drop his cigar ends in."

None the less Sir Alan Brooke, while censuring Auchinleck's policy on account of the resultant peril to beleaguered Malta, argued at the Chiefs' meeting on May 8th that they could not "order the Auk to attack about May 15th, against his advice." He suggested giving him a month's grace, and ordering him to co-ordinate his attack with the next Malta-bound convoy. Churchill, after asking everyone's opinion, drafted his own reply, stressing the "unanimous opinion that attack should be delivered, if pos-sible, before end of May."

"Two days later," says General Hollis, "the Cabinet and the Chiefs of Staff were summoned to discuss Auchinleck's reply. He refused to launch his attack until later in the summer, in Brooke's opinion overstating the danger to Egypt in case of defeat, and underestimating the plight of Malta. Still, the Chiefs decided that he was to have another chance: he was to be allowed to wait his opportunity, but not to delay beyond June, the scheduled date for the next Malta convoy. Brooke presented this decision to the Cabinet, who agreed, but the reply drafted by Churchill proved too strong for the taste of the Chiefs of Staff, and Brooke again toned it down."

Despite his own feelings in the matter, the C.I.G.S. continued in his endeavors to restrain the Prime Minister, telling him that Egypt would be lost if Churchill forced a precipitate attack. In fact, Egypt was being held, and Churchill was again all for action. Still more unpleasant wires were being intercepted by Brooke, who at last persuaded the Prime Minister to compromise by send-ing half of a wire to Auchinleck, and half to his Chief of Staff, General Corbett.

*   *   *   *

Churchill, having persisted in delaying the invasion of France until everything was ready, which he anticipated would be in 1943, in the meantime shifted the locale of aggression back to Norway, and again had the long-suffering General Brooke dis-cussing "Jupiter" into the small hours of the morning.

This project he advocated as not only direct combined military action to relieve the Russians, but also as a counter-measure to put a stop to attacks on the Murmansk convoys, and as a footing in Continental Europe from which British forces could work southwards. The absence of air superiority was to be no deterrent, since the importance of the objective outweighed losses estimated as high as one-fifth. Further, he considered the numbers of men and ships involved to be attractively small.

The aim was indeed simple enough: to destroy German garrisons on the airfields, and to capture them, with sufficient supplies to last them through the Arctic winter. Churchill believed then, as he did afterwards, that both "Jupiter" and the Algerian operation "Torch" were simultaneously possible.

Brooke and the Chiefs of Staff were unyielding. There were not enough ships left over from our transport commitments in the Middle East and India; shipping losses in the Atlantic were near their peak; and German naval units—the U-packs especially —were concentrated on Norwegian bases.

"Churchill, however, was determined to continue supplies of tanks and aircraft to Russia," Says General Hollis, "a generosity which Brooke considered to be madness, for many were lost on the way, maintenance by the Russians of those that survived the passage was primitive, and not only were they urgently required by the British, but further British shipping was lost in sending them. They did not even know, in the face of Russian secretiveness, just how urgently they were needed. Brooke, even now, was still fearful of a German invasion in England."

When the Prime Minister made his offer of material aid to Russia in 1941, the Soviet Union was on the brink of collapse. The Germans were thirty miles from Moscow, and the foreign embassies were about to be evacuated to Kuibyshev. No organized line of defense existed in the south. Coming at the lowest ebb in Russian fortunes, this offer had a tremendous actual and moral effect on the country's resistance. The British offer possibly prevented the catastrophe—even if in the long run the loss of life and ships on the Murmansk run exceeded the value of the goods thus carried.

Stalin's rough and surly letter to Churchill followed a decision announced to the Soviet dictator on July 17, 1942, that the Arctic convoys would have to be discontinued until arrangements could be devised which gave "a reasonable chance of at least a fair proportion of the convoys reaching you." Some of the ships, meanwhile, were to be diverted to the Persian Gulf, whence the supplies could be sent overland. Churchill added that, for the same reason, he would be unable to send land forces to Northern Norway.

Stalin declined to accept the arguments put forward for the discontinuation of the convoys, adding his unvarying and unconsidered demand for a Second Front.

Churchill and Roosevelt felt that it was not worth while arguing these points. Well aware of the ambivalent attitude of the U.S.S.R. towards its allies, the Prime Minister was secure in the knowledge that the British Government's contractual obligations were confined to the supply of war material; responsibility for their transport rested with the Russians. The tactful communique issued by Churchill and Molotov on "full understanding with regard to the urgent task of creating a Second Front in Europe in 1942" represented no commitment; for an *aide-memoire* personally presented to Molotov had stressed that such an assault was conditional on the availability of sufficient landing-craft, and the general feasibility of the operation.

This was the document to which Churchill and his colleagues were forced to refer frequently in the future whenever the Russians accused them of a breach of faith. It was, however, a little unfortunate that President Roosevelt followed up his guarded letter of April 12th to Stalin, in which he had suggested a Second Front "as the utilization of our armed forces in a manner to relieve your critical western front,"[6] with an open authorization to Molotov to assure Stalin that the Western Allies were preparing for a Second Front *that same year*. He took the further step—against Marshall's advice—of sending Churchill a telegram spe-

[6] *Stalin's Correspondence with Churchill, Attlee, Roosevelt and Truman,* 1941-1945. Foreign Languages Publishing House, Moscow, 1957, and Lawrence and Wishart, London, 1958.

cifically citing August as the latest date for a landing in Europe. The British remained non-committal, even when the Soviet Foreign Minister passed through London again on his way home. Brooke noted with approval that Mr. Churchill "carried the Cabinet with him . . . We do not move to France in strength except to stop there, and we do not go there until German morale is deteriorating."

In June, the Prime Minister asked Brooke to accompany him to Washington for the purpose of "talking him back on the rails" on the matter of a Western Front, and Brooke, who had slipped home in the hope of a quiet Sunday, was constantly on the telephone to answer questions about Rommel's ominous advance in North Africa. The Eighth Army, under General Ritchie, was retreating from Tobruk, and the situation was so serious that Churchill had to take the risk of flying the Atlantic so as to reduce the time taken to a minimum. He reached Washington with Brooke and Ismay on June 18th.

In the next few days Brooke, at Chiefs of Staff meetings, found himself in agreement with General Marshall, and even with Admiral King. He was now advocating an immediate build-up of United States forces in Britain ("Operation Bolero") with a view to an assault in 1943, and the Americans agreed to this, and also that a plan for immediate landings should be adopted "only in case of necessity or of an exceptionally favorable opportunity."

On the other hand, Brooke and his American opposite numbers feared the worst from the Prime Minister and the President, who had been conferring privately at Hyde Park, Mr. Roosevelt's home. This, they anticipated, might lead to a decision in favor of the diversionary operation "Jupiter," which together with "Torch," they felt would be impossible to achieve. But, in fact, Churchill had been counter-balancing an urgent plea to the President by Secretary of War Stimson for a "steady, rapid, and unrelenting prosecution" of the plan for an immediate invasion of Europe by a carefully reasoned exposition of the dangers of such a plan. Churchill questioned American planning—the points selected for beach-heads, and the supply of landing-craft. He argued again that success was conditional on a rapid loss of German morale, and insisted on the adoption of an alternative operation, to be prepared within the general structure of "Bolero." Understandably, he was not best pleased when he discovered that Brooke, for his part, had presented "Bolero" as an end in itself, and not as a means to some more ambitious scheme.

The fall of Tobruk, announced in the middle of a luncheon party at the White House, came as one of the "heaviest blows" Churchill could recall during the war.

"I did not attempt," he wrote later, "to hide from the President the shock I had received." The President and General Marshall's practical response was to work on the Prime Minister's request to divert the new Sherman tanks from the United States Army and send them to the Middle East.

Before the party left Washington, Churchill was introduced by Harry Hopkins to Generals Eisenhower and Clark, with whom he discussed the "Round-up" scheme. The Prime Minister was "immediately impressed by these remarkable but hitherto unknown men."[7] He also presented them with a copy of his memorandum of June 15th on the projected operation, in which he stressed its interdependence on other landings—"Jupiter" especially—and the need for effective air support.

Brooke, though he fell victim, unlike Stalin, to Roosevelt's personal charm, returned from Washington with mental reservations as to the President's military sense. He could not resist contrasting Roosevelt's reliance on Marshall with Churchill's obstinate support for plans which his C.I.G.S. considered wild. Sir John Dill, now head of the British Joint Staff Mission in Washington, was of invaluable help as a go-between with Marshall, who tended to suppose—erroneously—that Churchill and Brooke were in complete accord with each other. According to General Hollis, this appointment of Dill to Washington was "a stroke of genius on Churchill's part. His close association and friendship with General Marshall enabled him, in the last months of his life, to render an outstanding contribution to the Allied cause."

"Lloyd George left a legacy from the First War which Church-

---

[7] *The Hinge of Fate.*

ill put to good use," says General Hollis. "In Lloyd George's day, the Generals were all-powerful, for they had the King for an ally. Lloyd George used to say he was fighting on two fronts: the House of Commons was one, and the War Office another. Winston Churchill knew this history well, and he had no intention of fighting on these two fronts. When he became Prime Minister, he brought the Generals directly under his control by making himself Minister of Defense. In the Second World War, Buckingham Palace was not the ally of the War Office, as it had been in the First."

By July, with Churchill under fire in Parliament as a consequence of the Tobruk disaster, the British commanders decided finally that any cross-Channel invasion must be postponed until 1943. While "Sledgehammer" had been agreed upon by the War Cabinet, the Chiefs of Staff concluded that the conditions for a successful attack, in the form of invasion on a permanent basis, were unlikely to be fulfilled in 1942. Roosevelt was told that "no responsible British General, Admiral, or Air Marshal" was prepared to recommend "Sledgehammer"—which would interrupt the training for "Round-up," deplete the still restricted stocks of landing-craft, and accentuate the loss of imports caused by the diversion of shipping "for camouflage purposes." Mr. Churchill reiterated his faith in the "Gymnast" operation (the original name for "Torch," the North African landing).

This message was received unfavorably by Stimson and Marshall, who claimed that Churchill was now wriggling out of the decisions painstakingly reached at the Washington conferences. Stimson wrote in his diary that, if the British declined to go through with the agreed scheme, "we will turn our backs on them and take up war with Japan," thus, says Hollis, "emphasizing a lack of strategical grasp."

The Prime Minister still clung to his basic concept, viewing "Gymnast"—in conjunction with "Jupiter"—as the only great strategic stroke possible in the Western theater of war. "Jupiter" was making little progress, though at a meeting on July 12, 1942, the Prime Minister suggested that the Canadians, who were accustomed to similar climatic conditions, should be responsible for mounting this operation. He went out of his way to assure General McNaughton, the Canadian commander, that this suggestion did not stem from the idea that the Canadians should be given a task rejected as impossible by the British. Brooke, as might have been expected, briefed McNaughton with the full back history of the "Jupiter" project; and according to him, the Canadian Commander-in-Chief returned limp and exhausted from his week-end at Chequers, driven to confusion by the Prime Minister's command of the English language.

The appalling casualties that had forced the abandonment of the Murmansk convoys gave added stimulus to Churchill's Norwegian plans, for a successful attack on Norway would give Britain a defensive base from which the German depredations could be halted. "He has promised something of the kind to Stalin," Brooke commented acidly, finding his efforts at restraint unsuccessful.

All might be crystal-clear to Churchill, who knew what he wanted, and was now confining his plaints to Roosevelt's insistence on what—in a minute to General Hollis—he referred to as "this boastful, ill-chosen name (Round-up) . . . (I) hope it does not bring us ill-luck."

The American Chiefs, however, were divided. Marshall favored a European assault, and King was insistent as ever on priority for the Pacific. Churchill therefore sent a message through Sir John Dill stressing the value of "Gymnast" as being compatible with the continuation of the "Round-up" scheme, and also invaluable in that it would menace Italy and thus force the diversion of German air units from the Eastern front. True, this was to be a purely American operation, but only six divisions should be needed against Admiral Darlan's Vichy forces, and these, if replaced by new units as soon as the fighting was over, could be redeployed in time.

Churchill might tell Dill that in these circumstances "there could be no excuse for the switch of United States effort to the Pacific," but Admiral King's war was, as Dill commented on July 15th, strictly against the Japanese. The American arguments against "Gymnast" were: one, the diversion of King's ships from his beloved Pacific; two, the need for the creation of a new line of sea communications, and the inability of the new campaign to divert any Germans from the Russian front—plus the wastage of manpower which would be needed for "Round-up," the invasion of of Europe.

Dill reported that General Marshall was losing faith in the Allied invasion drive; the American Chief of Staff felt that it was being dissipated in talk. He shared with Beaverbrook the belief that Germany was too preoccupied on the Russian front to put up a decisive resistance in Western Europe. In the circumstances, Dill thought it wise to remind Marshall of Churchill's adherence to "Bolero," and, in the face of such threatened misunderstandings, a personal meeting was desirable. Marshall and King, accompanied by Harry Hopkins, therefore flew to London on July 18th.

While the American chiefs still favored attack in Europe, Roosevelt himself had some misgivings, and wrote a memorandum to his three delegates in which he made it clear that his concept of an alternative to "Sledgehammer" was another Western operation, and not the withdrawal of America to the Pacific. (This would have been an instance of engagement in a private war with a private enemy, a charge later levelled by Higgins at Churchill, but surely more applicable to Admiral King?)

General Brooke anticipated a "queer party" at the conference, with the three American delegates all holding different views—Hopkins supporting "Gymnast"; Marshall, "Sledgehammer"; and King, the Japanese theater of war. Brooke himself regarded 1942 as "dead off" for an invasion, and his fears of a Russian defeat in the meantime led him to support North Africa as a safer bet.

On the evening of Saturday, July 18th, the exhausted C.I.G.S. —just on his way home—was summoned to a Chiefs of Staff meeting at Chequers, where the expected lengthy discussions kept him working until 2:45 A.M. The official record states that it was unanimously agreed that "Gymnast" was the "only feasible proposition," and identified it as "the right wing of our Second Front," which must be extended to embrace Algiers and Oran as well as Casablanca.

The Americans had still to be convinced. Churchill wrote blandly that "we went over informally the divergence between us." Hopkins put it more strongly. He reported to his President: "The Prime Minister threw the British Constitution at me with some vehemence. As you know, it is an unwritten document, so no serious damage was done."

The Prime Minister argued that "Sledgehammer" might "delay, or even preclude 'Round-up,'" and that, in any case, the future operations of the Western Allies were geared to events on the Russian front. The delay enforced on "Round-up" by the abandonment of the preliminary Brest operation could profitably be used in the consideration of "Gymnast"—itself dependent on British progress in Egypt.

"The Americans were unable to co-ordinate their thinking," General Hollis recollects. "All fronts were inter-dependent for each other's success, and the Americans were, in their obstinacy, advocating the suicide of some six divisions with no hope of establishing a bridge-head to last through the winter."

For the next few days Hopkins, Marshall and King held out. King, of course, preferred the Pacific to "Gymnast," and complete deadlock arrived on the 22nd. Roosevelt expressed no surprise at this. There was no point, he held, in pressing for "Sledgehammer" against vehement British opposition, and he personally supported "Gymnast." The Prime Minister was anxious lest Brooke should "put Marshall off by referring to Middle East danger in 1943," but Brooke, ever mindful of the need for a defensive policy, replied that he had to give their allies "the whole strategical picture."

On July 24th, despite American disappointment, "Gymnast" was formally adopted, and rechristened "Torch." Roosevelt sent a cable on July 25th, requesting immediate plans for a landing not later than the end of October, and the American delegates left for home that evening.

Churchill had gained two of his points—the abandonment of "Sledgehammer" and the adoption of "Torch"—and still hoped to sell his allies the "Jupiter" plan as a complement to the latter.

The President was as delighted as Churchill at the success

of this meeting of minds (a favorite phrase of his), while Field-Marshal Dill admired the finesse with which the Prime Minister had handled the difficult negotiations.

The British Cabinet did not share these views. Brooke, on his own admission, perspired heavily in his attempts to straighten matters out, but commented that he was able to get his Memorandum on the discussions accepted without asking for any more concessions from the Americans, "who had gone a long way to meet us."

Thus was settled the vexed question of a Second Front in 1942.

    *   *   *   *

While at the top level the arguments on policy and strategy raged, under the general surveillance of Hollis the secret organizations were quietly working on ingenious devices to harry the enemy in smaller ways.

One was what General Sir Colin Gubbins now calls "a nice little thing" to be hidden inside an enemy airplane. At a certain height, when air pressure fell, a barometer-like device set off an explosive charge which destroyed the plane in the air. As soon as the existence of these time bombs was discovered, the Germans had to examine every plane before it flew, and double their guards on airfields.

On the eve of the outbreak of war Gubbins had been sent to Poland as Chief of Staff to General Carton de Wiart, who was Chief of the British Military Mission. He arrived in Warsaw on September 3rd, the Sunday that war was declared by Britain, but by then the war in Poland was already almost over. When Gubbins returned to England Dr. Hugh Dalton, the Minister of Economic Warfare, put him in charge of all operations and training for S.O.E., Special Operations Executive, which was to become another of the little-known organizations which had parts to play in winning the war out of all proportion to their size. At first Gubbins took charge of operations in Europe, but eventually his authority spread to all theaters of war. Dalton was in charge of S.O.E., and Mr. Eden was Chairman of the Political Warfare Executive—P.W.E.—which was run by Robert

Bruce Lockhart. There was much rivalry between some of these groups of dedicated men, for politically, the War Office was generally believed to be a Conservative stronghold; the Air Ministry was Liberal, and the Socialists controlled the Ministry of Economic Warfare. Eden, as Chairman of P.W.E., often adjudicated between the arguments of Dr. Dalton and Brendan Bracken, the Minister of Information.

"They would argue continually," recalls Hollis. "I remember how Dalton's face would go white with annoyance and the veins stand out on his forehead, and his eyes glisten as he strove to make his point."

Once Bracken accused S.O.E. of buying a newspaper in Buenos Aires so that it would print news favorable to Britain and help the British cause. This was indeed an admirable thing to do. The only snag he could find, indeed, was that his Ministry of Information had already bought it some weeks previously.

In the early days, because of the serious shortage of men in the fighting services, it was very difficult to recruit men and women for S.O.E., and the Chiefs of Staff were reluctant to believe that much good could come from such clandestine operations until they saw some results. These, however, could not be produced without the men to produce them. The deadlock persisted, and so S.O.E. began to use what contacts they had among the Allied Forces already in England, including Poles, French and Belgians, and some Greeks who had escaped to Cairo. The only inducement that General Gubbins could offer his personnel was immediate action, but this proved sufficient. In 1941, S.O.E. had only two airplanes; by June 25, 1944, seventy-six Flying Fortresses dropped arms and explosives to agents all over France, and on Bastille Day that year the number of Fortresses had increased to four hundred. Such was the measure of its growth.

Agents were equipped with radio sets, at first the size of a suitcase, which was the British idea of a portable radio before the war; but constant research and development produced sets with a range of 2,000 miles, yet no larger than a packet of ten cigarettes. The aerial could be a wire hung in a tree, or a metal spring mattress, if the operator was working in a town. The battery-charging mechanism was ingenious. For jungle use, the operators had minute steam engines which drove a dynamo. They filled the boilers with water; if they had none, they made their own. Other agents were supplied with a lightweight frame, and a wheel and pedals with which they worked a dynamo, lying on their backs.

Several devices now in wide use originated with S.O.E. One was the Corgi motor-scooter, which was dropped to agents; another, the frogmen's feet, which divers used when fixing limpet mines to the undersides of ships. A third was a gun used under water to rivet a mine to a ship, which is now used in salvage work; while the present popularity of midget radios owes much to their war-time development.

"Sometimes, in their enthusiasm, members of these little-known organizations became jealous of what they considered as their own personal preserves," writes General Hollis, "and sometimes, on further examination, ideas did not appear as good as they had done at first sight. An example of both these difficulties was the case of the Italian prisoners' letters."

The P.W.E. representative in Cairo sent Bruce Lockhart news of an S.O.E. scheme that was causing him some concern, feeling that since it was really a political maneuver it should be handled by P.W.E. rather than S.O.E. Apparently the Middle East S.O.E. team were considering asking Italian prisoners of war in Egypt to write letters home, saying how well they were being treated in captivity and how happy they were with the British, and advising their friends and relations in Italy to do all they could to stop this needless and senseless war. These letters would then be dropped "by chance" over Italy, to be picked up by the locals.

In London, the Chiefs of Staff, when informed of the idea, thought well of it, especially Portal, Chief of the Air Staff, who as the youngest was also the keenest on propaganda, realizing its enormous importance. It was not so simple, however, to decide whether or not S.O.E. should carry it out.

Sir Alexander Cadogan, head of the Foreign Office, and Mr. Eden, the Foreign Secretary, were away and the deputies, Sir Orme Sargent and Bruce Lockhart, were called to the Chiefs of

Staff meeting, timed for 11:30 A.M. in the War Cabinet room in the "Hole in the Ground." At the last minute Mr. Churchill wanted Sargent for a Cabinet meeting, and Bruce Lockhart had to go alone.

Sir Alan Brooke asked why the letters could not be dropped over Italy, and Bruce Lockhart replied: "Well, sir, if you will take the responsibility, I am willing to go back to the Foreign Office and persuade them to let it go ahead."

"What do you mean about responsibility?" asked Sir Alan quickly. "*Who* is responsible?"

"We are supposed to be fighting the war for decency and good behavior," replied Bruce Lockhart. "If we go breaking the Geneva Convention over mail and flouting postal conventions, the Germans might take reprisals."

"What kind of reprisals could they take?" asked Portal.

"They might decide to stop all letters to our prisoners in Germany and Italy."

"That would be a very wrong reprisal," Portal replied.

"Chief of Air Staff," asked Bruce Lockhart in surprise, "surely you don't mean to say that you think the Germans or Italians would be very particular about what was a *right* or a *wrong* reprisal?"

Sir Alan Brooke cut short the discussion by banging on the table.

"Lockhart," he said bluntly, "We're in a mess. Can you get us out of it?"

"If you give me till six to-night, I'll do what I can," Bruce Lockhart promised, and went off to contact Cairo. As he left, he heard Brooke say with annoyance to Admiral Cunningham: "It's a pretty bad performance on the part of Cairo to put you and me in a spot like this!"

In the end, the letters were never written.

❈   ❈   ❈   ❈

At the end of July, Churchill, depressed and infuriated by the inertia of the Middle East command, and Auchinleck's failure to drive the Germans back from El Alamein, determined to pay a personal visit to Cairo. The harassed Brooke, already on his way thither, met him at Middle East H.Q.

Brooke's Cairo diary is a document of dejection.[8] The Prime Minister fretted over delays in offensive action: he advocated, as a replacement for Auchinleck, General Gott, whom the C.I.G.S. knew to be very tired, and finally he suggested Brooke himself for the job. On the second day of his visit the measures necessary to protect Persian Gulf oil refineries at Abadan came under discussion; the Middle East commanders—Auchinleck, Tedder, and Admiral Leatham—all agreed that the defense of Abadan, with its oil refineries, had priority over Egypt. Churchill, however, held that Egypt must be of pre-eminent importance, and he wrote to R. G. Casey, Minister of State in the Middle East: "While Auchinleck fights . . . you should insist upon the mobilization for battle of all the rearward services. Everybody in uniform must fight exactly as they would if Kent or Sussex were invaded."

Brooke regarded Abadan as outstripping Egypt in importance because on it depended all the motive power of the fighting Services. The shortage of tankers would prevent the replacement of this supply from American sources. This obsession with Middle East oil was to dog British strategy again in the future.

The arguments continued; and Brooke persistently defended Auchinleck. Churchill was "pressing for an attack," he noted, "before Auchinleck can possibly get ready." It was suggested that Montgomery should be given command of the English Army, but the C.I.G.S. felt that "the Auk would ride him on too tight a rein." Montgomery would, however, in his view be the ideal commander for the job, so Brooke proposed transferring Auchin-

---

[8] "The surprising thing is that he still found time to write it," says General Hollis. "I was working from 7:30 each morning, week-ends included, until one or two o'clock on the following morning. Others were doing the same, yet the C.I.G.S., and General Sir John Kennedy, the Director of Military Operations, were still fresh enough to go back after meetings and write their own opinions of people and events of the day. This seems an astonishing performance to me. They must have been remarkable men to shape policy during their working hours and still be able to make such full and fascinating notes for their own use."

leck to another command. Churchill still wanted Gott or Sir Henry Maitland Wilson.

A few days later the irrepressible Prime Minister burst in upon Brooke while he was dressing, and told him "that his thoughts were taking shape." Brooke shuddered.

Churchill's thoughts formulated themselves into a proposed division of the existing Middle East Command into two areas: a Near East Command ending at the Canal, and a new Middle East Command covering Syria, Palestine, Persia and Iraq. This, Brooke protested, was an impossible boundary, since Syria and Palestine were administered from Egypt; to which Churchill retorted that he had lost confidence in Auchinleck, who was to be relegated to the new Middle East Command. Brooke was to have the Near East, and Montgomery was, after all, to head the Eighth Army.

Brooke, although offered time to consider this suggestion, rejected it on the spot. He was not anxious to abandon the limited measure of control he had established over the Prime Minister, and hoped that, by forcing Churchill to take his advice, he could shorten the war. And he stuck to his refusal despite the urgings of Field-Marshal Smuts.

The selection of a new team of commanders was, in any case, suddenly limited by General Gott's death in an air crash on his way to Cairo. It was finally agreed that General Alexander was to command in the Near East, that Montgomery would have the Eighth Army, and that Auchinleck was to be moved east of the Canal to the Middle East.

From Cairo the C.I.G.S. followed Churchill to Moscow, where the Prime Minister had the unpalatable task of putting the case for "no Second Front in 1942."

The first meeting of the two leaders was conducted in an atmosphere which Mr. Churchill recalled as bleak and somber. He again cited the Molotov *aide-memoire* in support of his refusal to make a specific promise, and reminded Stalin that they were not ready to launch an attack by September, the latest time in the year at which it would be feasible. He explained the strategic arguments, and followed on this defense by announcing the build-up for the invasion in 1943, by which time large numbers of landing-craft would have been built on both sides of the Atlantic.

Stalin dealt firmly with Churchill's arguments. He was un-convinced—as initially the Americans had been—by the Prime Minister's insistence on strong air support, and maintained that "there was not a single German division in France of any value," despite Churchill's assurance that there were in fact twenty-five.

After allowing the atmosphere to reach its depth of gloom, Churchill deftly produced his constructive offer. "There are other places," he said, "where an invasion could be mounted," and that was what he had come to discuss.

Stalin was roused to interest, and almost to enthusiasm. Churchill outlined the arguments—the need for victory in Egypt in September; in North Africa in October, while the Germans were still held down in France. He then produced his famous simile of the "soft under-belly" of the European crocodile, which the Western Allies were to attack while they also assaulted its "hard snout." If victory in North Africa could be consolidated in 1942, the following year could see a "deadly attack on Hitler." Stalin rapidly grasped the implications of "Torch"—a thrust in the back for Rommel, a warning for Spain, a provocation for Occupied France, and a threat to Italy. Even Churchill was startled by his masterly insight.

On the following night the Prime Minister seemed, in Brooke's eyes, to impress his personality even more forcefully on Stalin, when he countered the Russian leader's insulting questions, such as "When are you going to start fighting?" with a vehement tirade in which he expressed with savage cogency his views on fighting, on the uncomradely behavior of his host, and on the need for allies to co-operate for victory, and not to indulge in needling criticism. Stalin did not wait for the translation.

"I do not understand what you are saying," he commented, "But by God I like your sentiment!"[9]

Mutual respect had been won.

[9] *The Turn of the Tide.*

*   *   *   *

Before the Prime Minister and his party returned to England, the attack on Dieppe had been launched. This had, in fact, been planned since April, after the attack on St. Nazaire. It had been postponed because of bad weather in July, then cancelled altogether; and finally remounted in the greatest secrecy under a new code-name—for Churchill had regarded it as essential that a dummy run on a large scale should be made in Europe, as field training for the major invasion.[10]

He was later to affirm in the Commons, on September 8th, that he looked on Dieppe as an indispensable preliminary to full-scale operation—especially since the memory of Gallipoli, nearly twenty-eight years previously, still rankled and at this stage in invasion planning the capture of a substantial port was considered to pose a major problem.

The plan for Dieppe was basically simple: a frontal attack with flank support, plus Commando assaults on the surrounding coastal defense batteries. For the first time in a Combined Operations raid, tanks were used. The objectives were the destruction of the enemy defenses, the aerodrome installations at St. Aubin, the radar and power stations, with the docks, railways, and petrol dumps; and the capture of German invasion barges and secret documents.

"So anxious was Churchill over the success of this operation that he had called a special conference at the end of June," says General Hollis. "The Generals were, as usual, diffident: Brooke being responsible for the limiting of the scheme to an experimental scale, while Montgomery, who was responsible for the military side of the preparations, advocated its abandonment, as moon and tides were unfavorable, and to wait for more favorable conditions would be to incur immense security risks. The Prime Minister again stressed the need, at this conference, for *some* large-scale operation before the end of the summer."

In its revised form, the operation had to dispense with paratroopers and bomber support, while shipping concentrations were circumvented by the use of personnel landing-craft only.

[10] Col. C. P. Ismay, *The Canadian Army*, 1945.

Altogether, 4,963 Canadian and 1,074 British troops took part, with a handful of American observers.

Surprise was lost early on, for the force met a small German coastal convoy on the way to France. In the resulting action, some of the escort vessels were seriously damaged, while the craft carrying the Commando were scattered. The Group Commander's wireless was also destroyed, so revised orders could not be broadcast, and no signals went out until about six A.M.

The Germans, already on the *qui vive* for an attack, were further alerted for action by the noise of the engagement in the Channel, and several of the landings were opposed. Delays in landing tanks upset the attack on the aerodrome, for the Germans were still holding the river crossings, and for the same reason the infantry who made the central frontal assault came under heavy mortar and artillery fire. By the time the Calgary Regiment's tanks arrived, they found the way barred by heavy road-blocks, and could penetrate no further than the Promenade, although they were able to cover the infantry's retreat to the beaches. The arrival of the reserves did not bring the hoped-for success, and after withdrawal it was found that casualties were heavy: of a total force of 6,037, no less than 3,648 were killed, wounded, missing, or captured. German losses were estimated at some six hundred.

It was generally felt that, not for the first time in the history of British arms, the operation had been bungled. Tactically it was, indeed, an almost complete failure, and many lives were sacrificed for no tangible result. But some valuable lessons had been learned, although these are not immediately apparent to the critics. It was now recognized, for instance, that a frontal attack on a strongly-defended position was of little use, but that a series of flank attacks should be made round it. A permanent Naval assault force should be used—and alongside this Army units destined for amphibious operations must be trained. The operation had not been truly "combined." Timing must be more accurate, and information speedier, while pure tactical surprise was too unpredictable an element to substitute for a preliminary air or naval bombardment.

One of the basic faults of this excessive faith in surprise was its inability to cope with the incidence of inevitable and unforeseen delays. Tactical problems and lessons apart, the Prime Minister was satisfied that the demoralizing effect on the Germans had served to ease the situation in Russia. More important, the magnitude of the repulse and the numbers of casualties served for a time to still the popular, uninformed and vociferous outcry for a Second Front; dead men may tell no tales, but their death was itself a warning.

*　　*　　*　　*

On November 8th, 1942, all newspaper editors received from the Press and Censorship Bureau a notice marked "Private and Confidential, not for publication," which read: "It is requested that no mention be made of the unusual reception of broadcast programs, particularly in the South of England."

This instruction arose from the purchase in America, early in the war, of the world's most powerful radio transmitter.

"It was so large," says General Hollis, "that we had to ship it over in pieces and set it up on this side. We called it Aspidistra, after Gracie Fields' song about the biggest aspidistra in the world. But unfortunately when we got it over here we couldn't use it—because two of the ships carrying parts of the mechanism were sunk on the way."

Mr. Churchill was very anxious that this giant transmitter should be ready before the invasion of North Africa in 1942, so that it could be used to broadcast propaganda to the French in Algeria. He therefore sent a minute to Bruce Lockhart: "Please report to me every three days on this instrument, in not more than eight lines."

Lockhart explained that vital parts were missing, and that to replace them from America at that stage of the war, working through the official channels of the Ministry of Supply, might take months.

Mr. Churchill did not receive this information very kindly, and stumped off down the corridor to the little room with the clock with four hands in "The Hole" where his telephone was put through direct to Mr. Roosevelt at the White House. Within days the parts were sent over by special plane, and although the Aspidistra was not very satisfactory for long-range messages, it proved of very great value in the Normandy landings when its power completely blotted out enemy radio transmissions.

That same day, November 8th, was to be a busy one for the newspapers because its early hours saw the beginning of Operation "Torch," when British and American landings were successfully made in Algiers and along the coast on either side.

Even so, success was marred by personal and professional jealousy among those taking part. The Americans, against British advice, wanted to land *outside* the Mediterranean, well down the coast in North-West Africa because they feared a hostile Spanish reaction. The British wanted to land on African soil, as far inside the Mediterranean as possible, aiming for Sfax and Bizerta, because the country was easier there, with less chance of armor and vehicles being bogged down in the rains.

"Patton led the American onslaught; and I remember we had a British liaison officer in his flagship," says Hollis. "As this American armada approached Africa direct from the States, our man was horrified to find that there was no consultation between the Admiral in charge of the force, and the General in charge of the troops. When they drew near to the landing zone, he ventured to mention this to Patton and suggested that a discussion between him and the Admiral might iron out any difficulties.

"This very reasonable proposal enraged and astonished the fiery General Patton, who retorted: 'Discuss the plan with them? I'd sooner discuss it with a bunch of rattlesnakes!'

"In the event, many of the Americans who landed were actually slaughtered by their own guns, through lack of previous discussion of the plan."[11]

[11] Professor S. E. Morison, the American historian, lecturing on American contributions to the strategy of the Second World War at Oxford on May 16, 1957, said: "I can think . . . of one instance in World War Two where a strategic mistake by us can almost be proved, because if we had done the different thing the enemy had no means of meeting it. I refer to Operation

These landings, together with the rout of Rommel and the general loosening of the Axis stranglehold on the Mediterranean, showed that the war was now past the crucial stage.

"This must not be considered as the end," said Mr. Churchill at the Lord Mayor's Banquet on November 10th, "It may possibly be the beginning of the end, but it certainly is the end of the beginning."

That beginning had already lasted three years and two months; the end was not to come for another two-and-a-half years.

❖   ❖   ❖   ❖

Churchill was, as we have seen, already thinking in terms of an attack on the soft under-belly of Europe. As early as 1941 he had contemplated following up Wavell's conquest of Tripolitania with Operation "Whipcord," an assault on Sicily, and now he reverted to this idea. He hoped that Tunis would fall in about a month, and that a few weeks more would see the whole of French North Africa in Allied hands. If this happened, "Roundup," the major landing in France, was still a possibility for 1943.

He announced his plans to the Chiefs of Staff with the comment that "the interposition of 'Torch' is no excuse for lying down during 1943, content with descents on Sicily and Sardinia, and a few more operations like Dieppe." Knowing the predilection of the Generals for defense, Churchill feared that "Torch" might be made a pretext for locking up great forces for purely defensive purposes.

Trumbull Higgins, not altogether surprisingly, accuses Churchill of doing just this himself, pointing out that "it took an average of twelve divisions of the Western Allies some two-and-a-half years to push about the same number of Axis divisions . . . some two thousand miles. . . . At the end of several bitterly contested campaigns, the greatest natural barrier in Europe, the Alps, still lay between the Anglo-American armies

Torch—the landing in North Africa—in which it seems perfectly clear to me that the British concept of throwing the whole weight of our landings between Oran and Bizerta was better than the American concept of dividing between Casablanca, Oran, and Algiers."

and the Reich." And it must be remembered that each of the Allied divisions was several thousand men stronger than those of the German Army.

On November 18th the Prime Minister followed up his plan by pointing out that, under the "Bolero" proposal—the administrative preparations for the invasion of France—it had been agreed to prepare twenty-seven American and twenty-one British divisions with the appropriate landing-craft. "Torch" had siphoned off thirteen of these, however, and to operate against the enemy with such small numbers was hardly implementing the promises made to Stalin, who, he was sure, would notice the discrepancy. The virtual destruction of Rommel's army, he added, would appreciably reduce their Middle East commitments. "I never meant an Anglo-American army to be stuck in North Africa," he concluded. "It is a spring-board and not a sofa."

Churchill was anxious that the position should not deteriorate into the stalemate which was now, he thought, Germany's last hope—a delay of invasion which would waste another year and whittle down the effect of victory. In his memoirs he insists that he had no intention—as the Russians later tried to make out—of deliberately substituting "Torch" for "Round-up," with the object of postponing the Second Front for another year. Already the Germans were making propaganda capital out of the postponement of the Second Front, and the disagreements between the three Allies. Even after the invasion of Italy, William Joyce, in one of his "Views on the News" broadcasts, observed: "The Bolsheviks . . . are wasting no time on congratulating the Anglo-Americans on their so-called Second Front in Italy."

CHAPTER 8

That should be considered long which can
be decided but once.
(Deliberandum est diu, quod statuendum
semel).

PUBLILIUS SYRUS, *Sententiae.*

At this time, November 1942, a curious misunderstanding led to
a supposition that the Americans were staging a "go-slow" on their
objectives. General Hartle of the United States War Department
sent the Prime Minister a memorandum stating that, by order of
his Department, the British "must take sole responsibility for any
equipment requirements above those appropriate to a force of
427,000 men, for this was the limit of Lend-Lease." Since the administrative plans for an invasion of France had provided for a
force of over a million men, this was indeed a drastic cut, and the
Prime Minister, writing to the President at the end of November,
suggested that this could only be interpreted as a virtual abandonment of "Round-up." He stressed that "never was it suggested
that we should attempt no Second Front in 1943, or even 1944."
"Sledgehammer," the plan for attacking Cherbourg or Brest in
1942, had only been discarded because it would eat into resources
earmarked for a more serious operation. If the strength could not
be raised by 1943, then the operation must be mounted in 1944.
He begged Roosevelt to clarify the situation.

President Roosevelt replied at once that, in fact, the Americans
had no intention of abandoning "Round-up"; the cut in supplies

and forces indicated by General Hartle was only temporary, due to the immediate requirements of "Torch" and the Pacific war. Perhaps the Soviet Union, as well, had some share in this, if unwittingly, for on October 7, 1942, Stalin had written to Roosevelt that "our position in the south, particularly in the Stalingrad area, has deteriorated due to shortage of aircraft, mostly fighters." He was scathing about the contribution America had so far made, reminding the President that "the Kittyhawk is no match for the modern German fighter."[1]

Churchill outlined the necessary objectives of the extended Mediterranean campaign: consummation of the North African victory, and its exploitation by the bombing of Italy; and an advance into either Sardinia or Sicily, which would themselves form bases for air attacks on the Italian mainland.

General Brooke likewise was becoming critical of the Americans. He thought that Churchill was too sanguine over the ease with which Tunisia would be overrun, while in his eyes Eisenhower "seemed to be unable to grasp the urgency of pushing on to Tunis before the Germans built up their resistance there." Of Churchill's repeated talk of a re-entry to the Continent in 1943 the C.I.G.S. was equally intolerant. "He never faces realities," he lamented.

Brooke was also quite exhausted by the Prime Minister's talk of large armies, "for which there is no hope of ever finding the shipping." He looked upon his first year as C.I.G.S. as "quite the hardest year of my life," yet with true generosity of heart he conceded that "it is worth all the difficulties to have the privilege to work with such a man."

On December 3rd, at a Chiefs of Staff meeting, Churchill presented a long note on the Second Front, making liberal use of the springboard-versus-sofa metaphor. So far Brooke could see; but any talk of reopening a Western Front was anathema, and his original policy remained inflexible: to begin with the conquest of North Africa, thus reopening the Mediterranean and economizing on shipping by the elimination of the Cape route. He would follow this up by putting Italy out of the war; and finally, he would

[1] Stalin's Correspondence.

liberate France. Brooke still qualified his submissions by saying that his plan depended on Russia's remaining in the fight, but even the pessimistic C.I.G.S.'s doubts were now fast dispelling.

"Winston was suddenly swinging away." He was demanding more than Sicily and Sardinia, because, as he said, he had promised more to Stalin.

"No!" said Brooke meaningly. "*We* did not promise."[2]

He then pointed out the smallness of the forces available, and Churchill "inclined to agree we might perhaps do more in the Mediterranean unless there were signs of great weakness in Germany."

"Brooke was in difficulties now," writes General Hollis. "He was at the head of a dwindling minority. Apart from the irresponsible agitators of the Left Wing, there was Beaverbrook, with his intense faith in the Russian nation; Roosevelt, with his equally intense faith in the Russian system; Stimson threatening to divert American aid to the Pacific; and, in conversation with Sir Archibald Clark Kerr, the British Ambassador to Moscow, he had learned that Stalin was pinning his faith on a Second Front in 1943. Kerr even feared that a Russo-German peace might be negotiated.

"One odd outcome of the long discussions over Allied invasion strategy was that Churchill, who before the Americans entered the war was full of unorthodox plans for attacking the Germans although his military advisers—and particularly General Brooke —said they were impracticable, was now endeavoring to dissuade the Americans from projects that *he* thought impracticable! In the middle stood Brooke, backing Churchill against the often naïve ideas of the Americans, and backing himself against Churchill's own ambitious projects. In the middle of all this, Brooke still found time to keep his voluminous diary: truly a remarkable performance.

"An almost equally memorable performance was put up by the Director of Military Operations, General Sir John Kennedy, as has been proved by his excellent book, *The Business of War*, who also found time to make notes on contemporary events. I read

[2] *Notes on My Life,* VIII.

in a newspaper when this book was published, that General Kennedy was reported as saying he hoped that Churchill would not be offended by his disclosures. I do not expect he was, but I am sure he would have been most surprised at the time—as would many other people—had it become known that two men in such high office as the C.I.G.S. and the D.M.O., having access to all the most secret projects of the state, were in fact during the grave days of the war spending so much of their time making personal notes."

Mr. Churchill was now more or less in accord with General Marshall, who, as Dill informed the Prime Minister, wanted no time to be lost, after the enemy had been cleared from North Africa, before "we start pouring American forces into England instead of sending them to Africa for the exploitation of 'Torch.'" Marshall, however, based his calculations on "Round-up," whereas Churchill still preferred further Mediterranean operations as a springboard for the main attack.

Then things began to go wrong. The quick victory in North Africa did not materialize. Hitler's unexpected, and according to Churchill, strategically unsound transfer of almost 100,000 crack troops to Tunisia served to defer the Allied long-term strategy, though at the same time the Führer dissipated forces which he could have put to better use against Russia, or later, against the Allied landings in Normandy.

General Montgomery now joined the ranks of Brooke's opponents. A French invasion would, he admitted, be costly, but would "obviate all difficulties of shipping, air support, and so on." Montgomery, characteristically, considered that the German should be fought with, "because then you kill him."[3] He held that a successful invasion was possible by the following June provided enough American forces were available. Brooke laid stress in his typically terse reply on the fact that Montgomery was not "in possession of the full picture." Hitler's dispatch of reinforcements

[3] *The Turn of the Tide.* Montgomery's public utterances bore the same aggressive stamp. Speaking to Winchester College in 1943 he said, "I was pushed into the sea at Dunkirk. The only thing to do with the Germans is to find a good sea—and push them into it."

strengthened the C.I.G.S.'s position in the controversy, and in a paper aimed at dissuading Churchill from his French objectives, he pressed for a Mediterranean policy which should eliminate Italy from the war, and bring in Turkey.

"Always it was Churchill who pushed: always it was Brooke who admonished and urged caution," writes General Hollis. Yet Churchill was the man who, in Trumbull Higgins' eyes, was "the architect of stalemate."

Having, as he hoped, talked the Prime Minister out of impulsive steps with this paper, Brooke turned to convincing Stalin and the Americans. Always a realist over Russian opportunism, if not over their resilience, he expected—and got—nothing from the Soviet Union. He anticipated, equally rightly, a tough passage with the Americans.

Preparations now went ahead for a Conference of Heads of State, which Stalin contrived to avoid by refusing to travel outside the Soviet Union, backing his refusal with yet another insistent demand for a Second Front. The Conference duly took place at Casablanca on January 13, 1943.

The British Chiefs of Staff, under General Brooke's chairmanship, had drawn up a four-point plan, summing up their proposed policy as: first, the vigorous exploitation of "Torch" with a view to the elimination of Italy from the war; the inclusion of Turkey, and the denial of any respite to the Axis; second, increased bombing of Germany; third, maintenance of supplies to Russia; and fourth, the build-up of "Bolero" "on the greatest scale *that the above operations permit,* with the object of an invasion with twenty-one divisions in August or September, 1943," subject to the usual qualifying conditions.

The first three objectives were given priority as being of the maximum assistance to Russia: "Bolero's" comparative unimportance was ascribed to the fact that an up-grading of this project could add only four more divisions to the offensive's strength if the other plans were discarded. The main limiting factor remained, as ever, shipping, but by then American production of "Liberty" ships was beginning to catch up with the depredations of the U-boat packs.

The Americans were influenced by General Marshall's undiminished eagerness for an early "Round-up," and by their widely held view that the Mediterranean was a bottomless pit which would absorb their forces in the furtherance of British imperialist designs; for they were now convinced that the British had no intention of opening a Second Front. President Roosevelt shared this view. He had not committed himself on the Mediterranean question, despite a letter from Stalin on January 13th, regretting that "operations in North Africa have come to a standstill, and, I gather, for a long time, too. Would you care to comment?"

To meet the Americans, Brooke, after some argument, persuaded his fellow-Chiefs to accept Sicily rather than Sardinia as the next objective in the Mediterranean campaign. The only argument in favor of Sardinia, in his view, was that it was better placed for air action against the Italian mainland. This agreed, Churchill laid down the line of argument to be used with the Americans: a program of clearing North Africa, seizing Sicily, recapturing Burma, and launching the French invasion.

Brooke was consistently against a Second Front landing. In the words of the American historian Samuel Eliot Morison, he "gave the Americans the impression he didn't like it, didn't want it, and never believed in it." Indeed, General Walter Bedell Smith, Eisenhower's Chief of Staff, whose own unique contribution we shall be discussing later, wrote to Morison: "On one occasion (around January 10, 1944) during a conversation I had with (Brooke) in his office, shortly before I took over the Supreme Headquarters Staff, he expressed himself to the effect that it was not the role of the Western Allies to exert their power on land in Europe—that our power should be utilized in the air and on the sea and that the Russians should do the land fighting. He added that he had fought through the bocage country of Normandy and knew only too well how difficult this terrain was for successful offensive operations."[4]

In Beaverbrook's opinion, Churchill at this time was backing two horses. He was still against the launching of a Second Front, clinging to his idea of the probable success of an attack on the "soft underbelly" of Europe. His eventual acceptance of the con-

[4] Quoted by Morison in *"Strategy and Compromise."*

cept of a Second Front followed when it became clear that the
Americans would never be persuaded to the contrary.

During the days that followed, Brooke led the British Chiefs
in expounding to the Americans the advantages of their Mediterranean policy, and contending with American counter-arguments
in favor of the French project. The C.I.G.S. wrote despondently
that they seemed farther away than ever from agreement, and
that the Americans looked upon Japan rather than Germany as
the primary foe—and this at a time when they were accusing
Churchill and Brooke of pressing for a "localized" war in the
Mediterranean.

"Just as the worst stage of deadlock was reached," writes General Hollis, "Air Marshal Portal produced a paper, drafted by Air
Marshal Slessor, which, by an apparent miracle, the Americans
accepted with few alterations. This document followed suggestions made to Brooke by Dill, who insisted that settlement must
be reached without reference to the Prime Minister and the President. 'You know as well as I do,' said Dill, 'what a mess they
would make of it.' "

The paper authorized the continuance of operations in the Pacific and the Far East, but only within such limits as would not,
"in the opinion of the Combined Chiefs of Staff, prejudice the capacity of the United Nations to take any opportunity that may
present itself for the decisive defeat of Germany in 1943."[5]

Thus was clinched the matter of a Mediterranean offensive.
No new reasons were propounded, apart from the thesis that an
attack along the whole length of the Mediterranean would under-
mine one of the weaker links in the enemy's chain of communication—that south of the Alps. Once Italy had been forced out of
the war, Germany would be left with her fronts perilously
stretched.

A few days later, however, on January 21st, the Joint Planning
Staff again expressed a strong preference for Sardinia, thus tor-
pedoing Brooke's hard-won argument in favor of Sicily as the
next point of attack. Sardinia remained the subject of one of

[5] *The Central Blue*, by J. Slessor.

Brooke's strongest misgivings: he contended that the enemy could reinforce it from the North as easily as we could attack it from the South—whereas Sicily could be quickly captured, and had only one port, Messina, through which enemy reinforcements could come. This could be held without difficulty.

General Marshall, ever hopeful for the consummation of "Round-up" in 1943, was to a certain extent placated when it was agreed that American forces in Britain were to be built up as fast as possible to exploit any possible break-up of the Germans in Russia. An Allied inter-Services staff was also set up, under a British officer, Lieutenant-General F. E. Morgan, to work in London on an actual plan for the invasion. It was known by its initials, COSSAC—Chief of Staff, Supreme Allied Commander. In the months that followed, Sir Alan Brooke was to work in close liaison with General Morgan.

No official mention was made in the report of the Conference of the proposed invasion of the Italian mainland. Had it been, the Americans would have resisted it to the bitter end, and in any case, they would have insisted on Sardinia, half-way up the mainland, instead of Sicily, as the jumping-off point. Marshall, who now considered Churchill's policy as one of opportunity or expediency, pointedly asked whether the British Chiefs of Staff considered that an attack now against Sicily was a means to an end or an end in itself.

In Marshall's view, Sicily was a good place to *end* any Mediterranean operations, before concentrating on the invasion of Northern France.[6] In Brooke's opinion, it was a good place to *start* the invasion of Italy.

Just at this time the Russian war entered a new phase, when Marshal Paulus's army surrendered before Stalingrad, while the successes of the Eighth Army in Tunisia and of the Americans in Guadalcanal suggested more than a mere weathering of the immediate crises. The road to invasion was still blocked, however, for the U-boat battle was at its height. The March losses were a staggering 523,000 tons—400,000 tons of this in convoy. This, an

[6] Leighton and Coakley, *United States in World War II*, The War Department Global Logistics and Strategy (Washington 1955).

Admiralty report admitted, was the worst loss incurred by the convoy system since the outbreak of war.

Meanwhile, Stalin was by no means pleased with the outcome of the Casablanca Conference. "It is now, when the Soviet troops are still keeping up their broad offensive, that action by Anglo-American troops in North Africa is imperative," he wrote on February 16th, complaining of the delays in action. He added sarcastically that since the suspension of operations in Tunisia twenty-seven German divisions had been diverted *to* the Russian front. "In other words, instead of the Soviet Union being aided by diverting German forces from the Soviet-German front, what we get is relief for Hitler. . . ."

Both the President and the Prime Minister received copies of this vitriolic communication. The President's reply was abject, and blamed the hold-up on the weather; Churchill, in the grip of a high fever, was neither so polite nor so verbose.

"The battle of Tunisia is all right," he wrote shortly. "The enemy have shot their bolt, and will now be brought into the grip of the vise."

On March 15th, Stalin again urged that "the blow from the West should not be put off, that it should be struck in the spring or in the early summer. . . . The uncertainty of your statements concerning the contemplated Anglo-American offensive across the Channel arouses grave anxiety in me, about which I cannot be silent."[7]

"Fifteen days later, the Prime Minister was obliged to communicate with Stalin again, this time to break to him the Allies' reluctant decision to discontinue the Murmansk convoys until September, after the Sicilian assault had been launched, because they needed every ship they could find for the Atlantic convoys," recalls General Hollis. "He contrived to coat this bitter pill with assurances of the continued bombing of Germany and the resumption of fighting in Tunisia, and added his comments on Hitler's strategic error in diverting troops to North Africa."

Lord Beaverbrook, meanwhile, was again expounding the great deeds of the Russian Army, and on February 23rd in the House of Lords he summed up Stalin's enormous achievements against ap-

[7] Stalin's Correspondence.

parently insuperable odds: the loss of more equipment than had been sent to him by his Allies, of more than one-third of the country's industrial capacity, of nearly half the Russian farm lands, and of countless dead. Despite all these losses—the Ukraine, the Don basin, and the invasion of the Caucasus—Stalin had triumphed.

"How did he rally his armies?" asked Lord Beaverbrook belligerently, and then answered his own question.

"By persuading his tired people that the Second Front held out a prospect of victory, persuading his people that the Second Front was not far off."

The Germans were recruiting a million men, and the time for a spring offensive was near. Whatever offensive plan they chose, a speedy counter-attack was imperative.

"Time is the essence of the matter," Beaverbrook declared. "Consider the decision Stalin made before the ramparts of Moscow on the 6th of November, 1941. If he had withheld his stroke *for another day* the city would have fallen, and all the advantages won through the long months of retreat might have been dissipated in a single day . . .

"Such are the fearful hazards of war. It is the choice of the hour for staking all which decides the fate of nations. . . . The hour for decision presses upon us now. If we loiter and delay it may never come again: it may be gone for ever.

"I think that this nation will rise in all its lion's strength and seize the hour in that spirit of daring which has made us great. This should be the hour of British glory, the hour we have planned for and worked for, and striven for. Please God we shall not let it slip from us."

Stalin was not alone in his dissatisfaction. The Americans, since the Casablanca Conference, had felt that they were being outmaneuvered by the British. Continuous pressure from Admiral King had led to the deflection of more shipping to the Pacific, which General Brooke regarded as "breaking down over promises. . . ."

"Something," he recorded sadly, "has gone wrong with our Casablanca agreements."

On April 17th, Marshall proposed to Churchill that the Sicilian landings should be launched concurrently with the Tunisian campaign, thus fulfilling his cherished wish to wind up the Allies' Mediterranean commitments. This accelerated plan appealed strongly to the Prime Minister, and he at once telephoned his C.I.G.S. at his home.

"Quite mad and quite impossible," was Brooke's verdict. "I had half an hour's row with him on the telephone."[8]

"Within a fortnight, the end of the Tunisian campaign was in sight," says General Hollis. "This made a decision on future strategy—in the Mediterranean and the Far East—essential. Churchill proposed an early meeting with Roosevelt in Washington, though this time he had to travel by sea, as he was suffering from the after-effects of pneumonia. Brooke, who was to go with him, did not feel very hopeful as to results. 'Casablanca,' he wrote later, 'had taught me too much.'"

The voyage to America was spent in meetings and discussions among the Chiefs, the Joint Planners, and the other staff, which included Lord Beaverbrook, Lord Leathers, Professor Lindemann, and Field-Marshal Wavell. The C.I.G.S. continued to have unsatisfactory interviews with the Prime Minister, who was now considering an attack on North Sumatra or Penang—and this, Brooke reflected, at a time when they were on their way to Washington to plead the cause of "Germany First" against the inexorable Admiral King!

The British cause was strengthened by the Prime Minister's ability to show concrete results from his Mediterranean policy. A violent disagreement arose between the anti-British "Vinegar Joe" Stilwell and Lord Wavell, while Roosevelt added to the confusion by suggesting that priority should be given to aid to China.

Churchill said that we had not mastered the technique of cross-Channel invasion—although he still maintained his desire for an ultimate campaign in France, followed by an all-out concentration on Japan in 1945. The Americans, however, considered that they had been beguiled into accepting the Sicilian scheme at Casablanca, and now wanted to concentrate uninterruptedly on

[8] *The Turn of the Tide.*

the Pacific. They failed to see how a Mediterranean campaign could pave the way to a re-entry into France.

"Increasingly," says General Hollis, "recourse was being had to off-the-record meetings, confined to the Chiefs themselves, which avoided both the cumbersome mechanism and the ceaseless bickerings of plenary sessions.

"At the end of the Conference, it seemed that little had been resolved. King still thought that the Pacific alone was the pivotal point of the war; Marshall was wholly in favor of a cross-Channel invasion; Sir Charles Portal demanded a maximum concentration of aircraft in Britain before any invasion was mounted; Sir Dudley Pound stressed victory in the anti-submarine campaign as an essential prerequisite, while Brooke pinned all his hopes on the Mediterranean scheme, which he was sure would disperse German forces, help the Russians, and ultimately create those conditions he regarded as a *sine qua non* for an invasion of France. We were back where we started."

General Brooke put it in a different way.

The Prime Minister, he commented, "thinks one thing at one moment, and another the next . . ." He did not approve of the flexibility of Churchill's ideas for hitting the enemy where it hurt most—by area bombing, aid to Russia, or diversionary operations of the caliber of "Jupiter," the operation in Northern Norway.[9]

The President had a different problem. In the First World War America had been almost entirely dependent on her Allies. British ships ferried her troops across the Atlantic, and her airmen flew in British planes; the French gave 75's to arm the American artillery. Roosevelt was determined that such a state of affairs should not occur again.

At the last minute the Prime Minister saw a serious gap in the agreement so laboriously achieved between the Allied Chiefs. It had been accepted that twenty-nine divisions were to be prepared for an invasion in 1944, while the pressure on Italy was to continue. This, to Brooke, seemed a triumph, since no definite proviso had been made limiting Mediterranean operations, as Marshall wished, to Sicily. To Churchill, however, it was apparent that this

[9] *The Turn of the Tide.*

was merely a negative agreement; no definite plans had been made for the extension of the campaign beyond Sardinia at the farthest, thus leaving "a million and a half fine troops" kicking their heels till the early summer of 1944, while the Russians continued to bear the brunt of active fighting.

Again the situation was tense. Roosevelt was unwilling to press his Chiefs to accept the Italian scheme; and Hopkins warned the Prime Minister that agreement would prolong the Conference at least another week. Brooke maintained that Churchill "had done untold harm by raising all the suspicions, as regards ventures in the Balkans, which we had been endeavoring to suppress." The Prime Minister, for his part, considered that an independent agreement, reached behind the backs of himself and the President, smacked of a frame-up, and he anticipated that the American Chiefs might then influence the President on to their side, thus leaving him alone in defense of the Italian venture.

In the end Brooke achieved his objectives. The agreement on Italy was left vague, authorizing the Commander-in-Chief, North Africa, to plan for the Sicilian campaign in a way "best calculated to eliminate Italy from the war." Marshall was to fly to Algiers with Churchill and his C.I.G.S. to consult with Eisenhower and Alexander. Churchill, especially, welcomed Marshall's presence at these negotiations, as it would exonerate him from any American charges that he had exerted an undue influence.

"The meetings at Algiers began on May 28th, Churchill and Brooke being in agreement on the value of the Mediterranean operations in dispersing German forces," Hollis writes. "Brooke even foresaw an Italian collapse during the Sicilian campaign, and suggested that Eisenhower put his mind to the question of considering how far up into Italy we should go. It was calculated that there would be twenty-seven divisions available in the Mediterranean, and that the presence of such powerful forces rendered positive action mandatory before May 1944.

"The American antipathy to the British policy of hit and run and hit again was probably best expressed by General Marshall at a later Algiers Conference, in January 1944. Churchill, hands on the lapels of his jacket, as though he were addressing a member of the Opposition in the House, returned time and again to his proposal for an invasion of the island of Rhodes."

Both Roosevelt and Stalin had told him at Teheran the previous month—December 1943—that in their view it was not possible to land on Rhodes and still have the Second Front in the spring of 1944. Churchill was inexorable. "His Majesty's Government," he said, "cannot accept the consequences if we fail to make this operation against Rhodes."

This so infuriated General Marshall that he retorted: "No American is going to land on that goddam island!" And no American did.

About the Second Front, Stalin was, as usual, implacable, and on June 11th wrote to both Churchill and Roosevelt: "The decisions run counter to those reached by you . . . earlier this year concerning the date for a Second Front in Europe . . . and leaves the Soviet Army . . . to do the job alone." This in spite of the dispatch to Moscow of Joseph E. Davies, Russia's "great and good friend"—"a man familiar with the Soviet Union, and who can pass impartial judgment on things."[10]

Churchill replied patiently, reminding the Soviet dictator that the success of an early Second Front was more than questionable, and that a British defeat could not possibly aid Russia. Preparations for invasion in 1944 were being pushed ahead: but while the Americans had shown themselves capable of unparalleled levels of war production, they were still diverting too much to the Pacific, and out of 19,000 landing-craft launched in 1943, only 1,000 were allocated to "Round-Up."

By July 7, back in Downing Street, Churchill reiterated an offer to Brooke to relinquish his appointment as C.I.G.S., and take Supreme Command of Cross-Channel operations from Britain—though he was within a few days of his sixtieth birthday and, in normal times, due for retirement. Brooke did not accept.

Two days later, on July 9th, the assault on Sicily was launched. Syracuse fell the following day, and Brooke spent a pleasant Sunday at home, moving bookcases and helping in purely domestic

[10] Stalin to Roosevelt, May 26, 1943.

tasks, to keep his mind off Sicily. Then, within a few days, the worst cloud of mistrust was dispelled when Eisenhower recommended a follow-up of the Sicilian expedition into Italy. Marshall agreed, provided that the Sicilian operation went quickly enough, and "Round-Up" was not hampered. Marshall, King and Churchill all supported a bold attack on Salerno, south of Naples and a third of the way up the coast. "Why crawl up the leg," the Prime Minister argued, "like a harvest bug, from the ankle upwards? Let us rather strike at the knee."[11]

A shortage of assault-craft—many of which were either damaged or still engaged in the Sicilian landing—presented difficulties, but these were adjusted, although at the expense of operations in Burma or across the Channel.

"This will not be greeted with great joy by Marshall," wrote Brooke in his diary on July 20th. Indeed it was not, and, terrified that the British were after all trying to wriggle out of the "Round-up" timetable, the American Chiefs insisted on withdrawing a number of troops, bombers and landing-craft to Britain as an insurance for the future of the cross-Channel invasion. Here again the root cause was mistrust. Marshall still failed to understand either the value of Mediterranean operations, or their bearing on the future success of "Round-up"; while Churchill had "a hearty distrust of the lawyer's covenants with which his allies, attempted to bind him irrevocably to 'Overlord.'"[12]

Stimson, the American War Secretary, who was then in London, complained to the President that the Prime Minister seemed to regard Marshall's agreement to attack Salerno "as an endorsement of his whole Italian policy,"[13] whereas Marshall had merely agreed in the hopes of hastening the completion of the Italian adventure, leaving the way clear for "Round-Up." No more forces, Marshall argued, could be spared beyond the number agreed upon at the "Trident" conference in Washington.

Churchill, in view of the increased resistance expected in Sicily

[11] *The Turn of the Tide.*
[12] Higgins. "Overlord" was the name by which "Round-up" was later known.
[13] Stimson and Bundy, *On Active Service in War and Peace.*

since the arrival of more than three fresh German divisions, now proposed a direct attack on Naples and the west coast. Stimson, who had some acrimonious discussions with the Prime Minister, warned that the Americans "must be constantly on their guard against Mediterranean diversions."

The British Chiefs of Staff endeavored to explain to their American counterparts that the Washington Conference had expressly stated that the elimination of Italy from the war was one of the prime Allied objects. Once Italy was out of the way, a successful cross-Channel operation was assured. This the Americans now began to doubt. Stimson had hurried over to North Africa, and was now putting pressure on Eisenhower, warning him that Churchill was obsessed with the concept of a Balkan invasion. The situation was precipitated when news arrived that Mussolini had been arrested by his own countrymen on July 25th, and that the elderly anti-Fascist Marshal Badoglio had been charged by King Victor Emanuel with the formation of a new government.

In spite of this, the close of the Sicilian fighting was remarkably fierce, but on August 17th General Alexander cabled to the Prime Minister the news of the fall of Messina. The Allies had captured the island in thirty-eight days.

Churchill, who told Roosevelt that since Mussolini was out of the way he would "deal with any non-Fascist Italian Government which could deliver the goods," now advocated the President's policy of—in Roosevelt's own words—"the use of all Italian territory and transportation against the Germans in the north—*against the whole Balkan peninsula*," including, said Churchill, Sardinia, the Dodecanese, and Corfu. This seemed a simple policy. The problem, however, was how to exploit the fall of Fascism. Should the enormous forces available—nearly a million men—be landed in Salerno Bay? The Americans refused to make landing-craft available for the operation.

The actual terms of surrender which Eisenhower was to issue to the Italians were still under discussion. Brooke, by now suffering from the strain of the war, and from the after-effects of an illness in the spring, wanted to take this chance to "knock the props from under the Germans in the Mediterranean," but found himself forming the third angle of a triangle of which the other corners were represented by the Prime Minister and General Marshall, the American Chief of Staff being ridden, as ever at this time, by an obsession with Churchill's Balkan aspirations, real or imagined.

Before the final collapse in Sicily, the heads of Government and the Chiefs were meeting at Quebec for the "Quadrant" Conference to discuss plans for Italy, for the East, and for "Overlord," as "Round-Up" had now been renamed.

"On board the *Queen Mary*," says Hollis, "the British Chiefs worked over their case—supporting the elimination of Italy as not only pinning down German forces in the south, for already the Germans were withdrawing to the Dnieper along their whole South Russian front—but also as furnishing a base for air attacks on the German industrial potential in Bavaria.

"The Americans were now determined that the British would oppose an invasion of France; and Stimson therefore expressed the view that a British commander must not be appointed to lead 'Overlord.' He also stated that there was a 'vital difference of faith' between the two Allies, the British believing in a war of attrition on various Mediterranean and Balkan fronts, none of which 'methods of pinprick warfare can be counted on by us to fool Stalin into the belief that we have kept our pledge.'"

Stimson suggested Marshall for the post of Supreme Commander. Roosevelt and Churchill agreed.

The Allied Chiefs had a stormier passage. Neither Marshall nor King—both beating their respective and changeless drums—would agree on any extension of forces or supplies for the Mediterranean, although, as the British saw it, German troops in France must be whittled down by "diversions" to a maximum of twelve divisions. Even now the Americans were still unaware of the full implications of cross-Channel invasion, and Brooke, as he admitted, entirely failed to convey to Marshall the relation between the French and Italian operations.

"In my view," writes General Hollis, "the reasons for the clash between America and Britain over the best way to conquer Germany were really psychological.

"America, a large country, adopted—like a large man—frontal tactics. They wanted quick and terrible hammer blows that would speedily finish the fight: in this case, a very early landing in Europe, and then on down through France into Germany, and so over with the war.

"Britain, a small country, with a long history of frequently successful engagements against opponents that could have overwhelmed her with their numbers, adopted—like a small man faced by a large enemy—more subtle tactics. Over the centuries we had established an Empire by a policy of small operations which could be consolidated. Frequently we had gone in at the back door. For instance, we had beaten Napoleon by going through Spain. In Churchill's view (and mine) we could have destroyed Germany in the First War had the back door in Gallipoli been less ineptly opened.

"On the occasions when we have been forced to a large frontal attack against a larger force, a big good 'un had often beaten a good little 'un. And, as I have said, the memory of one million dead from the British Empire in the First World War—largely as a result of stupid frontal attacks and no imagination—hung heavily over every proposal. Their memory was the unseen visitor at every conference I attended."

On August 16th, Brooke, now aware that he was not to command the invasion forces after all, returned painstakingly to the attack, aided this time by the news that Badoglio had formed his Government, and was suing for peace. Churchill, however, was still insisting on his Sumatran plan, and shaking his fist in the General's face, he boomed: "I do not want any of your long-term projects: they cripple initiative!"

Churchill explained that he wanted an alternative, in case the Burmese campaign were slowed down by the difficulties of jungle warfare. This would make use of the dual elements of sea-power and surprise, which had paid such dividends in "Torch," and at the same time utilize the large forces available in India. In the end a compromise solution was achieved—but ultimately "Culverin," the Sumatran venture, was dropped. The proposals for "Overlord" were also thoroughly vetoed, the plan drawn up in

London by COSSAC approved, and a provisional date fixed—May 1, 1944. (In the event, the landings began five weeks later.) In any case, the most hotly debated issue of the war was settled.

"Now that the Italians had offered to surrender, once the Allies had landed, it was agreed that Naples and Rome should be occupied, and air bases established there," writes General Hollis, "Churchill insisted that he did not favor an advance north of the Ancona-Pisa line, though Sardinia, Corsica, and if possible, the Dodecanese should be seized, and, once the Adriatic was under Allied control, supplies should be ferried across to the Balkan partisans. This last suggestion, needless to say, evoked the bogyman of British imperialism in American minds, and as an alternative they demanded the mounting of 'Operation Anvil'—a landing on France's Mediterranean coast near Toulon.

"They were quite prepared to use the landing-craft for 'Anvil' which they grudged for Salerno—and, by shifting troops from Italy for this diversion, they gave the Russians a free hand in the Balkans.

"Brooke was dissatisfied, particularly with the endless and acrimonious conferences, which gave him no time for his hobby of bird-watching, such as he had enjoyed at Casablanca. Thanks to the withholding of landing-craft, it was not possible for General Eisenhower to invade the Italian mainland before the beginning of September, and so he offered armistice terms, which were accepted on September 3rd. In the meantime, he had lost the seven divisions withdrawn for the French invasion, and of the ten American divisions in Britain and the Mediterranean only four could theoretically be used against Italy—theoretically, because of the shortage of landing-craft.

"As the British had foreseen, the American refusal to follow up the victory in Sicily meant that many of the advantages so far gained were dissipated.

"On the night of September 8th the Germans surrounded Rome, and on the same night American troops of the Fifth Army, commanded by General Mark Clark, landed on the Salerno beaches; the British Eighth Army, under General Alexander, attacked Taranto.

"Thus began the costly, prolonged fight up through Italy, the long, slow way round."

*   *   *   *

"Who was right?" asks General Hollis now. "Churchill, Brooke, or the Americans?"

Beaverbrook, so often criticized, was undoubtedly right in that he acted as the spur to the war-horse, preventing the Prime Minister from succumbing to the over-cautiousness of his Generals, with their addiction to copy-book battles. He was the goad, either liked or loathed, but impossible to ignore.

"Throughout this period," writes Hollis, "Sir Alan Brooke appears as the apostle of caution, struggling on against the wave of restless energy, which kept him on his feet night after night—but which still left him time to keep his diaries—and against the ceaseless urge for action which, in his eyes, would be impossible and mad.

"Brooke opposed the Greek venture—yet it served to hold several German divisions in the Balkans, and thus gave the Russians several weeks' grace before the onset, of 'Barbarossa.'

"With the ominous echoes of the 1940 campaign still ringing a warning, the C.I.G.S.'s opposition to Churchill's Norwegian schemes is more understandable. It is by no means clear what the outcome of 'Jupiter' would have been, but, without doubt, had it been successful, it would have had far-reaching repercussions on the German position on their Arctic front, as well as impeding U-boat warfare. Hitler himself entertained the most serious apprehensions on this subject, which were strong enough to make him risk two of his biggest capital ships. Finally, it is curious that the impingement of the original Norwegian plan upon Brooke's purely defensive 'Exercise Bumper' should have conditioned to so great an extent his hostility to the operation."

Brooke's sympathy for Auchinleck, so concretely expressed in the toning down of Churchill's angry telegrams was also to be expected from one who, in 1942, entertained doubts on the Russians' ability to hold out, and apprehension as to the continued possibility of "Sea-Lion" (enemy invasion of Britain). But Auchin-leck wanted a pitched battle in conditions selected by himself, and this conventional attitude lost Britain the initiative in Egypt —and might have lost her the Middle Eastern war.

Brooke never welcomed aid to Russia, which he regarded as pumping oxygen into a dying and incurable patient. Beaverbrook, with his enthusiasm for the spirit of the Russian people; and Roosevelt, fatally fascinated by the Soviet system as a counter-blast to British imperialism, both ceaselessly advocated material and even military support for Stalin's armies.

Churchill struck a middle course. The Russians were Hitler's enemies, and, so far as the common aim—the destruction of Nazi-dom—went, aid to Russia was essential; but such aid must not be carried out to the exclusion of all other projects, nor must it be accompanied by concessions beneficial to the Russians alone.

Brooke and Churchill were not in such disagreement over Sicily. But again Brooke feared to antagonize the Americans by writing into the "Trident" agreement any concept for advancing into Italy; or, worse still, the Balkans. Here the Americans seem to have been guilty of obstruction, on the grounds that the Sicilian operation would divert troops from "Round-Up," or from the Pacific, and would give Britain a footing in the Balkans and thus further "British expansionism" at the price of offending the Russians. Certain it is that, even if British opinion did lay overmuch stress on shortages of landing-craft, and use this as a pretext for inaction, the Americans were not above doing the same themselves, and were prepared to create artificial local shortages to impede operations which did not meet with their approval.

Churchill almost certainly made mistakes, but he and Beaver-brook believed not only in action, but in the marriage of action to feasibility. Unwilling to risk a catastrophic defeat by launching an ill-prepared and ill-equipped force across the Channel, Churchill stuck inexorably to the principle of mounting less costly operations, which served to wear down the German defenses, and which also gave the Allies opportunities for positive action with tangible results. Some ventures, such as the area bombing of

Germany, did not achieve the results expected of them. Others—
Dieppe, for instance—provided invaluable experience which assured the ultimate success of "Overlord."

American policy, on the other hand, although favoring bold
attacks, was not always tempered with any deep awareness of the
implications or issues at stake, and was too often expounded with
sidelong glances at the Pacific War—and at the glowering features
of the men in the Kremlin.

"The true defense of Churchill," writes General Hollis, "is that
he always knew when to attack. He was not only the architect of
victory, he was also its accountant; he knew which attack would
bring the best dividend with the least risk of catastrophe."

CHAPTER 9

And so they gave their bodies to the Commonwealth,
and earned each for himself praise that will never die.
And with it the most glorious of sepulchres, not that in
which their mortal bones are laid, but a home in the
minds of men where their glory remains fresh to stir to
speech or to action as occasion arises.
For the whole world is the sepulchre of famous men,
and their story is not graven only on stone above their
native earth, but lives on far away without visible
symbol, woven into the stuff of other men's lives.

PERICLES' *Oration to the Athenian Dead*

By November, 1943, it became necessary to have a "Big Three"
Conference, but Stalin refused to go anywhere that involved more
than one day's flying from Moscow, and Roosevelt was not anxious
to come to England. Since Churchill had already been to America
on several occasions, it was decided that he and the President
would meet in Cairo, and then go on to Teheran to meet Stalin,
who eventually agreed to leave Russia for the first time since the
Revolution.

General Ismay sent his secretary, Paymaster Commander Maurice Knott, to Cairo to make arrangements for a full-scale Anglo-
American Conference at the Mena House Hotel,[1] eight miles out-

[1] Miss Joan Bright, who worked with Maurice Knott organizing the accommodation, was approached by one General who explained rather coldly
that he saw from the list of accommodation that she had put him down to
share a bedroom in Mena House with another General with whom he was

side Cairo, near the Pyramids. He was also empowered to take over local villas for the President and the Premier, and to make suitable arrangements for housing and feeding something like 600 other officers, secretaries and clerks.

"It was astonishing and shocking to see how these Conferences grew," says General Hollis. "The first Atlantic Charter Conference, for instance, involved only about fifty people. At each succeeding Conference—Washington, Quebec, Cairo, Yalta and Potsdam—the staffs multiplied like amoeba. It became a question of getting on the band wagon, for accommodation was always agreeable, free food and liquor were in abundance, and life was in every way more pleasant than in war-time England.

"Indeed, considerable rivalry grew between Departments over the size of the staffs they could take to these meetings. A First Sea Lord, for example, would require at least three or four Captains—the Heads of Admiralty Departments—to accompany him, together with their respective Staff officers, secretaries, typists, batmen, and other camp followers. Other Service Departments would not care to be outdone by the Admiralty, and so they would produce a similar or even larger quota. In this way a constant build-up went on which tended to make the Staffs increasingly large as the war proceeded. In my view, the majority of these officers and their subordinates could have been left at home without any detriment to the success of proceedings.

"Mr. Churchill was always trying to cut down non-operational staff, which grew to most shockingly large sizes as the war progressed. Only a month before D-Day, for instance, he sent me this memo:

> I certainly expressed myself strongly against these military missions to Algiers, from what I heard about them at the Gibraltar Conference, and I greatly regret that they should have

---

not on speaking terms. He trusted that Miss Bright would be good enough to alter this arrangement.

When she arrived in the foyer of the hotel on the day the Conference began she found him in a state of even greater fury.

"Not only have you put me down to share a room with General X," he said, "but instead of two single beds, there's only one double bed. I'm actually *sleeping* with the man. . . ."

piled themselves up and ensconced themselves at Algiers, where
they are not needed in any way, but only add to the horribly
bloated staffs which are lurking there, most of them away from
all participation in the war. I certainly wish this matter to be
taken up with a view to recalling and putting to some useful
work these highly paid and no doubt highly skilled and experienced officers. The best thing would be to form a Sacred Legion
of about 1,000 Staff Officers and let them set an example to the
troops in leading some particularly desperate attack. Anyhow,
the missions should be liquidated.

Early in November, Mr. Churchill's staff left London by special
train and travelled through the gray countryside to Plymouth,
where they embarked in H.M.S. *Renown.* The Prime Minister was
a little late, as he was far from well, and it was already dark when
he arrived. He came aboard slowly, with none of his usual "V"
signs and vigor.

Considering the importance of this Cairo Conference it was
surprising that no attempt at deception had been made.

"Sir Winston was a great stickler for security, and once taught
me a lesson I have never forgotten," recalls General Hollis. "He
asked me to render him a short report on a highly secret matter,
explaining that I was not to consult anyone. The matter in question was far beyond my ken, and I disregarded the Prime Minister's instructions to the extent of consulting three very high officials in three different Ministries. When I rendered my report, Sir
Winston inquired whether I had discussed it with anyone, and I
replied that I had spoken to these three senior men.

"He asked me for the name of the first official, and when I told
him he wrote a large figure 1 on his blotting pad. I told him the
name of the second, and he wrote another 1 alongside the first.
He acted similarly with the third. Then he asked: "*How* many
people did you say you had consulted?"

"I replied, 'Only three, Prime Minister.'

" 'No,' he said sternly, 'You did not. You consulted 111!' "

When the Prime Minister had sailed in the *Queen Mary* for the
Quebec Conference, for instance, only a few people knew until
the last moment that he would actually be aboard. To keep enemy

agents off the scent, the quarters he was to occupy were fitted with ramps, so that a wheelchair could be pushed up the steps. Notices in Dutch were fixed to the walls, and the rumor was spread deliberately that Queen Wilhelmina of Holland was paying a special visit to America as the guest of the U.S. Government. At the last moment, as the *Queen Mary* prepared to sail, Churchill arrived with his daughter Mary, then an officer in the A.T.S., who was traveling as his personal assistant. She had no idea about their destination, and it was not until the train drew alongside the ship that the Prime Minister explained to her that they were going to Quebec for a Conference.

"I'm supposed to be Queen Wilhelmina," he added, with a smile.

"If only you'd *told* me," replied his daughter at once, "we'd have made you up to *look* like her, too!"

❋   ❋   ❋   ❋

When the *Renown* arrived at Malta, Mr. Churchill, who had been poorly for the whole voyage, decided to stay with the Governor, Lord Gort, at the Valetta Palace, some way from the harbor.

Gort had lost nothing of the love for tiny detail that had marked his career as Commander-in-Chief in France in 1940, when he had taken up the major part of a Staff Conference trying to decide whether troops should wear steel helmets on their left or right shoulder when not actually wearing them on their heads. What now consumed him was a determination to live on the same low level of rations and comfort as the Maltese, in their state of continual siege and bombardment. To Hollis, Malta seemed to be little more than a ruin. Piles of rubble were all that remained of houses and shops; and little children, too thin and listless even to play in the bright sunshine, hung about the shabby, pitted streets. There were hardly any cars on the island, for gas was virtually impossible to obtain, and the general picture was one of extreme privation, far worse than anything in Britain. Food was very short and there were no eggs or butter, and very little milk available for anyone.

Churchill, nonetheless, took up residence in the Palace, a huge, cold barracks of a place, and soon after they arrived, Ismay and Hollis went to visit him.

"We found him lying in an enormous bed, looking like a pink wax cherub, and clearly feeling very unwell, and rather sorry for himself," recalls General Hollis. "He perked up when we brought him some cables, however, and suddenly made a most strange request. In a pathetic voice he asked: 'Could you please go back to that nice ship and bring me a little pat of butter?' "

They returned through the ruined streets with a pound of butter wrapped in brown paper for the Prime Minister, and also brought a message which had caused great concern: President Roosevelt had been advised by his Intelligence authorities that Cairo was unsafe as a meeting place. They claimed to have received information that an attempt would be made on his life. Was it possible to have the venue changed?

"Certainly," said Churchill at once. "We will have the Conference *here*. Pray have the necessary arrangements made."

So it came about that Leslie Hollis and Lawrence Burgis, who were also in the party, repeated their partnership of seven years previously, when they had worked together over the early arrangements for "The Hole in the Ground," and they set out to find accommodation for this Conference in Malta.

The task was formidable. First, they had to find living accommodation for the President and such senior colleagues as General Marshall and Admiral King and their staffs, as well as for the British Prime Minister and his Chiefs of Staff, and also accommodation for clerical staffs amounting to several hundred people of both sexes. All the accommodation had to be suitable from the security point of view, so that no attempt on their lives could be made by enemy agents.

Then arrangements had to be made for feeding and transporting this enormous contingent, providing offices in which to work, conference rooms, and such ancillary services as laundries and hospitals. In Malta at that time it was not possible to find even one hotel that could supply more than the barest essentials of shelter with the crudest service. Most of the hotels were in ruins, food was almost unobtainable, and even the water was suspect; it soon became apparent to Hollis that in these circumstances the whole idea was impossible to carry out.

The weather was unpleasantly hot, with a dry wind that blew the dust from the bomb-sites into their faces and aggravated his asthma. He and Burgis stood perspiring on a mountain of bricks, while hungry little children watched them expectantly and held out their hands for pennies.

"It just won't work," Hollis told Burgis. "We can't go to the President and say: 'You are sleeping in this cellar, and Admiral King can have the hole under the stairway, and General Marshall can have the bedroom that's got a bit of roof on it!' This just is not on."

Burgis was unwilling to accept this view.

"We've been given a brief to find accommodation," he kept repeating. "We must get the rooms."

"Then we'll have to build them ourselves," Hollis retorted. "I'm going back to tell the Prime Minister that the President will have to think again."

Before he went to Churchill he had a word with Ismay, who listened to him with a deep frown, and together they saw Churchill, who immediately agreed with them.

"This surprised me, for I expected an argument," comments Hollis. "Winston was usually a most exacting master. Nothing but the best was tolerated. Anything mediocre or makeshift was the signal for an outbreak of choler, and very fierce these outbreaks could be. I was sometimes at the receiving end, and I soon learned that the best attitude was to say as little as possible, but on no account to show fear or nervousness.

"During the height of the war, when we were working at the fullest pressure for anything up to eighteen hours a day, on a seven-day week, I recall that I submitted to the Prime Minister a rather loosely phrased minute. I opened a sentence with the words: 'Having regard to the fact that . . .' It was sent back to me with a stern comment: 'Colonel Hollis, you have used six words, where one word of two letters—namely "as"—would have sufficed. Pray remember that in an efficient Administration small things count as well as great.' . . ."

"I accept your decision," Churchill said at once. "I will inform the President accordingly."

On receipt of this news, Mr. Roosevelt thereupon decided to brave the risk of assassination, and come on to Cairo as had originally been arranged.

The meeting place was everything "The Hole in the Ground" was not: light, airy, warm and sunny. Residents of the Mena House Hotel had been evacuated to make way for the five-day Conference. Troops set up barbed-wire fences round the area, enclosing three square miles; and thirty-four villas in the vicinity were also commandeered in seven "defensive zones." They were surrounded with anti-aircraft guns, searchlights, pill-boxes, gun emplacements, and fire-watchers' towers. These villas were classi-fied as Super, First Class, and Ordinary.

Roosevelt arrived hidden behind the curtains of his bullet-proof Packard (which he called "my county jail"), and led in by two outriders, with two Jeeps, each containing four soldiers with submachine guns, and a command car armed with a machine gun. He brought with him his Chiefs of Staff, Leahy, Marshall and King, as well as Eisenhower, Stilwell and Chen-nault. Acting as semi-official photographers were Harry Hopkins' son Robert, and Elliott Roosevelt. Sarah Churchill was present as Churchill's aide and hostess.

The main subject of the Cairo Conference, at which rather less than half the world's population was represented, was the question of the Second Front. Towards the end of the agenda, China, Japan and the Pacific were also to be discussed. These plans, however, were immediately upset by the unexpected arrival of Chiang-Kai-shek with his wife and a party of twenty delegates, who were not expected until far later in the Confer-ence, but who actually arrived first.

In an attempt to keep news of the Conference and who was attending it from enemy agents in Cairo, all planes bringing delegates were supposed to land at a special airfield west of the Nile, twelve miles north of Mena, so that the passengers would not have to drive through Cairo, where they might be recognized. This plan was ruined by the arrival of the Generalissimo and Madame Chiang-Kai-shek, who, besides arriving two days before they were expected, landed at an airfield east of the Nile and drove through the center of Cairo looking for their accommodation. With a disturbing lack of wisdom Madame then decided to visit a hairdresser in the town, a circumstance that received much publicity and resulted in a crowd gathering to see her leave.

The British held that the Chinese theater of war was of very secondary importance to the European conflict. Roosevelt, however, thought the war in China served one essential purpose: it held down Japanese armies. This reasoning was clouded by the fact that Chiang's troops were not actually fighting the Japanese, for Chiang claimed that his men were untrained and unequipped. Like most Americans Roosevelt was fascinated by China, and very suspicious of British intentions in that country.

"Roosevelt's attitude towards Britain and the war was determined by circumstances out of his control, added to the fact that he had the instinctive American distrust of Imperial powers, which stems from their War of Independence," writes General Hollis. "These circumstances deserve study, for they molded Roosevelt's outlook during the years when he held the balance of power in the world: they are directly responsible for much that has overtaken the world since then . . ."

Even when France fell in June, 1940, and Britain was alone, Roosevelt could not face admitting to the American people that war was near. In July, however, he admitted to William C. Bullitt, U.S. Ambassador in Paris, who had just returned to the States, "that he could not get our defense preparations moving fast enough unless he should tell the country frankly that our very physical security was at stake."

It was decided that Bullitt should make a speech explaining the true and terrible position, and unless public reaction was very unfavorable, Roosevelt would follow this up with a "fireside chat," as his broadcasts were called, underlining what his Ambassador had already said.

On August 18, 1940, Bullitt announced in his trial speech: "America is in danger . . . It is as clear as anything on this earth that the U.S. will not *go* to war, but it is equally clear that war is *coming* to the American." He called for conscription and full aid to Britain. A poll reported that 97 per cent of the response was favorable to his sentiments. President Roosevelt was delighted, but even so he decided not to make his speech after all. It was the year of the Presidential election, and he did not want to risk losing.

That summer, however, Roosevelt turned over ships and armaments first to France and then to Britain, although some were too old to be of much use. He knew that America must quickly re-arm, and to do this they needed the shield of continued resistance by Britain. America just did not have the men and materials to face Germany alone, although time would speedily remedy this.

So weak was America then that on September 1, 1940, the U.S. Air Force had in hand only 53 modern bombers, and 187 modern pursuit planes. In these circumstances, Roosevelt's idea of Lend-Lease was a brilliant and friendly act. Bullitt thought that "In the invention of political mechanisms and expedients President Roosevelt was in a class by himself. In ability to handle American public opinion he was unrivalled. At his best he was a political genius, but his very ability enabled him to lead our country towards disaster when he was wrong."

America knew, too, in the spring of 1941, that Hitler was planning to attack Russia, and had already informed Stalin of the plan. Thus when the attack came on June 22nd, America— as the last great independent country not directly involved in the war—stood in a position to bring about an eventual and lasting peace. She alone had the power, independence and ability to achieve this end.

Stalin, on the one hand, had the men to fight the Germans, but almost no equipment. Britain, on the other, had far fewer

men, and although catching up in the manufacture of equipment of all kinds, willingly starved her forces of it to supply the
Russians. It was imperative for Stalin's survival that he was
given instant American aid, and in those circumstances Roosevelt could have dictated the terms on which this aid would have
been granted. More important, Roosevelt was in a position to
see that these terms were accepted and carried out. Indeed,
at that moment Roosevelt was the one man in the world who,
while technically remaining neutral, held in his hands the destinies of every other nation.

When the appeal for Russian Lend-Lease material came,
Roosevelt was warned by Ambassador Bullitt and others that
he must first obtain definite written public pledges about the
frontiers of Europe and the future of Asia, or else "the weight
of power in both Europe and Asia would have passed from the
U.S. to the Soviet Union. Stalin might mount the saddles of both
Hitler and the Japanese militarists."

Roosevelt, however, felt it futile to ask for any pledge from
Stalin, who he believed would break his promises as and when
it suited him. When Harry Hopkins and Averell Harriman went
to Russia to negotiate Lend-Lease, therefore, they were not told
to extract any pledges for a free Europe and China after the
war.

"Russia got more than one billion dollars worth of Lend-Lease
aid—but gave no pledges at all to America in return," writes
General Hollis. "While Roosevelt was doubtless right about
Stalin's ultimate intentions, such pledges could not have been
broken while Russia was still dependent on American aid for her
survival. Had she attempted to repudiate them, America would
have realized that here lay the seeds of danger which must be
stopped before they grew—as they have since grown—into Communist Imperialism all round the world.

"In fact, by December, 1941, only six months after Russia
entered the war, Stalin was already exploiting his freedom from
pledges by demanding from Mr. Eden a British agreement to his
annexation of parts of Finland, Roumania, East Poland, and
Baltic States. The American Government admitted to Britain

their opposition in principle to such action, but despite their position of immense strength in bargaining power, and Russia's equally immense weakness, the American State Department still sent the Lend-Lease supplies as agreed."

Now, at the Cairo Conference, Roosevelt complained of British imperialism. He said that the British were resisting building the Ledo road and were reluctant to drive an offensive through the Burma jungle. Mountbatten had spoken of starting a big offensive, but had not done so, and now the Prime Minister was talking of the need for landing-craft to attack the Andaman Islands.

"To hear Churchill talk," Roosevelt complained to his son Elliott, "you'd think they were the most strategic point this side of his beloved Balkans." In a sense they were, for from these islands the British-Indian armies could attack Rangoon.

"Their Empire ideas," Roosevelt continued, "are nineteenth century, if not seventeenth or eighteenth. And we're fighting a twentieth century war." This imperialist outlook, with which he credited Churchill, he had tried to discredit by explaining to him how wise had been the U.S. policy of giving independence to the Philippines—with the implication that the British ought to follow suit over the Empire.

"He (Churchill) says the Filipinos are a different breed of people, naturally ready to take responsibility," Roosevelt recounted naïvely. "He says we just don't understand the Indians, or the Burmese, or the Javanese, or even the Chinese."[2]

In his own mind, Roosevelt was quite sure that he understood *all* these races; and most important, the Russians as well.

He told his son, one night, that the British even opposed America's Pacific strategy of island-hopping.

"They don't begin to understand our thinking in terms of the Philippines as a future base for operations against Japan. Perhaps they don't appreciate the fact that the Filipinos will rally to our flag, inasmuch as they could hardly expect *their* colonials to rally to *theirs*."

The British argument for attacking Japan, said the President, was to concentrate on Malaya and then move on to the China coast. "Once again," he complained, "our Intelligence gives us a different picture from that of the British. They see only a Chinese coast infested with Japanese, while we are fully aware of the fact that much of that coast is in the hands of Chinese guerillas."

"These Chinese guerillas were, in fact, Communists. Chiang told Roosevelt so, and added that they were not fighting the Japanese either; but Roosevelt did not believe him," recalls General Hollis.

Elliott discussed with his father the withholding from the British of all American air reconnaissance photographs and the mapping of China which had been done under their guidance. The Chinese had made the Americans promise not to show these details to the British, before they would even agree to co-operate.

"It's not hard to appreciate their point of view," said the American President. "They're aware that the British want a look at them for commercial, post-war reasons. Chiang wants very badly to get our support against the British moving into Hong Kong and Shanghai and Canton with the same extra-territorial rights they enjoyed before the war. . . ."[2]

"Roosevelt further extracted from Chiang the promise that before the war ended he would form a 'unity national government' with the Yenan Communists, and guaranteed in turn that he would give the requested support against British claims to the ports," writes Hollis. "After the war, Roosevelt promised himself, no British warships should enter those ports. American warships would be allowed there, however. Chiang agreed to honor his side of the promise so long as the Soviet Government guaranteed the Manchurian frontier—a matter which was to be discussed at Teheran.

"The French, too, Roosevelt promised Chiang, should have no right to Indo-China after the war, and France would hold her colonies only as a trustee and be responsible to the United Nations with a view to their eventually becoming independent."

During the talks with Roosevelt and Chiang-Kai-shek, Madame Chiang acted as the interpreter; she and her husband were almost inseparable and used to talk over the day's events with

[2] Elliott Roosevelt, *As He Saw It*.

each other as they walked, hand in hand, in the garden of their villa.

Roosevelt privately thought she was an opportunist, a view since shared by others.

"I'd certainly not want to be known as her enemy, in her own country. But at the moment, who is there in China who could take Chiang's place? . . . With all their shortcomings, we've *got* to depend on the Chiangs."

Some of the friction caused by the China-Burma-India question seemed to have helped to harden the British attitude about "Overlord."[3]

Hopkins summed up the Roosevelt-Churchill arguments as "the old ones with a difference"—because by now America was producing war material at speed.

"The war from now on will be fought with equipment made in America," he said, "and by men born in America predominantly. . . . Who's senior partner, and who's junior? . . . And yet at the same time, Winston knows this Conference is taking place on Empire soil. That makes a subtle difference. . . ."

"When not conferring, the statesmen did a lot of formal entertaining, at functions ranging from small teas to elaborate dinners," General Hollis noted. "On Thanksgiving Day, for instance, the President gave the traditional feast of turkey and cranberry sauce, regardless of the climate. Afterwards, when they were posing for a photograph, he offered Chiang the seat in the center of the picture, which Chiang modestly refused, insisting that Roosevelt take it. Oddly, no one seemed to think of asking Churchill."

While austerity gripped Britain, entering her fifth year of wartime shortages, delegates at the Mena House were provided for the duration of the Conference with 22,000 lb. of meat, 78,000 eggs, 800 lb. of turkey, 4,600 lb. of sugar, 5,000 tins of fruit, half a million cigarettes and 1,500 cigars.

---

[3] Movement Control played a great part in the Overlord planning at Cairo, but Admiral Cunningham did not think very highly of all who made up this important branch. He said: "When we advance, it is all control and no movement. When we retire, it is all movement and no control."

The bar on the main floor was often doing business from nine in the morning until midnight, one result of which was seen during a long and involved discussion in the President's villa about the date of the proposed Second Front landings. Mr. Churchill sent Hollis back to the hotel to collect some details regarding tides in the English Channel, which were necessary for planning the Normandy landings.

"To reach the hotel, eight miles away, then find this information and bring it back, took me forty minutes," writes General Hollis. "On my return I was horrified to find that my American co-secretary had meantime fallen asleep, and had taken no notes at all of the war's most important discussion about the invasion of Europe! The possible consequences appalled me, and afterwards I tackled him with this unforgivable laziness. He had been drinking with friends on the previous evening and had a very bad hangover.

"Fortunately, when I showed General Ismay where my records had been interrupted, although he had not taken a single note during the meeting, he recalled with complete accuracy everything that had been said in my absence. . . ."

It was nearly winter, even in Egypt, but while the President appeared most of the time in a sober blue-gray suit, Churchill dazzled everyone by alternating between his zip-up siren suit and a brilliant white sharkskin suit, with a five-gallon cowboy hat on top.

Then, on November 27th, the Prime Minister and the President flew on to Teheran, where Stalin had already preceded them.

"At Teheran, with rather more than half the world's population represented," writes Hollis, "the object was supposed to be to end mutual suspicion between the three great powers. Roosevelt was suspicious of Churchill, and Stalin was suspicious of everybody. But outwardly they were all the greatest of buddies."

According to Roosevelt, "the biggest thing achieved at Teheran was in making clear to Stalin that the U.S. and Great Britain were not allied in one common bloc against the Soviet Union. I think we've got rid of that idea, once and for all. The one thing that could upset the apple-cart, after the war, is if the world is divided again, Russia against England and us. That's our big job now . . . making sure that we continue to act as intermediary between Russia and England."[4]

Churchill stayed at the British Legation opposite the Russian Embassy. Stalin had invited Roosevelt to stay at the Russian Embassy; Churchill had also offered him hospitality at the British Legation. At first Roosevelt refused both offers: the British on the grounds that he could not be a guest, and then the Russians because he did not wish to offend the British by accepting another invitation. In the end, he accepted Stalin's offer for convenience and security reasons—the Russian agents claimed they had already arrested three would-be assassins—and moved into the square, box-like Russian Embassy, while Stalin stayed some 150 yards off in another small Embassy building, blue-gray with a columned portico.

"For this first meeting with his two chief Allies Stalin had with him Molotov and Voroshilov, and although he was barely five foot five inches tall, despite his smallness and the ill-fitting Marshal's uniform he wore, his quiet, impassive figure with the bushy hair and iron-gray mustache had about it a magnetic, nearly majestic quality," General Hollis wrote later. "He was a living enigma. Only once did he become visibly angry when at a dinner given by Churchill at the British Legation on his sixty-ninth birthday, General Brooke remarked that the British had suffered more than any of the Allies in the war.

"Stalin at once stood up and replied that this was primarily a war of machines, and since most of the machines were produced by America, it was the Americans who were winning the war for the Allies."

Roosevelt had been banking a good deal on his first meeting with Stalin, "Uncle Joe" as he always called him to himself; and he did achieve a private meeting, as a gesture of confidence and informality. Stalin walked across the gravel path separating the two houses at three o'clock on the first afternoon and entered

[4] Elliott Roosevelt.

Roosevelt's sunny private sitting-room. He was wearing a camel-hair overcoat over his Marshal's uniform. For an hour the two men sat and talked, face to face, with an interpreter. Roosevelt's impression was very favorable.

"I'm sure we'll hit it off, Stalin and I," he told his son later on. "A great deal of the misunderstandings and the mistrusts of the past are going to get cleared up during the next few days—I hope once and for all."

Roosevelt discussed with Stalin the question of Russia's entering the war with Japan, and Stalin agreed on a date six months after Hitler's defeat. Roosevelt thought he agreed probably in order to gain a Western promise for a Second Front.

"He was willing to get in as soon as he could get troops to Siberia," the President told his son, "if we would just promise the May invasion in the West."

When Stalin was shown a copy of the "Overlord" plan, he asked a question or two, and then said just one word: "When?"

In the end, the "Overlord" question was settled, "for the fourth time," as Roosevelt said; and this time even the date, May 1st, was agreed. They also agreed on the Mediterranean thrust, but the American way—through France. Churchill had argued strongly for pushing through the Balkans, but Roosevelt, very pleased with his own perspicacity, said, "It was quite obvious to everyone in the room what he really meant. That he was above all else anxious to knife up into central Europe in order to keep the Red Army out of Austria and Roumania, even Hungary, if possible. Stalin knew it; I knew it, everybody knew it. . . ."

And Stalin was equally aware of his own motives, and equally tacit, when he argued for a western invasion and against a splitting into two of the Allied forces, an arrangement that also suited Roosevelt well.

"It's a pleasure working with him," he reported to his son, "There's nothing devious. He outlines the subject he wants discussed, and sticks to it."

The subject Stalin wanted discussed was, of course, "Overlord."

But Operation Anvil, the American attack on the South of France, planned in 1943 for 1944—"designed to split the enemy defense in France and facilitate Ike's attack"—in Normandy— did not appeal to General Mark Clark, who was earmarked to command it. Clark thought "Southern France looked like a dead-end street . . . or at least a very roundabout way of getting to Germany or the Balkans." In February 1944, to his relief, he was personally relieved of responsibility for Anvil; but his troops were still taken away from Italy to attack the South of France.

"Stalin was one of the strongest boosters of the invasion of southern France. He knew exactly what he wanted in a political as well as a military way; and the thing that he wanted most was to keep us out of the Balkans, which he had staked out for the Red Army.

"If we switched our strength from Italy to France it was obvious to Stalin, or to anyone else, that we would be turning away from Central Europe. From France the only way we could get to the Balkans was through Switzerland. In other words, Anvil (the American landing in Southern France) led into a dead-end street. It was easy to see, therefore, why Stalin favored Anvil at Teheran, and why he kept on pushing for it; but I could never understand why, as conditions changed and as the war situation changed, the U.S. and Britain failed to sit down and take another look at the overall picture. This wasn't done, although there was lots of talk about it, particularly by the British. I imagine that Churchill was responsible for this talk, and that it was not his fault that it never developed into anything more than talk.

"A campaign that might have changed the whole history of relations between the Western world and Soviet Russia was permitted to fade away . . . into much less than it could have been. The weakening of the campaign in Italy in order to invade southern France, instead of pushing on into the Balkans was one of the outstanding political mistakes of the war. I am firmly convinced that the French forces alone, with seven divisions available, could have captured Marseilles, protected Eisenhower's southern flank, and advanced up the Rhone valley to join hands with the main "Overlord" forces. The Fifth American

Corps, with its three divisions, could then have remained in Italy. The impetus of the Allied advance in Italy would thus not have been lost, and we could have advanced into the Balkans."[5]

Elliott Roosevelt asked his father whether Churchill might not have a case for a Balkan invasion, but his father argued, "Trouble is, the Prime Minister is thinking too much of the *post*-war, and where England will be. He's scared of letting the Russians get too strong. Maybe the Russians *will* get strong in Europe. Whether that's bad depends on a whole lot of factors. . . ."

Roosevelt also wanted to talk about China with Stalin, privately—"Couldn't do a lot of that talking while Winston was around"—and put to Stalin the wish of Chiang-Kai-shek to end British rights in Chinese ports and to have a Russian guarantee of their frontier.

"Uncle Joe," he told Elliott afterwards, "agreed that, of course, Manchuria would remain with the Chinese and agreed to help us back Chiang against the British."

The Russians, Stalin had said unctuously, were anxious for world recognition of Soviet sovereignty, and therefore they would certainly respect the sovereignty of other countries.

"Shortly after this," says General Hollis, "Stilwell called on the President, dissatisfied that Chiang seemed to be storing up his strength to use against the Chinese Communists after the war. Roosevelt diplomatically said little, knowing that he had separate commitments now to both Chiang and Stalin. He did not seem to see any irony in this double-think. . . .

"Two incidents, unrelated to the strategic discussion, remain very clearly in my mind. The first was the presentation to Stalin of a beautifully jewelled and inscribed sword, the Sword of Stalingrad. After a general salute of Russian and British Guards of Honor, Mr. Churchill advanced, and with a bow handed the sword to Stalin, who raised it to his lips and kissed the bright blade, and then passed it over to Marshal Voroshilov who, to my mind, had been drinking. Voroshilov fumbled with the sword and dropped it on the ground. Stalin withered him with a look.

[5] General Mark Clark, *Calculated Risk.*

The Marshal picked it up shamefacedly, and the ceremony went on.

"I've often wondered what Stalin said to him afterwards.

"The second incident took place at Mr. Churchill's birthday dinner party in the British Legation. This followed lavish dinner parties by both Roosevelt and Stalin, and the Russian speeches were interpreted by a Mr. Pavlov, who spoke English well, but in a most stilted and copybook manner. No rhetoric, no fervor of the speeches could survive his curiously artificial translation.

"During the first of Stalin's speeches, I noticed that a mountainous ice cream about three feet high, and of the most complicated design, was being served. The room was very warm, and as the waiter gave us each a portion, his hand trembled, and the gigantic confection began to slide from the plate. For a moment we thought with horror that it would land on Stalin's head, but it just missed him and fell over Mr. Pavlov in a cascade of cream and melting mush.

"Mr. Pavlov was quite equal to the disaster. He did not even wipe the mess from his hair. He stood erect as ever. "Mr. Stalin," he continued, "he says . . ."

On the morning after Churchill's birthday party, both the British and American delegations returned to Cairo to wind up the Conference, and there Mr. Churchill gave a final dinner party to the Combined Chiefs of Staff and the Secretariat. Just before it began, Hollis heard that General Ismay had been taken ill in Cairo.

"When I saw him in his room I was horrified to see how ill he looked. He had been working regularly up to eighteen hours in each twenty-four for the previous three years, and exhaustion had finally overcome him. I went to the Prime Minister's dinner party with a heavy heart, for, as next senior to Ismay, I realized that all his responsibilities would now rest on me, as well as my own.

"I told Mr. Churchill about Ismay's illness and he was obviously grieved, but during the dinner he kept looking fixedly at me in a strange and ruminative way. I could not understand the reason for this, and it disturbed me, for every time I looked up from my plate I saw his eyes fixed on me in a way I had never seen before.

"At last, after the meal, he asked me: 'You aren't ill, are you?'

"I replied, 'No, Sir, I am perfectly fit.'

" 'Hm,' he said, piercing his cigar. 'Hm. You'd better be!'

"After the Cairo Conference," continues General Hollis, "Churchill decided to visit the battlefields in Italy. I was to follow him later, and embarked at Alexandria in H.M.S. *Penelope*. While actually at sea I received a cipher telegram with news that he had fallen ill in Carthage and was staying in—of all places—a pre-war swimming chateau, placed at his disposal by the American Government. My presence was required immediately.

"The *Penelope* meanwhile had been ordered to Bizerta, where the Flag Officer Commanding ordered her to anchor well outside the harbor because of the danger from sunken ships. The Captain told me this, but I replied that these orders would not help me to visit the Prime Minister speedily, and so I asked him on my own authority to disregard them, and go right into the harbor and get alongside.

"This he agreed to do, and as we sailed in further signals from the Flag Officer arrived thick and fast, for he could not understand why the Captain was deliberately disobeying his orders. Eventually I could see a figure climb into a car and be driven to the quayside to await our arrival: the Flag Officer himself.

"Fortunately we avoided all the sunken wrecks, and when I came down the gangway in military uniform and saluted him, my reception was cold in the extreme. As soon as I was able to explain the circumstances that necessitated our disobeying his orders, however, he did all he could to help me.

"I was given an American car and a British R.A.S.C. driver, and for the next few days I commuted morning and evening between Bizerta and Carthage, a distance of seventy miles each way. One night, an American military police patrol waved our car to a standstill. The driver wound down the window.

" 'I don't want any trouble, mate,' he said. 'I'm on a rush job with a Brigadier in the British Service.' The policeman looked in and I corroborated what the driver said, and the M.P. waved us on our way.

"'That was lucky, sir,' said the driver to me over his shoulder as soon as we were moving. 'I'd no pass, no identity card, no driving license, no number plates. If you hadn't been here, I'd have had no luck, either!'"

Although Mr. Churchill was seriously ill with pneumonia, he still kept at close grips with the war situation, and his interest presented Hollis with grave difficulties, for the telephone service to the bathing house was crude, and all secret messages had to be brought and sent by despatch riders.

When at last the Prime Minister began to mend, it was decided by his doctors that he should spend some weeks' convalescence in Marrakesh. It was obviously necessary for him to have a complete cipher staff there, for Marrakesh would now temporarily become the nerve center of the war; and so Hollis suggested that he should fly home and return with the cipher officers.

Mr. Churchill was not at all pleased at the prospect of being left alone. Since Hollis made the proposal on the Monday of Christmas week, he rather uncharitably assumed that Hollis had only made it so that he could spend Christmas Day—the Friday —in England with his wife. He therefore asked Hollis when he thought he could return, and Hollis, knowing quite well what was in the Prime Minister's mind, promised he would be back at four o'clock on Christmas Eve. On this understanding it was agreed that he should go. The only problem was—how?

Sir Alan Brooke, who was passing through Marrakesh that evening, gave him a lift in his own airplane. Instead of the bad weather usual for that time of year, everything was clear, and they reached England late on Tuesday afternoon. By Wednesday evening Hollis was ready to return, with a number of W.A.A.F. cipher officers. Then fog came down over British airfields, and flying was cancelled. Only one airfield was in use, in Dorset, and there they had to drive by motor-coach. They arrived at midnight, and took off in a bomber.

The first step was Casablanca, controlled by the Americans; and here some doubt arose as to whether they could proceed. Hollis saw the Commanding Officer and explained the urgency of their journey, and within half an hour the plane was refuelled. They reached their next stop, Tunis, at half-past three on Thursday afternoon. Commander Thompson, one of Churchill's personal staff, was anxiously waiting for Hollis with his car, and by driving furiously all the way to Churchill's villa, they managed to arrive at three minutes to four.

Hollis went straight into Churchill's bedroom, where the Prime Minister, still abed, had called a conference with Field Marshal Wilson, Air Marshal Tedder, Admiral Cunningham, and their advisers. These officers were sitting round the room waiting for the discussions to begin, and looked at Hollis's arrival with some surprise.

"Ah, Hollis," said Churchill from his bed. "I *knew* you would be back. *Now* we can begin."

"I was very touched at this faith in my ability to make a double journey of some 5,000-odd miles so punctually," writes General Hollis, "for literally dozens of circumstances could have made me days late."

Marrakesh was a hiatus between conferences and battles. On the surface it seemed as remote from war as from the blackout and austerity of Britain; in the courtyard outside their offices, Churchill's staff could pick oranges from the trees, or sit in the sunshine and enjoy the sharp Algerian wine. But against this strange background of warmth, of lizards basking on warm stone, of the sea and the sun and the wine, the old arguments for and against a landing in Italy as against a landing in France still remained unchanged.

"Churchill wanted to land at Anzio, but to do this he needed American landing-craft," wrote Hollis later on. "The Americans pointed out that all their ships were needed for the French landing. Churchill promised to send them back to England *after* Anzio so that they could be used to carry the forces to France. He produced set after set of calendar dates to prove that this could be done quite easily, but still the Americans were unwilling to risk it; they had already privately decided that there would be no landing in Italy. Lord Beaverbrook was asked to be ready to go to see Roosevelt and explain to him the need for an Italian landing, a task he faced without great enthusiasm, for he had all along pressed for a Second Front.

"Such was the rather strained position when Eisenhower arrived. But with his genius for compromise and adaptation, he reconciled both points of view. There would, after all, be a landing in Italy. . . .

"I first met Eisenhower when he was the American equivalent of our own Director of Military Operations (General Kennedy), on a visit to Washington. Admiral Stark, Generals Marshall, Arnold and Bedell Smith were with him in the room.

"Eisenhower struck me as being impressive physically—alert and tireless—and also very quick to grasp a point that the others, his seniors, would like to argue about. He did well in all the posts he was given, and was an obvious nominee for Supreme Commander for 'Overlord.' The only other possibilities were Marshall and Brooke. It is doubtful whether the Americans, Bradley and Patton, would have served willingly under a British Supremo. Also Churchill did not want to lose Brooke, and Roosevelt needed Marshall, so Eisenhower got the job.

"I remember him, not as a strategic man, or as a planner, nor as one who could initiate strategy, but as a very able conciliator. For instance, although Britain had been two years longer in the war than America, the weight of arms in 'Overlord' was predominantly American: this position led to friction at many levels, for experience and strength are not always good mixers.

"Eisenhower, however, promulgated an order to the effect that if any serious dispute broke out between an American and a British officer under his command, he would not investigate it or take sides but both officers could pack their kit immediately and would be returned to their home units. This had the effect of making them sink their differences and work in greater harmony than would otherwise have been the case."

Eisenhower's aide, Captain Harry C. Butcher, tells the story of an American and a British officer who got into a severe argument which reached such proportions that General Eisenhower sent for both officers and talked to them in the interests of unity. After giving both of them a lecture he dismissed the British officer, but kept the American for further words.

"I don't mind your airing your differences with this British officer," he said. "I don't particularly mind that you engaged in fisticuffs with him. I must say that I think you were right in your position. Ordinarily I don't condone cursing and name-calling, but I forgive you for calling him a son-of-a-bitch. But I cannot forgive you for calling him a *British* son-of-a-bitch. Consequently, I am sending you home on a slow boat, un-escorted."[6]

Eisenhower took advice from everyone, but the final decision was always his own—as when he gave the order to sail on D-Day. Rough weather had postponed the assault once already for twenty-four hours when the ships were already at sea. If it were postponed again, the men would have to disembark, for they could not stay indefinitely aboard their cramped craft; and if they all went ashore then all hope of keeping their objective secret would be lost.

Eisenhower decided to sail. Had he not done so then, the invasion of France would have been postponed, perhaps for another year, perhaps for ever.

And London would have been destroyed, not only by the V-1 and V-2 rockets but by the V-3, the most sinister weapon of all: long-range guns with barrels 500 feet in length. These were constructed barely eighty miles from London, just behind Calais, in blockhouses with roofs twenty feet thick, and walls so strong that no bomb in use at that date could crack them. From behind sliding steel doors, these guns could fire six shells a minute on London; 1,200 tons of explosives every day. Within a fortnight as much high explosive as was rained on Berlin during six years of war, would have fallen on the capital.[7]

---

[6] *"Three Years with Eisenhower,"* by Harry C. Butcher.

[7] Professor S. E. Morison said at Oxford on May 16, 1957, "If we had not invaded northern Europe in 1944 London would certainly have been laid flat by the V-1 bombs and V-2 rockets. War with Germany would not have ended until 1946."

"This saving of London we owe to Eisenhower, above all others at this point of war," writes General Hollis. The debt was recognized by King George VI, when he gave Eisenhower the Order of Merit, the only British military decoration that a monarch can give without recommendation or approval of his Government. When Eisenhower was granted the Freedom of the City of London on June 12, 1945—a year and six days after he took the decision to sail to France—he spoke to a crowd of 30,000, and added, almost jokingly: "Whether you know it or not, I'm now a Londoner myself. I've as much right to be down in the crowd yelling as you have!"

Then, only a handful hearing him knew the significance behind his words.

But to return to Marrakesh: Montgomery was another of the visitors, and was shown the draft plan for "Overlord" drawn up by General Sir Frederick Morgan. He did not appear very happy with it, and in his blunt, direct way he told the Prime Minister so.

"Very well then," replied Churchill at once. "If you don't like Morgan's plan, do one of your own!"

Some of those with Churchill in the Villa Taylor in Marrakesh rather resented Montgomery's attitude, and felt that this challenge would show whether he was as good a tactician as his friends would have them believe. They did not have long to wait for their answer.

"Montgomery retired with his staff to his rooms, and all through that night, against the drone of mosquitoes and night-moths, we heard the noise of sustained typing," Hollis says. "Only at dawn did the clatter of the keys cease. Later that morning he expounded his plan, which contained an immense expansion of the original rather limited frontal attack. Thereafter, even Montgomery's former critics had no doubt of his ability as a General. . . .

"In one corner of the grounds stood a tower like a minaret, and here Churchill, Beaverbrook, Montgomery and I would sit and watch the evening sun go down over the desert in all its glory and splendor. For a few moments, our conversation would turn to this astonishingly beautiful sight, and then back it would go to the unending topic: the impending Second Front, which Churchill was convinced was the only way in which we could lose the war."

Mr. Churchill's doctors had advised him to spend as much time as possible out of doors, and so he would travel almost daily to the Atlas Mountains, driving with his staff in several cars, and there the discussions would continue in the open air. These outings were enjoyable only for those fortunate enough to be with the Prime Minister in the leading car, for those who drove in the cars behind were smothered in dust.

On arriving at the place selected, Churchill would often climb down into one of the valleys on some expedition of his own, and then, since his doctors had forbidden him to exert himself in his convalescence, he would have to be hauled up again. Two British soldiers would go down after him with a tablecloth, brought for a picnic lunch. They would fold this lengthways, and then, putting it behind the Prime Minister, would pull him up, one on either side.

On one of these occasions, Churchill's party stopped for a meal in a field which a Moroccan farmer was ploughing with oxen. His dog, rather like an Alsatian, viewed their arrival with much interest, which increased when Mr. Churchill sat down in a large camp chair, and began to eat a wing of cold fried chicken. The dog grovelled towards him on his belly, with pleading eyes. Mr. Churchill looked down, and spoke thus to the beast:

"O, dog," he said, "when you woke up this morning did you really think you were going to have the most wonderful feast of your life?"

And he handed the dog the remainder of the wing.

"At Marrakesh, de Gaulle held his first military review, a rather sad performance, for his men were armed with English guns and American tanks," writes General Hollis. "They had no French arms at all. French children, evacuated from their Motherland, sang the '*Marseillaise*,' and de Gaulle put on as good a show as he could—although some of us suspected that he must have marched the same men round and round the square to make them appear more than they were!"

One night at dinner, Mr. Churchill put before Hollis a plate covered with a table napkin.

"Your hors d'œuvre," he said quietly. Hollis lifted the napkin and saw, glittering on the white plate, the polished brass insignia of a Major-General.

The Prime Minister had gone to enormous trouble to procure these almost unobtainable emblems from Algiers; he had even greater difficulty, however, in getting the approval to Hollis's promotion from London, for his wishes reached the Royal Marines Office on Christmas Day.

A junior officer, who had been left in sole charge, communicated the contents of the cable to the Admiralty branch that dealt with the promotion of officers to the Marines equivalent of Flag Rank. There, an equally junior Civil Servant, left on duty over Christmas, gave it as his opinion that such matters could not be conducted in an arbitrary and hurried fashion. They should wait until after the holiday. Such was their youth and inexperience that they sent a signal to this effect to Marrakesh. This aroused Churchill to retort: "Have you no motor cars, or airplanes, or telephones in the U.K.?"

To this, answer came there none, and Hollis was immediately promoted to Major-General, a promotion recorded in London by two very shaken young men.

Although the Marrakesh sunshine was helping Churchill in his recovery, the doctors were very strict in their orders that nothing should be allowed to excite him, as this might well bring on a relapse. One morning, when news arrived from General Alexander that Allied forces had landed at Anzio, Hollis measured the distance on the map and found that they were thirty-five miles southeast of Rome. He went in and reported the fact to Churchill, whose face glowed with delight.

"We have landed at the mouth of the Tiber," he announced with satisfaction. "We have landed at the throat of Rome."

Hollis replied that this seemed rather optimistic, as they were still thirty-five miles from Rome. Mr. Churchill's face clouded, and he suggested sharply that the General should take the trouble to measure the distance on a map before supplying him with such false and disturbing information. As he spoke, Hollis noted with some alarm that the color in his face had deepened. There was no doubt that Mr. Churchill was becoming considerably excited.

Hollis therefore retired to the Map Room, waited for a few minutes, and then reappeared in Churchill's presence.

"You are quite right, Prime Minister," he said soothingly. "I was wrong. We are *not* thirty-five miles from Rome. We are thirty-four-and-a-half miles away."

"*Exactly*," replied Mr. Churchill beaming, all annoyance gone. "I *knew* I was right."

After dinner in the Villa Taylor it was customary for a fairly fierce poker game to start up.

"Usually," writes General Hollis, "I managed to avoid being drawn in by pressure of work, but one night Lord Beaverbrook pressed me to join. With great misgivings I did so, and being at best a poor gambler with little card sense, I drew the most terrible hands and lost what was—for me—a very considerable sum of money—something like a month's pay. To the others, of course, such a sum was nothing at all.

"In due course, Winston totted up the score, and before I had time to calculate myself exactly how much I was down, he said: 'You needn't worry, Hollis, it's all divided by two hundred and forty-four!'

"I am sure that Mr. Churchill did this division sum purely for my benefit. And perhaps one of the nicest features of his kindness was the casual way in which he did it."

※   ※   ※   ※

"In the autumn of 1958," continues General Hollis, "more than 14 years after all these discussions and arguments took place, Field Marshal Montgomery published his memoirs, which aroused great interest. He claimed, in my view, however, more for himself than was justified by his admittedly excellent record in the field.

"One such instance, which stands particularly strongly in my mind, concerns the drive towards Berlin. On September 4, 1944, only four days after his promotion to Field Marshal, Montgomery wrote to Eisenhower that the Allies needed 'one really powerful and full-blooded thrust towards Berlin.'

"On September 15 he urged taking the northern Ruhr route to Berlin, arguing that time was the vital factor, but Eisenhower, although assuring him that he was 'completely in agreement,' still insisted that 'one single knife-like drive towards Berlin' was out of the question.

"By September 22, Eisenhower, by Montgomery's account, agreed with Monty's plan, but Montgomery writes that 'he had taken the decision exactly one month too late . . . Berlin was lost to us when we failed to make a sound operational plan in August, 1944, after the victory in Normandy. . . . The way things were being handled was going to have repercussions far beyond the end of the war; it looked to me then as if we were going to "muck it up." I reckon we did.'

"The inference to readers who have not access to all the facts is that Montgomery was right, and, as he claims so often in his book, others were wrong. Looking back over the events of the intervening 14 years, with a divided Germany and the relentless march of Communism in so many other countries, it appears that only the folly of others prevented the brilliance of Montgomery from winning the peace as he had won so many martial victories in the war.

"With a lack of frankness surprising in such a frank and outspoken character, he does not say that the whole future of Berlin had in fact been agreed months earlier in London by the deliberations of an almost unknown body called the European Advisory Commission, *and that there was therefore no question of him being able to make his drive on to Berlin.*

"He briefly mentions the E.A.C. twice in his book when he explains that they had not decided on the boundaries of the French zone until after the Potsdam conference.

"These references, meager and passing though they are, show that he was aware of the deliberations of this almost unknown body which, meeting in private in Lancaster House, St. James's, has had an incalculable influence on all our lives, and on the lives of generations still to come.

"While Churchill, Beaverbrook and the rest of us were at Marrakesh, the E.A.C. were preparing for its first meeting. . . .

"The formation of this unusual Commission had been suggested during the Moscow Conference in October 1943, and in the following month Mr. Eden told the House of Commons that it would be 'an advisory not an executive body . . . a piece of machinery set up for the convenience of the three Governments . . . not an instrument for imposing their views on others. On . . . these three Powers principally . . . will lie the responsibility for ensuring that this war be followed by lasting peace.' As such, its organization and the men who ran it, deserve some study. . . ."

John G. Winant, the American Ambassador to Britain, who represented America on the Commission, presided over their first meeting. The Russian Ambassador, Mr. Feodor Tatasovitch Gusev, appeared for his country. Britain was represented by William Strang. When Strang's appointment was announced and since it carried ambassadorial rank, he was created a Knight Commander of St. Michael and St. George, to be on an equal footing with the others.

In looks, the sandy-haired Gusev was the antithesis of the black-haired Winant; in outlook they were also a world apart. Where Winant was casual, Gusev was tense; where Winant was friendly, he was withdrawn; where Winant was expansive, Gusev was a man who lived to rules. Not quite forty, short and stubby, the son of a municipal official of a small town near Leningrad, he had succeeded the veteran Maisky as Russian Ambassador to Britain and shared with him an inscrutability of face.

"He could say nothing in several languages with unruffled immobility," General Hollis wrote later.

Gusev studied law and political science at Leningrad University, then served a useful apprenticeship in the N.K.V.D., the Soviet Secret Police, and joined the Foreign Office in 1937, where he made a special study of British institutions. It was not widely known whether his connection with the N.K.V.D. was severed or strengthened as the years went by.

Before coming to Britain, he had been Russian envoy to Canada, where he did not mix much with Canadians. Indeed, a Canadian diplomat said afterwards: "We always had the impression that he really rather despised it all."

He certainly wasted no time on small talk and pleasantries. At the opening meeting of the European Advisory Commission he nodded twice and said: "Good morning." After about ninety minutes, he interrupted proceedings to shake his head and say: "No."

And at the end of the meeting he said: "Good afternoon," and left.

The British delegate, Sir William Strang's career had been varied in scope and success. He had joined the Foreign Office after the First World War from London University and the Sorbonne—a change from the majority of entrants who came by way of Oxford or Cambridge—and within two years was acting Chargé d'Affaires in Belgrade. In 1930 he was appointed Counsellor at the British Embassy in Moscow, and acted as Chargé d'Affaires three years later during the trial of the British engineers. In the same year he succeeded Alexander Cadogan as head of the League of Nations Department in the Foreign Office.

Strang was a man of dry humor. When he accompanied Eden to Moscow in 1935, they lunched at Litvinoff's country house, where on a plate at each place at table was a pat of butter with Litvinoff's favorite and much publicized motto: "Peace is indivisible." As Mr. Maisky, then Russian Ambassador to London, prepared to cut his butter, Strang startled him with the warning, "Be careful how you cut that!"

Strang first came before the public eye in June 1939, when the Chamberlain Government decided that since "the points of difference between Britain and Russia were so few, an agreement between them could be signed very easily." As head of the Central European Department of the Foreign Office and therefore intimately connected with the pacts with Poland, Roumania and

Turkey—which Britain had not the military means to honor—
Strang was sent to Moscow to speed up this Russian agreement.

"Britain," Mr. Chamberlain told the House of Commons, "has
made it clear that we are ready immediately and without reserve
to join the French Government in giving Russia full military
support in the event of aggression against her, involving hostilities with a European power."

"Strang carried out his duties in Moscow to the best of his
very considerable ability," writes General Hollis. "But a Civil Servant was not the right man to send to deal with the Russian rulers
at that time. Lord Halifax had gone to Germany: a Minister of
equal rank should have gone to Russia. Strang did not even see
Stalin, who was in fact busy signing a non-aggression pact with
Germany. He therefore had to return home with nothing at all."

Lesser men might have faded into oblivion after such a journey,
but not Sir William. He stayed with the Foreign Office, and on his
appointment in 1943 as Britain's representative on the European
Advisory Commission, *The Times* commented: "The choice is admirable . . . his knowledge of the new Russia is particularly
intimate. . . ."

The European Advisory Commission met at Lancaster House
from February 1944 until its last meeting in the following July.
In that month they finally agreed on the conditions by which the
three Powers would accept Germany's surrender. There were to
be sixteen conditions for the so-called "unconditional surrender,"
and more time was taken up in discussing them than had been occupied over the Versailles Treaty twenty-five years previously, for
Gusev could not agree with Winant on any point without first
referring the matter to Moscow. Usually he received a Soviet
counter-proposal on which Winant had to stall until he, in turn,
could hear the views of the President in Washington.

As at so many international discussions, the delegates all wanted
to discuss different things. Russia, who proposed to turn the whole
German army into reconstruction gangs, would never submit
military plans for discussion. Britain put forward for discussion
civil and economic matters as well as military ones. America offered only general observations.

The small nations, Belgium and Holland among them, felt that they had been ignored in not being invited to sit on the Commission, although they had their own plans for the future of Germany; and France was particularly resentful that she had not been included among the major nations. Finally, despite the machinery of the European Advisory Commission, the last word in any decision obviously remained with the three heads of the Governments involved.

Eventually, after many meetings, certain conditions were agreed. The three zones of influence were based on a map of Germany that had appeared in the *New York Times*. President Roosevelt had marked this map in what he proposed should be a distribution of zones. The U.S. Army then photographed the map and enlarged it, and the Commission members based their deliberations upon this.

Both Churchill and Roosevelt, being the leaders of maritime nations, wanted the northern territory of Germany, which included the great ports of Hamburg and Bremen. The Russians were more concerned with land than sea, and did not dispute the Western claim. Gusev sat in silence while Winant and Strang disagreed over the carving up of the still undefeated Germany. Neither Gusev nor any of his Russian advisers made any comment while the American and British delegates—both conscious of the naval advantages in having the ports—argued passionately for their control. Finally, after much discussion and some acrimony, the Americans gave way to the British on the occupation of the North for, in fact, the American Army preferred the Southern area of Germany. They asked for, and got, however, an enclave at Bremen.

At last the post-war map of Germany was settled and agreed, but not the conditions of occupation.

"At that time the American policy was 'to make the Russians trust us,' and the implementation of this policy sometimes necessitated the cutting of the throats of the British," writes Hollis. "This the Americans were quite prepared to do, believing that the end would justify the means, but in reality the British and Americans cut their own throats, so far as the post-war control of Germany was concerned. Both had been so eager for the ports that they had entirely neglected to safeguard control of the capital—Berlin! It was agreed that a Ministry of Communications would be tripartite in each of the three zones, but while free access to Berlin, which was in the Russian zone, was mentioned, it was not discussed in any detail.

"The reason no one at the Commission asked for a corridor to reach Berlin was that there was then no suggestion that any of the Allies would hold on to the land in Germany that they had conquered, for no dispute between the victorious Allies was contemplated. For obvious psychological reasons Berlin, the capital, was to be the center for negotiating a peace. No one thought about permanent occupation there. The enclaves were originally intended only for a peace treaty, but in the event, they were both left with enclaves in Berlin, and they could not retreat. And after the British General Election in 1945, which the Socialists won, the Russian attitude hardened, and they became more intractable and held on to East Berlin."

There is an odd postscript to this work of the European Advisory Commission,[8] concerning General Bedell Smith, Eisenhower's Chief of Staff in Europe from January 1944. Bedell Smith had signed the Italian armistice in September, 1943, and when he went to sign the German surrender on behalf of Eisenhower, he met the German negotiator, General Jodl—who had been Hitler's personal military adviser—and Friedeberg, at Eisenhower's advance headquarters in Rheims, a red brick building, formerly a technical school.

Discussion lasted right through the afternoon and evening of May 6th, and finally, at 2:41 A.M. on May 7th, the unconditional

[8] Echoes of European Advisory Commission decisions also rebounded on Eisenhower during the 1952 American Presidential election, when his political opponents blamed him for not continuing the drive East across Germany and so capturing all Berlin. Seven years before, on April 18, 1945, Harry K. Butcher, his naval aide, had written in his diary: "Ike went to Downing Street to see Churchill. The Prime Minister wants him to take Berlin, but Ike sees no military sense in it. He thinks it more important that we clear our flank . . . cut north to Lubeck, south to the so-called Redoubt." *Three Years with Eisenhower.*

surrender—for which the European Advisory Commission had so painstakingly prepared sixteen conditions—was signed at a long wooden table in a sparsely furnished war-room with the maps of the front still pinned to the walls. Then a forgetful side to Bedell Smith's character was suddenly and embarrassingly discovered. Almost unbelievably, he had mislaid the list of sixteen conditions of surrender on which peace would be declared! He could submit only four of them from memory.

The Russians were more careful. They stuck closely to the sixteen conditions—and added some more of their own for good measure, which were agreed.

Fate has since touched the lives of all these four men, who all received honors for their services. Winant, a great friend to Britain, was admitted to the Order of Merit. Shortly after his return to America, he took his own life. Sir William Strang became head of the Foreign Office, and is now a peer; General Bedell Smith was appointed American Ambassador to Moscow and then Director of the Central Intelligence Bureau. But Gusev, the little Russian who had said so little but observed much during the meetings in Lancaster House, received recognition of his services to his country more speedily than any of the others. On November 4, 1944, barely four months after the last meeting of the European Advisory Commission, he was awarded the Order of Lenin for "eminent services to the Soviet State and exemplary carrying out of the Government's instructions."

Just how well Gusev had carried out these instructions was soon apparent. By reaching Berlin—and staying there—the Russian Armies captured upwards of 50,000 German technicians, scientists and electronic experts who had been working on the V-1 and V-2 guided missiles near Berlin and transported them to Russia. The emergence of Russia as a space-power barely thirteen years after the war owes much to the "eminent services" of Feodor Gusev.

CHAPTER 10

I know the warning song is sung in vain,
That few will hear, and fewer heed the
strain.

COWPER *Expostulation*

Early in 1945, further Three-Power talks were necessary, and a
site for these had to be sought. Stalin, as before, refused to move
very far from home, but Moscow would be too cold in the winter;
and Teheran had been an inhospitable capital. Roosevelt, always
eager to appease Stalin, therefore suggested that they should try
Yalta, which he described as "a pleasant resort on the Crimean
Riviera." At first there was some confusion as to whether Roosevelt
had meant *Malta* and not Yalta, but Churchill settled it with the
phrase: "Yalta, not Malta: don't alter or falter."

Pride in their country prevented the Russians from explaining
that the whole of the Crimea was a waste land, burned, blackened
and ruined by the Germans; that thousands of unexploded mines
were still embedded on and off the roads. And while the eastern
side of the protecting mountain range was warm, west of it lay
a morass of mud, deluged by sleet and snow, and raked by
continual bitter winds. This was the site chosen for the Conference.

The Russians, with their usual thoroughness, detailed thousands
of Red Army soldiers to restore the roads, filling in bomb-holes,
and redecorating and refurnishing the houses for the three Delega-

tions. No less than 1,500 railway coaches were run from Moscow—
four days' journey north—with supplies of food, drink, bedding
and other stores. They also brought Moscow's best hotel staff and
carpets, and so extensive had been the devastation that thousands
of panes of glass had also to be replaced before the houses were
habitable. Hardly one unbroken window remained in Yalta.
Finally, 30,000 Russian troops arrived to guard the roads and the
houses of the Delegations. Saki airfield, where the advance parties
landed, was little better than a snowy field, rutted and pitted by
the wheels of lorries, with a huddle of shabby tents, and a control
tower built from lengths of unplaned wood, surmounted by a
wooden hut like a sentry-box.

By this time, both the American and British Conference teams
had swollen to such numbers that special ships had to be char-
tered to carry them, with the equipment needed for such a meeting, which as Joan Bright told General Hollis, was "at the end of
nowhere." It was impossible to anchor these vessels in Yalta
harbor, which was full of mines and sunken ships, so they lay
off Sebastopol, on the other side of the peninsula, ninety miles
across the mountains from the ruined palaces where the delegates
lived. These ships were their sole link with their home countries,
and all messages in and out were transmitted through them. Now,
instead of being within walking distance, as they had been at
Cairo and Teheran, the delegations faced between four and six
hours of travel between the shambles of Saki airfield and the
ruins of Sebastopol; Yusupov Palace, where the Russians had their
headquarters; Livadia Palace, at Yalta, the American center; and
Vorontzov Palace, at Alupka, headquarters of the British.

Only the most senior members of the delegations had a bedroom to themselves. As many as twenty Generals would be
sharing one bathroom, so that scenes at Vorontzov Palace reminded many of the British delegation of their younger days at
boarding-school. Lord Portal, Chief of the Air Staff, felt that it
was unco-operative to lock the bathroom door when beyond lay
an even more important room. Joan Bright did not share his view.

"What if there is a woman in the bath?" she asked.

"That makes no difference," he replied. "If a woman is in

the bath, then, obviously, the man backs out. If it's a man, no
harm is done."

One morning after this she saw him on tiptoe, trying to peep
through the fanlight above the bathroom door to see who was
taking so long in the bath. He turned away, his face a study.

"It's Jumbo," he explained, and went back to wait in his room.
Moments later, Field-Marshal Sir Henry Maitland Wilson, holding his dressing-gown, sponge and huge bath towel, hurried away
down the corridor.

Mr. Eden was surprised to find that not only were he and his
staff going to be very cramped for space, but also all the windows
of his room on the first floor had been tightly sealed. He was told
that a special train from Moscow was awaited, bringing the
special tools needed to open them. He accepted this with the
same good grace with which he accepted the fact that, instead of
a proper desk at which to work, all that could be found was a
small French table with unequal legs. The Russian Commandant
was approached with a request for a larger table or desk, but he
pointed out that to get larger furniture up to the first floor they
would have to break the windows to pull it through, because the
staircase was too narrow for it to be taken up in the usual way.
Mr. Eden kept his shaky table.

Mr. Churchill liked to sleep in a large bed, and it was discovered that the one supplied to him was extremely narrow.
President Roosevelt and his Foreign Secretary, Mr. Stettinius,
however, had each been given a double bed, and so Joan Bright
suggested to the same Commandant that the double bed of Mr.
Stettinius should be moved into Churchill's suite, so that the Big
Two at least would have a large bed apiece.

The Commandant shook his head; it could not be done. Instead, a special train was dispatched on the four days' run to
Moscow to fetch a larger bed, which arrived in Yalta on the same
day as the Prime Minister.

In the small villas outside, the British staff lived under barrack-
room conditions. As many as twenty would be queuing every
morning to use one wash-house, while Russian girls, who had arrived with bath-brushes to scrub their backs—seemingly an old

Russian custom—were surprised that their services were not required.

Nevertheless, despite the discomfort, the British Delegation retained its characteristic phlegm. Looking out from the one sitting-room that had been allotted to the senior members, across the thousands of newly planted flowers especially brought from Moscow for the occasion, Field-Marshal Sir Harold Alexander would stand, legs apart, back to the roaring fire, his glittering leather riding-boots reflecting the red tongues of flame. Sir Archibald Clark Kerr, the British Ambassador, sat apart from the rest, his back to the room, reading some obscure book on Chinese philosophy. Field-Marshal Sir Henry Maitland Wilson would make do with a week-old edition of *The Times;* and, on a sofa, Lord Moran and Admiral Somerville would sit discussing medicine and techniques of healing which the war had accelerated.

The main purpose of Roosevelt at Yalta was to gain Russian agreement for an attack on Japan. The Russians, for their part, wanted to get as much as possible out of the Americans. The meeting was, therefore, mainly between Russia and America, with these two aims in view, which dominated whatever else was discussed.

Roosevelt's great weakness—and one shared by the band of "tragically ignorant progressives"[1] who guided American policy in the crucial years—was a passion for flirtation with the Kremlin. His clique of faithful supporters—General Marshall, Ambassador Joseph Davies, Harry Hopkins, and his own son Elliott—missed no opportunity to praise the Soviet Union, in and out of season.

The history of Roosevelt's sympathy towards Russia went back a long way. With General Marshall's promotion to Chief of Staff in 1939, over the heads of twenty Major-Generals and fourteen senior Brigadiers, the way was further paved for the pro-Soviet policy that the President, a man always prone to act on his own initiative, was destined to inflict upon his country. From Pearl Harbor onwards, streams of American equipment were shipped

[1] F. Wittmer, *The Yalta Betrayal,* Idaho, 1954.

to Russia, over 2,500 ships delivering more than fifteen million tons. According to Felix Wittmer, "tons of atomic bomb materials" were included in these shipments—along with aircraft, tanks and other military vehicles.

Worse than an infatuation with Russia, however, was the belief of Roosevelt and Hopkins that they could conduct any kind of advantageous deal with the Soviets. In March 1942, the President wrote to Churchill: "I know you will not mind my being brutally frank when I tell you that I think I can personally handle Stalin better than either your Foreign Office or my State Department."[2] This credulous attitude surprised Stalin and Molotov, who, needless to say, wasted no time in exploiting it to the full.

The downhill rush that led to the Yalta "Bargain" was not so precipitate. In 1942, Roosevelt still held out against the suicidal cross-Channel operation propounded at Stalin's urging by Marshall, citing in defense of his views the poor showing of American troops in the North African campaign. But the infatuation progressed. General Stilwell, whose sympathies were Left rather than Right, was appointed to the Far East command; and the secret American Advisory Committee on Post-War Foreign Affairs attracted not only such recruits as Dean Acheson, Harry Hopkins and General Marshall, but also more sinister figures of the stamp of Alger Hiss and Harry Dexter White.

The tortuous line of Russian policy passed by the "liberal" American politicians. At Casablanca in January 1943, Roosevelt propounded the doctrine of unconditional surrender as the minimum acceptable from a defeated Germany. Stalin, however, published a statement a month later to the effect that "it would be ridiculous to identify Hitler's clique with the German people and the German state." He did not want to stir up a spirit of last-ditch *German*—as opposed to Nazi—resistance, by talk of unconditional surrender. This could wait until the Nazis were crushed for all time. Two years later the Soviet dictator was cheerfully proclaiming his Government's "inflexible purpose . . . to disarm and disband all German armed forces . . . remove all Nazi and

[2] W. Churchill, *The Hinge of Fate.*

militarist influence from public office," and so on; but in 1943 he deemed it politic first to divide the Germans and then to conquer.

The breach between Russia and the London Polish "Government in Exile" was blamed by Sumner Welles on the Poles for their protest over the Katyn Massacre which then, as throughout the war, was shrugged off as "German propaganda." Poland was an issue the Americans preferred to evade. Much against Churchill's will, Stalin insisted on moving the Soviet frontier to the Curzon Line, and fobbing off Poland with some former German territory as compensation.

Churchill and Roosevelt hoped that this concession might preserve a completely free and undominated Poland, but Stalin's ambitions embraced a larger area of Soviet military control, and he ultimately achieved a puppet Polish government, with seventeen Russian headquarters in the country, from which the suppression of Polish nationalism could be directed. Stalin also insisted that Anglo-American support in Yugoslavia should be transferred from General Mahajlovic's Cetniks to Tito's Partisans. This undoubtedly produced a more cohesive resistance against the Germans, even if it did play straight into Soviet hands, and immeasurably aided their post-war policy.

The path of appeasement was accelerated by the fact that the Western Allies had become uncomfortably aware that there might be a German-Soviet peace—as had happened in 1917—and up to Yalta, Roosevelt's main objective was to keep Russia in the war. At the Quebec Conference, an American document, sanctioned, though not drafted, by Marshall, was produced, stating that "Since Russia is the decisive factor in the war, she must be given every assistance, and every effort must be made to obtain her friendship. Likewise, since without question she will dominate Europe on the defeat of the Axis, it is even more essential to develop and maintain the most friendly relations with Russia."[3] This document further commented that it was imperative for Russia to be brought into the Pacific war, to ensure a speedier and less costly victory.

[3] F. Wittmer.

Stalin had told Cordell Hull in October, 1943, that the Soviet Union would join in defeating Japan, and fortified with this promise, the Americans sidestepped the issue of Poland as being a question that could wait until after the war.

"Up to Teheran, however, the door was still open for Western participation in the liberation of East Europe; and to defeat this concept—one always supported by Churchill—Russia relied upon her American sympathizers," writes General Hollis. "Not content with mere appeasement, Left wing newspapers in the U.S.A. denounced the idea of piercing through the soft underbelly of Europe as another British imperialist project. When the Teheran Conference opened, Roosevelt was duly converted to the plan for a 'Third Front' in the South of France, and Stalin pounced upon the converted President. As we have seen, Roosevelt was prevailed upon to divert part of General Clark's army from Italy, thus ruling out an Anglo-American landing in Yugoslavia, and leaving the way open for Soviet liberation and the establishment of a string of People's Republics in the Balkans."

The consequences of Teheran, which cemented American acquiescence in Soviet expansion, and even active support of it, were far-reaching. In 1944, Soviet Legations were opened in Cairo, Beirut, Damascus and Baghdad, which were to become fertile sources of anti-Western propaganda, under cover of their legitimate role of supervising the flow of American Lend-Lease to Russia. In Persia, the Soviet-financed Press was already denouncing the British and Americans in the jargon of *Pravda*—Fascists, reactionaries, imperialists. The Americans, for their part, were equally busy destroying files on Communists and subversives.

Teheran had marked the culmination of Roosevelt's long and hitherto unsuccessful endeavors to arrange a personal meeting with Stalin. For the last Conference, however, he was forced to go to the Soviet Union. Already he was tired and ill, a dying man. According to W. H. Chamberlin, in *America's Second Crusade*, he had shown signs of loss of memory at Teheran, but at Yalta he experienced difficulty in both the formulation and coherent expression of his thoughts. Appeasement, however, was still uppermost. The British had by now resigned themselves to the fact that, owing to American industrial superiority, Roosevelt was the pre-eminent influence in Western diplomacy. Churchill had, therefore, grudgingly to submit to any deal between America and Russia.

The physical conditions under which the Yalta Conference were held helped still less. The American and British delegations were a tedious journey apart, with the Soviet headquarters between them. Even the private American cable service, linked with Washington, was not as secure as it seemed, for their cable ship lay eighty miles off Sebastopol and the overland cables were guarded by Soviet riflewomen.

Roosevelt, however, scattered concessions wholesale. He allowed the Ukrainian and White Russian republics, provinces whose autonomy existed only on paper, to enter the United Nations as independent States, thus trebling Russia's voting strength at the stroke of a pen. Roosevelt also agreed—and his successor Harry Truman later ratified—that a Polish government would be accepted whose character met with the Soviet's approval.

Despite the absence of any Russian steps to implement Stalin's promise to Cordell Hull in 1943, Roosevelt made far more dangerous concessions in the Far East. In November 1943, he had pledged Chiang Kai-shek that Britain and America intended to deprive Japan of all the Pacific Island territory she had appropriated since 1914, and further, that all the territory she had seized from China should be restored.

But at Yalta this pledge was broken. Behind China's back—and after the American Press had announced that "China was now to be treated as an equal and no longer 'kicked around' "—Roosevelt signed an agreement with Churchill and Stalin which gave Russia pre-eminent interests in the Manchurian port of Dairen, and Port Arthur, its naval base, with control of access to both by railway. This disastrous promise was given simply in exchange for Stalin's undertaking on paper to fight Japan—already conceded *gratis*.

"Roosevelt's Service advisers," General Hollis wrote later, "had assured him that even though the Western Allies possessed the atomic bomb and were prepared to drop it on Japan, they could still expect a million casualties before they completely subdued the Japanese islands. The garrisons on these islands were expected to fight on relentlessly to the last man, regardless whether the main body of Japan military and politic, had surrendered or been overwhelmed.

"Obviously, this supposedly expert information—which, in fact, turned out to be quite wrong—colored the President's outlook and made him more anxious to be sure of Russian help in the conquest of Japan than he might otherwise have been."

In effect, American interests were ill-served by the inclusion of Russia in the Far Eastern war, since, as Bullitt claims, had Russia not invaded Manchuria "we and China together could have brought a rapid and just peace to the Far East."

Stalin also persuaded Roosevelt to agree to the Soviet annexation of the Kurile Islands, thus cutting the air route from Alaska to Japan, and to the detachment of the Russian-sponsored state of Outer Mongolia from the Chinese Republic.

A month after Yalta, the President was "disappointed and offended" by the behavior of Russian agents in Poland, and by an insulting personal message from Stalin alleging secret negotiations in Berne for a separate peace. Yet the dying man stuck to his guns, although more frustrations were to follow. The Russians refused to broaden the base of the Lublin Polish Government, to make it more representative in answer to a Western appeal. On April 1, Roosevelt complained to Stalin that he was "tragically disillusioned" at Russia's "apparently indifferent attitude" to the Yalta agreement. But an hour before his death, eleven days later, Roosevelt was telegraphing Churchill in answer to a request for advice:

> I would minimize the general Soviet problem as much as possible, because these problems in one way and another seem to arise every day, and most of them straighten out as in the case of the Berne meeting. We must be firm, however, and our course thus far is correct.

Thus Stalin quietly gulled Roosevelt at Yalta, and the policy of ruthless expediency paid its dividends. On April 12th the President died, and, as Bullitt says, "President Truman inherited an American foreign policy in bankruptcy."

❋　　❋　　❋　　❋

"The Conference between Britain, America and Russia at Potsdam in July 1945, was the last big Conference of the war," says General Hollis. "I remember it especially for many things. First, Roosevelt, who had looked so ill at Teheran, was no longer with us, and his place was taken by President Truman, who, in my view, had a greater grasp of the essentials that faced us. Then the Conservative Party lost the 1945 election in the middle of the Conference, and Mr. Churchill was replaced by Mr. Attlee. Next, Stalin, who seemed inestimably harder to deal with than he had appeared in the early days when he had needed our aid, had also aged. In the eighteen months since I first saw him at Teheran his hair had gone as white as the tunic he wore.

"Lastly, Operation Terminal had about it an atmosphere of reaction. The war was virtually over and with it had gone the speed of urgency, and the need to sink our differences and concentrate on defeating our enemies."

The Conference opened in the Cecilienhof Palace, which had belonged to Kaiser Wilhelm II. Truman crossed the Atlantic in the U.S.S. *Augusta,* transferring to the Presidential aircraft at Antwerp; Churchill flew in on July 14th, and was greeted by a British Royal Marines band wearing white helmets and playing *Rule, Britannia.*

The Palace lay on the outskirts of Potsdam, a comfortable country house built by the Kronprinz Wilhelm, the Kaiser's son. There were still signs of hand-to-hand fighting in the grounds, but the small graves amid the shabby flower-beds were only those of the Kaiser's dogs.

The Russians had planted a courtyard with red flowers in the shape of a huge red star in the grounds; it showed up brightly against the short cropped lawn.

"Inside," writes General Hollis, "was a large room panelled in dark wood, furnished with a crimson carpet, overlaid with a red and purple Oriental rug. This room also contained a twelve-foot circular table and fifteen chairs, and desks for secretaries and ste-nographers. From this main meeting room, arched hallways led to private suites. The main dining-room was also nearby and here President Truman, who really preferred bourbon, had to drink many a toast in vodka. The dining table was large enough to seat thirty-one people.

"In the ceiling above it was a galleon sailing majestically under white clouds, picked out in plaster bas-relief. In the plaster sky the Russians had gone to great trouble to paint a huge red star, which shed its rays on the galleon's sails. This struck me as being symbolic, for their politics were also coloring the voyage of our own ship of state."

The other furnishings, too, were strange; the chairs of the dele-gates were decorated with carved angels, and Truman's quarters had dark wallpaper in the living-room, with pictures of a dead rabbit, a bright red lobster and half a cantaloupe in his private dining-room.

Business proceeded fairly briskly, despite language difficulties and almost constant diarrhea caused by the bad water, polluted by corpses.

Three interpreters and nine other subordinates sat at the table with the Big Three, where Truman's mainstays were James Byrnes, his Secretary of State, and ex-Ambassador Joseph Davies. Thirty or more experts sat at little tables around the room. Churchill, while he was there, often consulted Attlee, though it was noticeable that when Attlee took over, he had rather less to say to his Foreign Secretary, Ernest Bevin. Truman, a brisk and affable chairman, did not wander from the point as Roosevelt used to do.

"When Mr. Bevin replaced Mr. Eden, Ernie swiftly became a very popular figure," writes General Hollis. "I remember once how his household staff had prepared some magnificent sand-wiches with fine slices of bread and succulent fillings to eat when he returned from the Cecilienhof late at night, but he brushed these aside. Instead, he drew up his chair to the kitchen table, and cut himself enormous slices of bread, on which he laid pieces of cheese, and washed down this simple meal with several glasses of beer."

Each Delegation could call upon the services of various military bands, dance bands and musicians who were in the Services. The American pianist Eugene List played for President Truman; Stalin held a concert in honor of the British and American Delegations, who heard recitals by Moscow's most eminent musicians. The British had a Royal Marines band as well as the string section of the Royal Air Force Symphony Orchestra, and Denis Matthews, the pianist.

Amusements and recreations were virtually non-existent and there was indeed little time for them, but the two Field-Marshals, Sir Alan Brooke and Sir Harold Alexander, asked the Russians if they could fish on the Griebnitzsee. They were told that the lake was full of dead, the water was polluted, and that even if fishing were possible, it was forbidden for any craft to sail on the lake. Furthermore, the Russians, who were guarding the other shore, would shoot.

"Ah, the bitterness of victory!" observed General Hollis.

About an hour afterwards, however, the attention of those in the Palace was drawn to Field-Marshal Alexander, who was gesticulating at the end of the small jetty that thrust out from the foot of the garden into the lake. He appeared furiously angry.

"We looked out towards the lake," writes General Hollis, "and saw a small canoe in which sat two of the most distinguished Service men of our generation: Field-Marshal Sir Alan Brooke and Marshal of the R.A.F. Sir Charles Portal.

"Brooke was holding a fishing-rod and looking very pleased about it. Portal was holding a paddle, and looking most unhappy. By the time they changed jobs, and Brooke had the paddle and Portal the rod, Field-Marshal Alexander had left the end of the jetty. Someone suggested that he had gone to tell the Russians to shoot. . . ."

Against this background of ceremony, protocol, and the depressing reminders of a war that was still fresh in everyone's memory, the future was to be decided. Already the effectiveness

of the United Nations as a force for world peace had been weakened by the decision of the San Francisco Conference to accord
powers of veto to the permanent members of the Security Council. These powers presupposed a sense of responsibility on the
part of the major nations; for the right of veto gave any unscrupu-
lous Power the mandate to torpedo any international police
force.

The policy of appeasement continued. Even the successful
atom bomb tests in New Mexico, just completed, did not deter
Truman from agreeing to the Soviet annexation of Koenigsberg
and parts of East Prussia. The Soviets also did well out of reparations: Edwin Pauley, the President's Reparations Representatives,
was deceived into parting with all German assets in Austria.
Russia was also authorized to take reparations as required from
her own zone of occupation in Germany, plus "ten per cent of
such industrial capital in the Western zones as is unnecessary for
the German peace economy."[4] The consequence was a wholesale
seizure of German industry, on the pretext that it had been Nazi-
owned.

This principle was a legacy from Roosevelt, who had approved
a plan suggested by Henry Morgenthau of the U.S. Treasury,
whereby the industrial plant and equipment of the Ruhr should
be dismantled and removed to Allied countries. Cordell Hull had
vigorously opposed this action on the grounds that German industry was integral to the European economy, and should be
conserved: further, idle coalfields and factories would bring
starvation, which could only be alleviated by American charity.

The Conference produced "surprisingly little news," a fact
that should not have seemed surprising because so many of its decisions had been predicted or pre-arranged.

The declaration of terms for Japan—no longer unconditional
surrender—was issued from Potsdam, indeed, but it was not a Big
Three document: it was an American document, and Truman's
signature on it was the one that counted. True, Chiang Kai-shek
had approved it in Washington, and Churchill and Attlee had

4 Bullit.

both signed, but this was America's war; Stalin as a nominal neutral, did not sign. He had won all he wanted, in any case.

"On the day the war ended, back in London, Churchill gave a small luncheon party, to which he invited his Chiefs of Staff, General Ismay and myself," recalls General Hollis. "Afterwards he walked round the table, raising his glass to each one of us in turn, and at the end of the toasts, he suddenly paused and pointed upwards to the ceiling.

"'This is all very well, gentlemen,' he said, 'But we mustn't forget the One above.'

"Sometimes, in the years since then, when the peace we all worked and fought for so hard, seems to be what Dryden called 'war in masquerade,' I remember these words.

"For afterwards, in 'The Hole in the Ground,' it certainly seemed very easy to forget so much that had happened. Gradually the activity slowed, officers left on other postings, the great engines that blew in the filtered air from the Horseferry Road stopped and were still, the Royal Marines Guard stood down, and within months the 'Hole' was virtually deserted. . . ."

Now it remains, a shell that carried the spirit of victory; empty rooms left as they were on the last day of war, with pinpricks still in the wall maps and red tags on Churchill's table marked "Action this day." The red and green telephones are silent; in the smallest room where the Prime Minister would telephone President Roosevelt, even the clock with four hands has stopped.

Yet in the long, silent corridors, the dim lights still burn ceaselessly under their china shades, like lamps lit in memory of great men and great deeds that changed the world.

ACKNOWLEDGMENTS

We would like to acknowledge the very great help and co-operation so many people have so generously given in connection with the preparation of this book. Our debt of gratitude is particularly heavy to the following:

The Rt. Hon. Lord Beaverbrook, P.C.

The Rt. Hon. Lord Hankey, G.C.B., P.C., G.C.M.G., G.C.V.O., F.R.S.

The Rt. Hon. Admiral of the Fleet Viscount Mountbatten of Burma, K.G., P.C., G.C.S.I., G.C.I.E., G.C.V.O., G.C.B., D.S.O.

Marshal of the Royal Air Force Lord Portal, K.G., G.C.B., O.M., D.S.O., M.C.

Sir Robert Bruce Lockhart, K.C.M.G.

Major-General Sir Edward Spears, Bt., K.B.E., C.B., M.C.

Major-General Sir Colin Gubbins, K.C.M.G., D.S.O., M.C.

Air Commodore H. V. Rowley

Colonel Dudley Clarke, C.B.E.

Mrs. Joan Bright Astley, O.B.E.

Colonel S. J. Bassett, C.B.E., R.M.

Mr. Lawrence Burgis, C.M.G., C.V.O.

Rear-Admiral A. D. Nichol, C.B., O.B.E., D.S.O.

Mr. Stuart Anderson, M.B.E.

We would also thank Miss Mary Cosh and Mr. Michael Sedgwick for their research, Mr. Edwin Merrett and the staff of the *Daily Express* Library for their willing help in checking so many references, the Admiralty Librarian, the Press Officer of the London Transport Executive, and Mrs. Eileen Rufus for typing the manuscript.

Any errors remaining are our own.

BIBLIOGRAPHY

THE SECOND WORLD WAR, Vols. 1-6, Sir Winston Churchill, Houghton Mifflin.

TURN OF THE TIDE, Sir Arthur Bryant, Doubleday.

THE BUSINESS OF WAR, Gen. Sir John Kennedy, Morrow.

CRUSADE IN EUROPE, Gen. Eisenhower, Doubleday.

THREE YEARS WITH EISENHOWER, Harry C. Butcher.

THE CIANO DIARIES, Dutton.

BRITISH WAR PRODUCTION, M. M. Postan.

THE GOEBBELS DIARIES, ed. L. P. Lochner.

PANZER LEADER, H. Guderian, Dutton.

A SAILOR'S ODYSSEY, Lord Cunningham of Hyndehope, Dutton.

IT COULD HAPPEN AGAIN, Lord Chatfield.

PRELUDE TO DUNKIRK, Sir Edward Spears, Hill & Wang.

DON'T TRUST TO LUCK, Lord Beaverbrook.

LEND-LEASE, E. R. Stettinius.

STRUGGLE FOR EUROPE, Chester Wilmot, Harpers.

WHITE HOUSE PAPERS, R. Sherwood.

ONE MARINE'S TALE, Gen. Sir Leslie Hollis.

ORGANIZATION AND EQUIPMENT FOR WAR, Gen. Sir Ronald M. Weeks, Cambridge Univ. Press.

ON ACTIVE SERVICE IN PEACE AND WAR, H. L. Stimson & McG. Bundy.

U.S. OFFICIAL WAR HISTORIES.

ATLANTIC MEETING, H. V. Morton.

HANSARD.

SUPREME CONTROL IN WAR, Lord Hankey, Cambridge Univ. Press.

AS HE SAW IT, Elliott Roosevelt.

THE ROOSEVELT LETTERS, Duell, Sloan & Pearce.

THE YALTA BETRAYAL, Wittmer, Caxton.

HITLER, A. Bullock, Harpers.

THE WAR AGAINST JAPAN, Gen. Woodburn Kirby.

U-BOATS AT WAR, Harold Busch.

FUEHRER'S NAVAL CONFERENCES.

U.S. STRATEGIC BOMBING SURVEY, U.S. Govt. Printing Office.

INVASION 1940, Ronald Wheatley.

OPERATION SEA-LION, Peter Fleming, Simon & Schuster.

EUROPEAN THEATER OF OPERATIONS—Cross Channel Operations, U.S. War Dept.

HITLER'S STRATEGY, Hinsley, Cambridge Univ. Press.

WINSTON CHURCHILL AND THE SECOND FRONT, Trumbull Higgins, Oxford Univ. Press.

STALIN'S LETTERS, Dutton.

GLOBAL LOGISTICS AND STRATEGY, U.S. War Dept.

CALCULATED RISK, Gen. Mark Clark, Harpers.

LIFE IN OUR HANDS, Pamela Bright.

STRATEGY AND COMPROMISE, Samuel Eliot Morison, Little, Brown.

THE CENTRAL BLUE, Air Marshall Sir J. Slessor, Praeger.

Files of: *Daily Express, Daily Herald, Daily Mail, The Times, Time, Life, Sunday Express, Sunday Pictorial, The People, The Observer, The Sunday Times, The American Weekly.*

INDEX

Abadan, 220
Absenteeism, 107
Acheson, Dean, 290
Adam, Col. R. (General Sir Ronald), 29
Admiralty, 24, 29, 46, 65, 71, 74–75, 79–80, 92–93, 117–20, 129, 131–33, 237, 252, 277
——, Plans Division, 117
Adriatic Sea, 247
aerial bombardment, 33, 61, 73, 80, 108, 114–16, 184, 224
Africa, 44, 140–41, 144, 172, 226
——, North, 13, 82, 86–87, 111, 141–42, 151–52, 176, 185, 189, 194, 196, 199–201, 204, 210, 212, 214, 222, 225–28, 230, 232, 234, 237, 241, 244, 290
air conditioning, 39, 56
Air Force, Royal, 6, 28–30, 42–43, 45, 48–49, 73, 88, 97–98, 113, 115, 117–18, 201, 297; Bomber Command, 170; Ferry Command, 11, 17, 20; Fighter Command, 19, 114, 116, 136–37, 170; No. 10 Fighter Group, 19, 20; W.A.A.F., 271
Air Intelligence, 79
Air Ministry, 29, 71, 76–77, 99–101, 110, 115–16, 129, 173, 217
air raid warnings, 108
air support, 193, 203, 204, 212, 232
air-sea rescue craft, 118
aircraft: Beaufighter, 115; Beaufort, 115; Berwick, British Airways Boeing flying-boat, 11–21; Flamingo, 83, 89; Flying Fortress, 217; Gloster Gauntlet, 43, 116; Hendon bomber, 43; Hind bomber, 43; Hurricane fighter, 114–15; Kittyhawk fighter, 230; Oxford, 115; Spitfire fighter, 83, 89, 202; Stirling bomber, 115; Wellington bomber, 115
Aircraft Defense Police, 113
aircraft factories, hours worked in, 101–104, 106–108; inspectors, 103–104;

protection of, from aerial attack, 112–16
Aircraft Production, 98–104, 106–108, 111–12, 186; Ministry of, 98–103, 113, 174, 179
Alamein, El, 141–42, 200, 219
Alaska, 294
Alexander, Rt. Hon. A. V. (Viscount Alexander of Hillsborough), 7
Alexander, Gen. Sir Harold (Field Marshal Earl), 138, 169, 206, 221, 241, 245, 247, 277, 289, 297
Alderney, 203
Alexandria, 205, 270
Algeria, 141, 196, 208, 225
Algiers, 214, 226–27n, 241, 252–53, 277; Conference at, 241–42
All Fools' Day, 31, 189
Allied Forces in Britain, 217
Alps, 235
aluminum, shortage of, 99; supplied to Russia, 159, 178–79
Alupka, Crimea, 287
Amatol, 50
America, South, 98
American Advisory Committee on Post-War Foreign Affairs, 290
American Chiefs of Staff, 121, 167, 184, 188, 191, 197, 213, 241, 243–44, 257
American War of Independence, 258
amphibious operations, 117, 128, 175, 185, 197, 224; see also Combined Operations
Ancona-Pisa Line, 247
Andaman Islands, 261
Anderson, Rt. Hon. Sir John, 108
Anglo-Russian Treaty of 1942, 202
anti-aircraft gun, 43
anti-tank gun, 96
Antwerp, 189, 295
"Anvil," Operation, 247, 267
Anzio, 272, 277
Arcadia Conference, see Washington
Archangel, 142, 157–58, 160, 184